TRADITIONAL ARCHERY

TRADITIONAL ARCHERY

Second Edition, Revised and Updated

Sam Fadala

STACKPOLE BOOKS

Published by
STACKPOLE BOOKS
5067 Ritter Road
Mechanicsburg, PA 17055
www.stackpolebooks.com

Printed in China

10 9 8 7 6 5 4 3 2 1

First edition

Cover design by Caroline Stover

Photos by Nick Fadala except where otherwise indicated.

On the cover: Series IV tapered laminated all-glass-limb bow with gray actionwood riser and red elm bow with shedua riser, both handmade by Herb Meland of Pronghorn Custom Bows, Casper, Wyoming. Arrows made by Rusty Izatt of Warrior Archery. Photo by Nick Fadala.

Library of Congress Cataloging-in-Publication Data

Fadala, Sam, 1939–
    Traditional archery / Sam Fadala. — 2nd ed., rev. and updated.
        p. cm.
    ISBN 978-0-8117-0673-5
    1. Archery. 2. Archery—History. I. Title.
    GV1185.F33 2011
    799.3'2—dc22
                                                    2010026234

For
Herb and Norla

Contents

1

Traditional Why

Tipi rings lay before us, large round rocks placed in a circle to hold a no-madic dwelling in place a long time ago. We found and examined plains Indian artifacts, then returned them to their resting places. How long ago did those Native Americans live and hunt in this vast mountain valley? No one could say for sure. Even more fascinating than the arrowheads and spear points were what my companion and I chose to call "mystery rocks." They were watermelon-sized and laid out in straight, long rows, obviously placed neatly for a reason. Alongside some were manmade depressions. Could they have been used to direct buffalo? Could be. The shaggy beast is known to turn aside when it comes across slight impediments. I got down into one of the pits. The vantage point provided a perfect view of a well-worn trail. If bi-son charged along that lane, guided by the rocks, a hunter would have a

The lure of traditional archery is partly romance—like that in the story called to mind by this American bison. The intrepid Indian of the plains procured meat, hide, and numerous other products from this animal, most often armed with nothing more than a "bent stick" and a stone-tipped arrow.

1

Bows of yore were very simple "machines," working tools that were invented in various parts of the globe along a similar time line. The traditional archer today can shoot replicas of the finest bows of any era.

bowshot from ten paces. Any brave in the tribe could make a certain hit with his natural-handling bow at that distance.

The brave hidden in the pit, if indeed it was a pit for buffalo hunting, probably had a very simple bow (I have never seen sights on an American Indian bow, not that it would surprise me if such a bow existed at some time), somewhat short with greatly varied draw weight, firing an arrow tipped with a carefully and even beautifully chipped broadhead of stone—perhaps flint. At some point, Indians on the plains discovered that discarded metalwork left behind by white pioneers could also be worked into broadheads. But I doubt that any of these cut the same as the glasslike obsidian head. The hunter of the high plains drew his bow and sent that sharp-tipped shaft on course by instinct (see chapter 13).

"Going back to our roots" has become a cliché, somewhat boring to hear at times. But all clichés are true. That is how they got to be clichés. Like many other archers, when I got into traditional archery, I was returning to roots planted when, as a little kid, I cut a nice strong branch from my grandfather's favorite oleander, making a bow out of it with simple twine for a string. Time passed, but I never tired of bows. Then, shortly after the first compound hit the sporting goods shop, I joined the ranks of wheel-and-pulley shooters. These bows had just one advantage at that time—the relaxation factor. They might draw at 60 pounds, for example, but hold back at only 40. The chronograph proved that my glass/maple laminated 75-pound Ben Pearson longbow shot just as fast an arrow as a compound. The Black Widow recurve shot faster yet.

I enjoyed the compound shooting machine at the time and find no problem with the many archers who prefer that type of bow today. They're better than ever, shooting arrows at high velocity with super accuracy. But I was through with it after a while. I had the hottest compound going, but happily gave it away to a cousin who coveted that wheelbow. I was out of archery for a spell, although I always had an old longbow handy that I would "plink" with from time to time. Then, almost overnight, it seemed, longbows and recurves were back. The "traditional why" was being asked and answered. Initially, most of the bows, as I recall, came from custom shops. But in time, companies that offered stickbows in the past, such as Bear Archery, were back at it again.

The distilled joy of archery had become but a memory for older archers and a never-done for younger bow shooters. The older set fanned a tiny ember glowing in a dark recess of past experience until it rekindled into bright flame. The strung stick was back. But not just back; it was better than ever. Bowyers had not been asleep in the cabbage patch. They had, all along, been perfecting their trade. Now longbows and recurves were not only easily

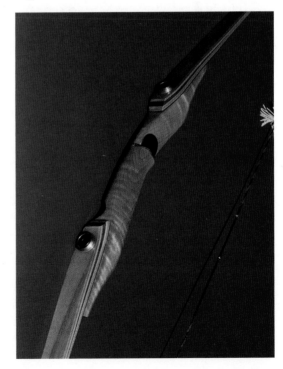

Almost overnight, it seems, traditional bows made a comeback. Bows like this one are as beautiful as similar bows of the past—but with improved performance.

Today, archery "shoots" and gatherings are well-attended by the traditional clan. At some events at least half of the tackle is traditional.

obtained again, they were the best longbows and recurves ever. They could not compete in arrow velocity with the mechanical advantage of the compound, of course, but 190- to 200-feet per second was not uncommon for the better sticks. And this was with "real" arrows. Not soda straws, but arrows heavy enough to penetrate the biggest bull, buck, or boar.

The last several state archery gatherings I attended found approximately one-half of the members shooting longbows and recurves. That number could be skewed because many compound-shooting members may not have attended, the gatherings holding more attraction for the traditionalist. But there is no mistake that today the stickbow is a force in twenty-first-century archery. But why? It's easier to master the compound bow. After all, it's high-tech. Let-off is higher than ever. It's not impossible to find compounds holding at 35 pounds marked 70-pound draw weight. And they have sights—all kinds of sights. What will they think of next? I once came across an advertisement for a bow sight promising rangefinder ability.

More practice time is necessary with a traditional bow than with a compound. Sure, the compound demands some practice. But with sights—and don't forget let-off plus the release device designed to eliminate fingers on the string—just about anyone can put arrows into the gold at reasonable ranges. And the best compound bow shooters can cluster their arrows into the mark from pretty far off! Meanwhile, stick shooters better practice if they want to be proficient. As Maurice Thompson said, the successful archer shoots to the point where no overt conscious effort is demanded to put his or her arrow on target. In fact, when the instinctive archer tries to put too much conscious effort into launching that arrow, it may go awry often as not.

While compound bows are very accurate, so are traditional bows. When a good traditional bow is "locked up" in a shooting rest, it will put arrow after arrow on target; the traditional archer does not have to worry about the accuracy of a chosen bow. PHOTO COURTESY OF THE BOHNING COMPANY, LTD.

Ask any ten traditional archery fans why they shoot longbow or recurve and you may get ten different responses. But here are some that I got when I asked. One archer told me that it was the advancement of the compound bow that made him abandon the wheels and pulleys. It was "too good" for him. He wanted more challenge. "I woke up one day," he said, "and my latest compound bow looked like something from *Star Wars*. I said enough. And that was that. I began searching for a recurve. I used to shoot recurve bows." Another said, "Something was missing. I used to have fun shooting my longbow. I wasn't really having that much fun with my compound. As soon as I got back into shooting a longbow, I started having a lot more fun." A game warden said, "Since we try to manage game more than hunters in this state, I suppose it doesn't really matter how a tag is filled. The hunter is finished either way, whether he gets that deer or elk with a bow or a .300 Magnum. But it does sort of bother me that we gave, and still give, bowhunters special seasons, longer and in ideal habitat, because they're 'handicapped.' And then they turned around and did everything possible to eliminate the handicap with their compound bows."

"I got so tired packing that compound around. It was more trouble than my 9-pound .30-06. At least I could sling the rifle, but so-called slings I found for the compound didn't help at all. They were still bulky. My longbows—I shoot longbows now—don't even weight two pounds. Sure, I have a quiver to pack now, but I got one of those Catquivers and it carries my lunch, fire-starter, and other gear as well as arrows." This last speaker ended by echoing what a previous person said in my informal survey. "And I'm having a lot more fun with my longbows than I ever had with the compound." Another told me, "Sam, it was the technology. I had to get into the computer and

The traditional bow, like the one carried here on a back-country rove, embodies not only the history of yesteryear, but beauty and grace as well. It is much more than an arrow-shooting machine.

e-mail and iPods and Palm Pilots for my work and I'll be darned if I am going high-tech in my archery."

But are there any real advantages to stickbows over compounds? Those who fire darts from sticks think so. But at the same time, any traditional archer who thinks he can do better at forty yards putting arrows into a bull's eye the breadth of a teacup had best be Stacy Groscup, Byron Furguson, Howard Hill, or one of the other greats. At the same time, I'm waiting to see a wheelbow shooter snick aspirins out of the air. Maybe there are those who can. Perhaps I missed them. But the natural fluidness of longbow and recurve does not seem to reside in the compound. Also there are a few, very few, traditionalists who fire a fast and accurate arrow in the field. They are not handicapped with the longbows they shoot. I have watched Vern Butler skewer a cow pie at 75 yards and farther. I have watched Bob Taylor, at close range, stop shooting at a mark because his group was so tight that he would break arrows already in the target.

And yes, there is the romance factor. Maurice and Will Thompson shot the longbow. So did Pope and Young. Fred Bear had his recurve. Before the wheelbow mob finds a lynching rope, I acknowledge another cliché that bears repeating: beauty is in the eye of the beholder. Many archers see a beauty in the intricate workings of their compound bows. True, but Zebrawood, cocobolo, Tonkin bamboo, Osage orange, bloodwood, shedua,

The traditional bow embodies, in most cases, art as well as function. That in part is due to the many exotic wood choices available to the bow maker of the day.

bocote—these beautiful woods are not too often found in compounds. I doubt, however, that many archers would stay with longbows and recurves if they had no success with either. In other words, why carry a stick when the wheelbow holds all four aces in the performance deck?

Tradition for its own sake. Why not? Light in the hand. Pretty. But when it comes to traditional going up against primitive, how the picture changes. We laugh at compound bows because they are mechanical, but now the compound lover gets his chance to laugh, since the gap between primitive and modern traditional bows is just as wide as that between compound and traditional. The modern longbow or recurve is built on principles of working geometry with laminated limbs—one bow with all-glass limbs—impregnated risers full of synthetic glue-like stuff infused at high pressure to make them almost unbreakable, epoxy this and epoxy that, arrow speeds in the 200 foot-per-second domain, the list goes on and on. A good primitive bow can be made to launch a surprisingly fast arrow. But not as fast as the modern longbow or recurve.

The modern stick is no more closely related to the primitive bow than a lizard to an alligator. These short-legged creatures are both reptiles, but oh how different they are, especially if the latter has a grip on your tennis shoe. Likewise, the modern composite bow built of state-of-the-art materials by a gifted bowyer is just barely cousin to the old self-bow (bow made of a single

The modern composite bow, now crafted by a number of talented bowyers not only in America but also abroad, has taken a grip on the sport of archery. The stick is back and back to stay.

My "finest moments" in the bow-shooting have been on roves and survival hunts when I backpacked into wilderness areas. One of the reasons for the comeback of the traditional bow is its connection with simpler times.

wood) of yesteryear that Geronimo may have carried, or for that matter the simple sticks carried today by natives of the Amazon forest.

I seem to be following the cliché trail these days. But another that fits this chapter is the saying, "one man's meat is another man's poison," along with its relative, "to each his own." Fully explaining the "why" of traditional archery to a newcomer in the archery circle, or a full-fledged compound archer, or someone who has never even shot a bow, is like describing the flavor of mopane worms, which I ate once in Africa. They taste like, well, I can't think of a comparison. The best I can do is relate a personal anecdote. Some of my favorite hunting memories are the survival hunts I used to go on, sometimes for weeks at a time. My partner and I did so many that I lost count of the longest ever. Just before his passing I mentioned our "month-long" Mexico, which I have always referred to as that length."Sam," Ted said, "We were gone just short of *two* months. That's how I lost my job at the mine." Then I remembered. What we could carry on our backs was our gear. Where we ended up at day's end was home. My fine Cabela's lightweight Hunter's Bivy shelter was not yet invented, nor my Coleman's Cloudcroft mummy bag, good for 20 below with sweat suit and watch cap on; our sleeping bags were army-issue made mostly with feathers donated, no doubt with protest, from chickens. Ground pad?

Older bows like these were not nearly as efficient as the traditional bows we have today, but they served many very well and today are often collected by archers who revere the past.

One of the joys of traditional archery is its "naturalness." Shooting off the shelf in an instinctive manner is not only successful, but rewarding in a world where everything else seems to be high-tech.

What was that? And our bows on those treks were grim by comparison with today's fine sticks. But we didn't know our tackle was mediocre, so we made up for lack of excellence with everyday shooting familiarity.

My partner's 55-pound all-fiberglass bow drew like 70 and fired arrows like 35. It stacked like a big pile of buckwheat pancakes (difficult toward the last few inches). Mine was better, a 75-pound longbow that pushed a fairly fast arrow (25 feet per second slower than my current 57-pound Pronghorn Three-Piece Takedown longbow, or any Black Widow of my acquaintance). But our arrows flew like those of Tommy the American Indian and Maurice Thompson. On some of those adventures the nights were cold but we dug a trench, started a fire in the length of the trench, let it burn to coals, covered the coals with the excavated earth, and spread out our sleeping bags on top. Maybe the experience would have been just as rich with compound bows. But I don't think so.

And so I have a challenge for the reader who is not yet into stickbows but thinking about it. Try one. Try a good one. Don't latch on to a 70-pound stick or even 65 or 60. Go with light draw to begin with. Shoot up close only—and target size is not important. Don't try too hard. Relax. Tilt the bow

Going back can be rewarding. Here, one of the members of the traditional archery party enjoys a nighttime campfire on a rove.

to angle to form a V for the arrow to rest in. Determine an anchor point. Make it a little high; you can always lower it later. My anchor point is with the right hand knuckle of my index finger touching my right cheekbone. The corner of the mouth works better for others. Keep the bow arm just slightly crooked at the elbow. Unlock your knees. Bend a little, just a little. Later you can modify the "squat." Don't look at the bow. Don't concentrate on the arrow, I know. The great archer Howard Hill was supposed to use point-of-arrow almost as a sight. But for now, just burn a hole in the center of the target with both eyes open. Let the arrow "escape" from the bow. First time around, sort of draw your bow hand back a little during the release, a pull-through method. Later, if you like, you can switch to the flower petal where fingers sort of "lose control" of the string and the arrow "escapes" almost of its own volition. The big thing is to not drop the bow arm. Keep it as close as possible to the position it was in before the arrow flew. And now watch that dart sing into the straw bale, burying itself deeply. Do it again. And again. And again. And don't worry about score as long as you're observing form.

OK. Maybe it's "not your cup of tea," as an old friend used to tell me when I didn't like something. But maybe, just maybe, it will take only one short session for you to understand what I cannot explain in words—sort of like what mopane worms taste like.

2

Beginnings

Longbow and recurve history is not only fascinating to a few million of us, but also appropriate for understanding our roots. And so this chapter on that history serves as a foundation for chapters to come in this book.

Not everyone agrees on where to start the timeline, but in my opinion, the history of the bow begins with the *atlatl*, a name coined by Professor Nuttal, a renowned naturalist, in 1891, who apparently formed it by combining two Aztec words meaning *throwing* and *water*. Pronunciation was supposed to be *aht-laht-il*, the first part like saying "ah" for a doctor's throat examination, with a "t" on the end of it. It's been written as at'latl as well as atlatl. It is thought to have been first used in Peru, but nobody really knows. Some sharp individual figured out that he could multiply his own strength in throwing a spear (not yet an arrow)—possibly with two hundred times the power.

The atlatl has also been known as spearthrower, throwing stick, throwing board, spear sling, dart thrower, Woomera (in Australia), hul-che in a 1935 *Poplar Mechanics* magazine, and other names, according to *All About the At'latl* by Gary Fogelman. I like throwing stick or, better yet, casting stick, for that's what the atlatl is, a stick designed to launch a dart. (The weapon launched by the atlatl is sometimes called a spear, but I prefer to call it a dart. The long dart of the atlatl has fletching: it is, therefore, not a spear in my estimation, but a very long arrow.) The atlatl casting stick was often around fifteen to twenty-four inches long, while the dart could be four or even five feet long. Fogelman states that the atlatl developed around 12,000 B.C.

We could examine countless niches in time where the bow made a difference in cultures, but that would be a book. So, skipping a huge span of centuries, let's look at the bows and arrows that had the *most* influence on the fathers of modern longbow/recurve shooting, such as the Thompson Brothers. One of these would be the bow used by Robin Hood and his merry band of men in Sherwood Forest: the English longbow. Robin's bow was a rather

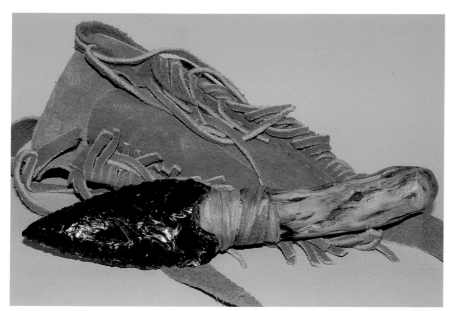

This flint knife was crafted in modern times, but in the style of early knives.

Flint was was used not only for ancient arrowheads and knives, but also, in a much later time, flint to ignite the powder charge in a flintlock firearm. Certainly, flint deserves center stage in a chapter on beginnings.

amazing instrument. Very early firearms were neither accurate nor long-range capable, and they were slow to load and to reload after firing. At the time of these early guns, Robin Hood's longbow had excellent range, being capable of casting a heavy arrow at least two hundred yards, with a starting speed of around 160 to 170 feet per second. Furthermore, a practiced archer could fire many arrows in the time it took the rifleman to reload his musket only once. The longbow may not have exceeded the crossbow in extreme range, but it was far more practical in that it did not have to be "cocked" and therefore could shoot more arrows than the crossbow in the same amount of time.

The longbow put England on the map in the fourteenth and fifteenth centuries as Europe's foremost power. Even when English troops were outnumbered, the day was often won for the English because the longbow could shoot an arrow far and with enough force to penetrate steel when it arrived on target. A story from around 1300 A.D. says that a Welsh archer pierced an English knight with an arrow that pinned the latter to his horse, the arrow passing through thigh, chain mail, and wooden saddle. This story is quite possible because a heavy arrow cast from a strong bow is capable of similar penetration today. Dr. Saxon Pope investigated what a longbow with a strong broadhead could do against a mail coat of the era. In *Hunting with the Bow & Arrow*, he writes:

> To test a steel bodkin [broadhead] pointed arrow such as was used at the battle of Cressy [Crecy], I borrowed a shirt of chain armor from the Museum, a beautiful specimen made in Damascus in the 15th Century. It weighed twenty-five pounds and was in perfect condition. One of the attendants in the Museum offered to put it on and allow me to shoot at him. Fortunately, I declined his proffered services and put it on a wooden box, padded with burlap to represent clothing.
>
> Indoors at a distance of seven yards, I discharged an arrow at it with such force that sparks flew from the links of steel as from a forge. The bodkin point and shaft went through the thickest portion of the back, penetrated an inch of wood and bulged out the opposite side of the armor shirt. The attendant turned a pale green. An arrow of this type can be shot about two hundred yards and would be deadly up to the full limit of its flight.

The English longbow was responsible for the Thompson Brothers, Pope and Young, and every other force in the continuance of the bow as a powerful tool. It was Robin's bow that Maurice and Will relied on. It was this bow that Pope and Young adopted.

So where did this English longbow come from? Records put it in the hands of Welsh archers fighting against the English (prior to the Norman invasion of 1066). The English picked up on the bow and used it to such great success that it carried the English name henceforth. As with almost all history, historians find it difficult if not impossible to agree on who invented the longbow, and when. And so it's wise to add that perhaps the longbow, although certainly not in the final form employed by the Welsh, may have been used by German archers, or perhaps Scandinavians, around 500 B.C. While I

have no data to either confirm or re-
ject this idea, it is plausible to doubt
the power of these early bows compared to the true English longbow
that came along in the hands of the
Welsh.

Real English longbows have
been discovered and are still around
today. Pope reported that in the recovery of the *Mary Rose*, "sunk off
the coast of Albion in 1545 and
raised in 1841, only two longbows
were recovered, unfinished staves at
that." These were taken to the Tower
of London for safekeeping. The
"staves were six feet, four and three-
quarters inches long, one and one-
half inches across the handle, one
and one-quarter inches thick," according to Pope. Dr. Pope is not to be
blamed for what was probably mis-
information at the time. The *Mary
Rose*, named for Henry the Eighth's
favorite sister, Mary Tudor, was in-

*This handmade steel broadhead was
crafted after the fashion of metal heads
used in the era of the longbow.*

deed sunk on 19 July 1545 in the Isle of Wight. In the 1830s a few guns were
raised to the surface (we believe) and possibly bow staves at the same time.
The ship was not completely salvaged until 1982. On board, it is reported,
were 172 bows and 4,000 arrows (some reports say 3,500 arrows).

Since the Welsh-English longbow (or possibly the lesser form invented
around 500 B.C.) is the very basis of the traditional bows we shoot today, its
history is relished by modern archers of longbow/recurve bent. We enjoy
learning of its prowess, especially in battle. Possibly the first major English
longbow war showing was the Battle of Falkirk on April 1, 1298, when England invaded Scotland. Edward I defeated William Wallace in that battle due
to a sky filled with deadly arrows raining down on the Scots from the longbows of Welsh archers, historians believe.

The English longbow was a very important part of England's military
power. The medieval English government had rules regarding the longbow
and its use, including compulsory ownership of bows by a certain class of cit-
izen. When King Henry II was in power, all who earned two to five pounds
per annum were literally forced to own a longbow. Many archers were
required by law to practice on Sundays. These rules made sense because, as

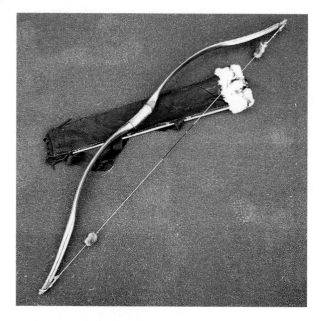

*Ed Scott's traditional
self-bows "shoot hard"
and have proved
themselves in the big
game field.*

we traditional archers know today, meaningful practice keeps those arrows zapping into the target.

The English longbow was a self-bow—a bow made of one material only, in this case, wood. Yew was a popular wood for the longbow, although it is believed that English yew was not preferred. Rather, yew from Spain and Italy was sought by the British to make their bows. Apparently, a regular supply was ensured because for each ton of imported goods from these countries, including wine, the importer had to promise a number of yew staves for bow-making.

Ease of manufacture was another reason why the longbow was so popular. In medieval times when the bow was employed in warfare, a bowyer could build an English self-bow in a couple hours. Imagine trying to make a Mongol bow that fast. In more modern times, as traditional archery was poised to rise again, the Thompson brothers, Pope and Young, and other pioneers could make an English longbow in the backyard. And that was very important.

Draw weights for the English longbow fell in the 80- to 120-pound range, according to some historians, but of course they may have varied greatly, as they still do today. The draw length of these bows is calculated at 29 to 32 inches. That tells us that the archer of Olde England was not drawing to an anchor point at corner of mouth or cheekbone. If armor is any indication, the knight of the era was no taller than we are and perhaps even shorter on the

Left: In the beginnings of archery there were hundreds of variations, not only of bows, but also of arrows. This handmade arrow was made from a piece of square-shaped wood, as you can see by looking closely. It has three small notches cut near the self-nock so the archer can tell the direction of the cock feather by feel.
Right: This handmade wooden arrow has a self-nock cut right into the back of the shaft. It also has a tiny nail to be used as a tactical indicator to note the direction of the cock feather.

average. If he did the Howard Hill anchor point, the bow's draw length would probably run around 26 inches. So his draw was probably "to the ear" or "to the breast." An illustration in *Sport with Gun and Rod*, 1883, in an article by Maurice Thompson, "Bow-Shooting," shows an archer drawing his bow to the ear, as I believe Maurice did. Like Maurice, medieval archers would have used their own judgement in determining where to make an anchor point.

The American archer also inherited the English arrow. It was made of birch, ash, elm, witch hazel, yew, and other woods. The English longbow arrow had to be tough, with draw weights of 80 to 120 pounds. Known also as livery, sheaf, and standard, these arrows were thick. That they were the "clothyard shafts" of three feet plus one inch is probably not true—at least in terms of today's twelve-inch feet. One source says that at the time "natural feet" were 9.9 inches long, so three times 9.9 plus 1 would be 30.7 inches. Actual arrows from the Mary Rose are reported to be 30 to 31 inches long, which makes more sense.

From some of the stories you hear, you'd expect the old English longbow to all but penetrate modern tank armor at 200 yards or better. Pope surely proved that at close range the English longbow could, and did, penetrate a mail coat, but some of these other stories may be more fanciful. Taking nothing away from these bows, the problem with history is the story goes through a lot of people, who sometimes alter the facts, instead of "telling it like it is," telling it the way it sounds better or pleases more *important* people. The point is, we have to study archery from what the historians were able to save for us, even if sometimes the facts are not as factual as they could be. But most of the information from the past is interesting and useful to the modern traditional archer who has an interest in the forerunners of his or her bow.

The English longbow was only one of many excellent bows of the past, though the others had a less profound effect on the comeback of traditional archery. The Mongol bow is one of the best. In point of fact, this bow was, and still is, superior to the English longbow, and one of its type can be purchased today from Recurvebowshop.com. This company offers Hungarian, Roman, Hunnish, and other unique bow styles. The Mongol bow is included here because it represents a piece of archery history that has come down to us sparingly, although not lost. As I am able to understand the dynamics of this bow, they are of symmetrical limb design, both limbs being of the same length (not true of all bow types). As I point out in Chapter 16, one way to quiet a recurve bow is to include a buffer where string meets limb. The Mongol bow has similar "string pads" for stopping the string almost immediately after the arrow is away. These were not for quietness, however, but to immediately stop string motion.

Unlike the English longbow, the Mongol bow is composite, constructed of mixed materials. The core is wood but the belly of the bow (the part facing toward the archer) is composed of horn, and the back of the bow of sinew. These bows were glued (possibly with fish glue), as are the composite traditional bows of today (with modern adhesives). The Mongol bow also has a string-run or string bridge made of horn, leather, or wood, which supports the string. The limbs, when unstrung, face forward in an amazing arc for energy storage. While not a direct ancestor of today's mainstream traditional bows, the Mongol bow deserves inclusion in this book because of its advanced design.

Though the longbows/recurves used today in the United States are usually descendants of the English longbow, the American Indian bow no doubt also had some influence in the return of traditional archery. After all,

everyone who has seen even a single "Cowboy and Indian" movie has watched arrows flying on the screen. And certainly the Indian bow is of all types the "most American."

Before the coming of the Europeans to the vast territory ruled by the Native American, the major hunting and war tool was the bow and arrow, although the tomahawk ranked high in the Indian's arsenal along with clubs and spears. The bow accounted for most game. Bison (American buffalo) *were* stampeded over cliffs, but not in the numbers some conclude from bone graveyards found today; with a vicious winter coming on, securing robes, tent material, and meat put any relative of "sportsmanship" into the shade. The bow was the only weapon of those days that had any real range. It was a prime weapon of war for the same reason.

Ed Scott of Owl Bows creates extremely fine examples of self-bows in the style of the American Indians.

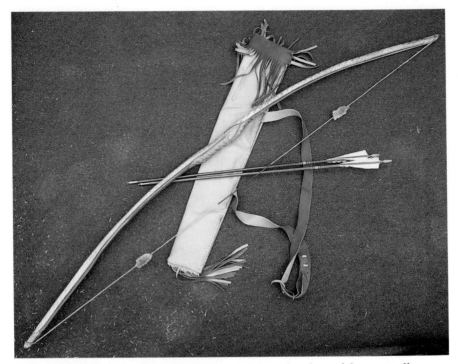

The simple self-bow, made of a single material, served archers of the past well.

Osborne Russell, in his *Journal of a Trapper*, printed by the University of Nebraska Press, describes some handsome examples of Indian tackle he saw working as a trapper from 1834 to 1843. "They were well armed with bows and arrows pointed with obsidian," he wrote in his journal. "The bows were beautifully wrought from Sheep, Buffaloe, and Elk horns secured with Deer and Elk sinews and ornamented with porcupine quills and generally about 3 feet long." Russell's work is a reliable report of the fur trade era, confirmed by historians and archaeologists.

While records are sketchy at best, making the assumption that some of the mountain men (fur trappers) in the far west of the 1800s used bows part of the time makes sense. They certainly adopted most of the Indians' means of survival or they would have perished in their first winter. The first Americans on the plains knew how to survive. The white settlers knew how to survive too—but their practices were better suited to survival back east. Burn up your powder and ball for a rabbit or grouse supper? Or even a deer or antelope? Maybe, but you wouldn't have a new supply of lead or propellant until rendezvous time when you traded your beaver pelts. And though the

A self-bow launches an arrow. While not as fast as a modern composite traditional bow, the self-bow still gets the job done.

territory was vast, firing a shot needlessly might bring in Bug's Boys, as trappers called the dangerous Blackfoot tribe. A mountain man with a bow could accomplish a lot.

Though records of the fur trapper carrying bows and arrows are slim, modern-day renactors of the fur trade era have bow shooting contests as part of the fun. I had a chance to try out the bows present at one rendezvous. Most were self-bows, a few with composite backing to increase efficiency, all strictly modeled after the Indian sticks of yore. A dedicated buckskinner by the name of Jack "Traveling Dog" Tripp allowed me to shoot some of his handmade bows of primitive design made of oak, Osage orange, and hickory, some backed with sinew or snakeskin. Jack's arrows were made by Mrs. Tripp to match the bows, each in traditional Indian style and marked to show ownership.

While we "owe a debt hard to pay" to the fathers of the American archery comeback, they would not have built a single bow without their predecessors leading the way with examples, especially the English longbow, which remains the cornerstone of this return. Fortunately, very few bows of

The Indian-style bow continues to prove its mettle in the field, just as it provided for the American Indians long ago. This modern-day bow was handmade by Ed Scott of Owl Bows.

the past are gone forever. There are finely made Indian-style bows available today, as well as Eskimo bows and of course the interesting Mongol bow. The Howard Hill–type longbow, so reminiscent of its English parent, is also far from gone. Mostly, however, longbows and recurves coming from today's custom archery shop are of composite design, with laminated limbs capable of casting an arrow far downrange. And of course, as we know, that means good initial arrow speed because speed is cast.

3

Fathers of
Traditional Archery

An entire book—a rather large and interesting book—could be written about the archers responsible for the great popularity of traditional bow shooting today. The names engraved in this hall of fame would not all be from the distant past either. How many present-day traditional bow shooters have been influenced by the great magazine *Traditional Bowhunter*? We will never know the number, but we do know that T. J. Conrads, the pub-lisher, took a chance in turning dream into reality. And his gamble paid off. What influence did Stacy Groscup have as admirers watched his arrows smoking aspirins out of the air? Did onlookers decide to in-vestigate the traditional bow after witnessing this traditional bow shooter's skill? The great Byron Fur-guson's arrow from his longbow snuffs a candle flame. That has to stimulate the imagination.

And so this chapter begins with an apology to the many greats who I could not include in this short chap-ter, people like Glenn St. Charles, Bob Swinehart, and the unbelievably gifted Howard Hill. How about Fred Bear, who put affordable bows into the hands of thousands of archers? Ben Pearson championed good bows—thanks, Ben, for my 75-pound longbow that gave me so

The great Byron Ferguson wows crowds with his unerring ability to send arrows straight to the mark. Here, he fires an arrow behind his back as he looks into a mirror. A great influence on all who see him shoot, he can be considered one of the fathers of traditional archery.

Archery legend Howard Hill shooting a bow. PHOTO FROM T. J. CONRADS'S PERSONAL ARCHIVES.

much pleasure. And we must honor all those unsung heroes, the bowyers whose talents continue to bring forth the finest longbows and recurves of any era.

But narrow down we must, and so we turn to two brothers who took up the longbow more out of necessity at the time than desire. Return to the American Civil War. Georgia, one of the original thirteen states, joined the fray on January 19, 1861, seceeding from the Union to join a losing cause. General Sherman marched across her beautiful landscape in 1864, capturing Atlanta on September 2 and Savannah on December 21, leaving a swath of grave destruction in his wake.

Among the homes leveled was that of Will and Maurice Thompson. These two brothers were not Georgians by birth; both were born in Fairfield, Indiana—James Madison Thompson in 1844, (he later changed his name to James Maurice), and William Henry Thompson in 1848. Their father, a Baptist preacher, moved to the Cherokee Hill country of Georgia in 1853. He produced cash crops on three hundred acres of farmland to augment his meager salary as a man of the cloth. Maurice (who never went by James) and his brother Will grew up best friends, making their own bows and arrows as youths often did before the electronic age. Of course, they crafted their own tackle. A few bows and arrows could be purchased at the time, especially in New York, but not in Georgia. The boys learned the art of shooting through the taskmaster called experience and with the help of a mentor named Williams, a hermit and also an archer in the best English classic tradition. It was Williams who taught the brothers proper employment of the strung stick.

Meanwhile, Mother Thompson tutored her sons in the art of clear thinking through diligent reading, a legacy that favors us to this day because both boys became authors, especially Maurice. Father Thompson owned no slaves. He even belonged to a Yankee group in Georgia. But when it came time for his sons to choose sides, the brothers went with the South. After all, the South was their home. Maurice joined first in December of 1862, signing with the 63rd Regiment of Georgia Volunteers. He was eighteen years old. Will joined the Fourth Infantry of Georgia in 1863. He was only fifteen. Little is known of

Maurice (left) and
Will (right) Thompson.
PHOTO FROM T. J. CONRADS'S
PERSONAL ARCHIVES.

Will's service. But we do know that Maurice was wounded and taken prisoner of war. Eventually, he was granted a parole pass issued in Hampton, Georgia, on May 12, 1865, which read, "The bearer 3d Lieut. J.M. Thompson of Co. D Johnsons Regiment of Ga. Cav. C.S.A. a prisoner of the army of North Ga. has permission to go to his home and there remain undisturbed." But there was no home to return to after Sherman's "march to the sea."

The farmland lay in ruins; the treasured library was burned to the ground, the domicile itself all but unlivable. Maurice and Will kept the vultures at bay by raising a few crops, making cider, and selling squirrel tails for ten cents apiece. But there was a catch. As defeated Southerners they were not allowed firearms on pain of imprisonment. And so they returned to their first love—the longbow. Archery became much more than sport. In 1866 the brothers hunted the swamplands with a black friend named Jordon; their first outing ran a full month. Their small game bows, as they called them, drew 40 to 50 pounds and their big game bows drew 60 to 70, except for one special "snakewood" stick that pulled 90 pounds. (How draw weight was assessed is not revealed in Maurice's writing.)

This illustration from "Bow-Shooting," by Maurice Thompson, printed in Sport with Gun and Rod, *shows Thompson stringing a longbow using the push-pull method.*

Otter skin belt quivers bore their arrows. Some of these arrows were made of reeds for small game and birds. Others were stouter darts for big game. The brothers would shoot three hundred arrows, sometimes more, on a single hunt. Their quarry included deer, black bear, pumas (cougars), wild turkeys, bobcats and other animals. But it was birds that brought in the cash. Herons and other feather-bearing avians provided the fantastic plumes that graced the hats of the fashionable ladies of the period. And so the young men were essentially professional hunters. Maurice never ventured outside the United States. But Will did. He hunted in British Columbia in 1911, ten years after the passing of his older brother. Of course, he was allowed to carry a firearm by then. But it was the bow that remained his favorite for life. Will was National Archery Champion five times. It was he who influenced the great archers to follow: Chief Compton, Saxon Pope, Arthur Young—all of whom came to him for instruction.

While Will worked as a lawyer for the railroad, his brother Maurice, also a lawyer, became a national figure in the field of literature. He was also a poet

This illustration from "Bow-Shooting" shows Maurice Thompson drawing and anchoring a longbow with a broadhead arrow. Thomspon's anchor point is just below eye level, just like those of many archers today.

and a novelist. His pen poured out words for *Scribner's Monthly, Harper's,* and *Appleton Journal,* prestigious periodicals. He wrote about natural history, science, and adventure. But for us, his archery articles and one great book rise above the rest of his efforts. *The Witchery of Archery,* first printed in 1878, with another printing in 1879, and still available in reprint today (from Three Rivers Archery) resides on my bookshelf among books intended for rereading. My favorite chapter, "Three Weeks a Savage Life," describes Maurice's days hunting with Tommy, an American Indian archer.

"What days spent coasting about the fingers of the inlets for wild-fowl," Maurice wrote, "or stalking the thickets and savannahs for turkeys! When I think of it now, I can hear the dull 'flap' of Tommy's bow and the 'tshe-e-e-e' of his deadly arrow, ending with a 'chuck,' as it puffed feathers from a duck or struck a turkey through and through, and I live those days over again." It was *The Witchery of Archery* that prompted me and my bow-shooting partner, the late Ted Walter, to go afield for days on end with nothing but bows and arrows—what we called "survival hunts." Our bows alone provided us with

A depiction of shooting for distance from "Bow-Shooting."

meat. Our longest trek was two full months spent living off the land. Looking back, I know the time could have been spent seeking a fortune. But I have no regrets.

Sport with Rod and Gun, printed in 1883, carried a section by Maurice Thompson entitled "Bow-Shooting." The author explained how to make bows and tackle, along with illustrations of both. He also gave interesting advice on practice, writing, "If you begin your practice for the purpose of learning to shoot wild game by 'flood and field,' you must not use a target at a fixed distance. [The archer] gets used to a certain size, color, and condition of *background,* and when he gets into the woods and lifts his bow to draw on bird or hare, his accustomed rings and dark background are not there." It is better, Maurice suggested, to shoot at "a black rubber ball four inches in diameter, suspended in mid-air by a string fastened to the low limb of an apple tree." The times were different, of course, and the brothers were fond of shooting targets we eschew today, including woodpeckers, a favored mark.

The brothers shot instinctively, with no bow sights at all, just as we manage longbows and recurves today. "You will never be a good shot," Maurice taught, "till all of the operations of archery are performed as naturally and almost involuntarily as your breathing." He went on to say, "A meadow-lark shows its yellow breast in a bunch of clover blossoms thirty yards ahead—you pause instantly, throw up your bow quickly, gracefully draw an arrow to the head, let go sharply—all with little effort. . . with which you take so many steps in walking." (They did shoot at everything!) Maurice was not the only instructor; in fact, Will was probably more the teacher. But it was Maurice who could weave a beautiful fabric with words.

"I well remember," he wrote, "an old curmudgeon whom we ran across in a Florida woods. He carried a flint-locked rifle, nearly six feet long, and wore what, some twenty years before, had been a beaver tile [high silk hat]. He helped himself to an enormous quid [cut] of smoking fine cut, and forthwith began to ply us with questions about our weapons." Will and Maurice proudly displayed their bows and arrows, but the old gentleman only remarked, "Ye couldn't gi' me a thousand o' them 'ere bows!" The Thompsons did not consider their handcrafted bows the finest. As Maurice said, "No home-made bow or target-arrows can half-way equal those beautiful weapons made by Philip Highfield of London, England."

No one will know how many archers were touched by Will directly through his target shooting and the close personal contact he unselfishly gave to all who showed interest in drawing a good bow. Nor can we assess the value of Maurice's writings. What we do know is that the brothers were the first Americans to lift bowhunting from historical to a present-day activity and a new level of favor. They gave the bow the status it deserved then and deserves now. They were true fathers of modern traditional archery, influencing the greats to follow. Saxon Pope summarized it perfectly when he wrote," To Will and Maurice Thompson we owe a debt of gratitude hard to pay."

Now we turn to a man who lived in a modern era, but whose way of life came from a time long ago, his tribe relying on Stone Age survival skills to make a living as hunters and gatherers. He was named Ishi, a name bestowed by Dr. A. L. Kroeber, head of the University of California Department of Anthropology. (Kroeber took the name from the Old Testament book of Hosea, chapter 2, verse 16: "And it shall be at that day, saith the Lord, that thou shall call me Ishi [husband]; and thou shalt call me no more Baali [master].") Ishi also meant *man* in Yana. Ishi was said to be the last member of his Yana tribe, all others pursued to their destruction in the mountains of Northern California. Recent and perhaps more reliable scientific investigation informs that the Ishi story is faulty at best. He probably was not the last member of his tribe, nor even a full-blooded Yana. So the inscription etched

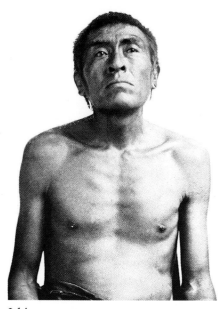

Ishi. PHOTO FROM T. J. CONRADS'S PERSONAL ARCHIVES.

into the little black jar containing his cremated remains, "Ishi, the Last Yana Indian, 1916," is at the very least suspect.

We know very little for certain about Ishi's life. He is believed to have been born some time around 1860. According to one version of the story, he was found in a corral, naked, shivering, exhausted, and hungry. Another version has Ishi located by butchers outside a slaughterhouse near Oroville, California. Historians think he was found on August 29, 1911. He was jailed. Kroeber, along with T. T. Waterman, another anthropologist, befriended the lonely man, giving him a place to live in the anthropology museum. We do know he died, probably of tuberculosis, on March 25, 1916 (he was guessed to be in his mid-fifties at this time).

Regardless, this man (who never revealed his real name), this Ishi, had a great impact on archery. Without Ishi, we might never have known, or even heard of, Saxon Pope. There never would have been a Pope & Young Club. Pope was a physician called in to examine Ishi, whose immune system must have been weak, as he had had no contact since birth with mumps, measles, T.B. and other ailments. We do know for certain, as one biographer wrote, that "Ishi, like other California Indians of his time, was an excellent archer." Pope took great interest in Ishi's bows and arrows as his new friend took interest in him as a white man. It was Ishi who taught the doctor how to make primitive tackle. The two hunted together in the mountains of Northern California. Ishi's impact on Saxon Pope led him into a world of archery that lasted a lifetime.

Pope's *Hunting with the Bow and Arrow,* a book that played a large role in the return of archery to its former glory, begins with "The Story of the Last Yana Indian." Pope was an instructor in surgery at the University Medical School when Ishi was employed as a janitor at the nearby museum, Pope says, "to teach him modern industry and the value of money." Pope also assesses that Ishi was "perfectly happy and a great favorite with everybody." And then came the bows and arrows. "He taught me how to make bows and arrows, how to shoot them, and how to hunt," Pope writes. Back in his own mountain territory, Ishi demonstrated many outdoor skills. "We swam the streams together, hunted deer and small game, and at night sat under the stars by the camp fire," Pope continues. Saxon was with Ishi at his passing, directing his medications "and gently stroking his hand as a small sign of fellowship and sympathy."

Saxton Pope kneeling to shoot. PHOTO FROM T. J. CONRADS'S PERSONAL ARCHIVES.

The second chapter of *Hunting with the Bow and Arrow* deals with "How Ishi Made His Bow and Arrow and His Methods of Shooting." Chapter 3 continues with "Ishi's Methods of Hunting." Being of a scientific mind, Pope asked questions about archery, such as, "How would an arrow fly if the bow were held in a mechanical rest and the string released by a mechanical release?" And "What is the effect of placing the cock feather next to the bow?" Interestingly, in answer to the last query, Pope said that placing the cock feather inward rather than outward caused the arrow to divert and drop lower, which is contrary to my own findings. But then I do not know what arrow Pope was shooting, with what fletching, or with what kind of riser.

After teaming up with Art Young, Pope followed serious hunting trails, even facing the mighty grizzly with nothing but a bow and arrow. After a study of the big bear's anatomy, the two archers agreed that, "after all, he was only made of

Ishi dressing game. PHOTO FROM T. J. CONRADS'S PERSONAL ARCHIVES.

Art Young with a lion. PHOTO FROM T. J. CONRADS'S PERSONAL ARCHIVES.

flesh and blood, and our arrows were capable of solving that problem," the problem being how to get the bear rather than the bear getting you. And so the hunters—"Mr. Compton, Mr. Young" and of course Pope—went to test this conclusion. A photograph appearing on page 237 of my copy of *Hunting with Bow and Arrow* has a caption reading, "The Great Kadiak [*sic*] Bear Brought Low."

Another book by Saxon Pope, *The Adventurous Bowmen* (published in 1926), deals with hunting in Africa with bow and arrow. I know of no other books by this traditional archer. But these two certainly had an impact on bow shooting. In the foreword of *Hunting with Bow and Arrow,* Joe St. Charles writes that Pope's work "served to inspire and create the hundreds of thousands of bowhunters who later were able to put the bow and arrow in its rightful place." The links are there. From prehistoric times, the history of traditional archery goes from Otzi the Ice Man wandering the high country of the Italian Alps, to a much later Maurice and Will Thompson, onward to Ishi crafting his own archery tackle as Otzi had to, followed by the likes of Fred Bear, Ben Pearson, Howard Hill, right into the 21st century—to us.

Ben Pearson (left)
PHOTO FROM T. J.
CONRADS'S PERSONAL
ARCHIVES.

Howard Hill
PHOTO FROM T. J.
CONRADS'S PERSONAL
ARCHIVES.

4

Bows that Came Before

Before going into bow geometry, draw weight, setup and tuning, testing, and other aspects of traditional archery, a short journey into the past is not only interesting, but also helpful in understanding the evolution that brings us to our longbows and recurves of today. Moreover, traditional archery is much more than simply seeing how fast an arrow can be sent downrange, or how further mechanical manipulation can make longbows and recurves easier and easier to shoot, bringing them further and further away from stickbows. The traditional archer is deeply interested in the history of the sport

We are not interested in strict chronology here, just in touching on bows that came before ours, for a fuller understanding of archery in general and our bows in particular. Archaeologists place the first bows as far back as 40,000 years ago. The raw mechanical function of these machines was, as it still is with our bows, a sort of lever system, the hand being the fulcrum for the bending limbs, since the midsection of the bow does not flex (or if so very

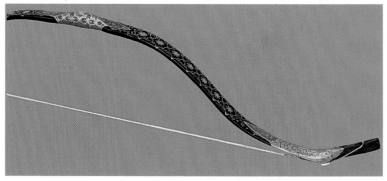

A master bowyer in Hungary, Csaba Grózer, has recreated many bows of the Turks, Mongols, Scythians, and others. This photo illustrates the beauty of these bows of the past. PHOTO COURTESY OF HUNARCHERY.

little). While early bows, like that of the Ice Man, which we will talk about in more detail later, had to be quite long to function fluidly, composite examples came along later to allow much shorter bows, especially important for archers on horseback. Egyptian soldiers had composite bows. So did Chinese soldiers. The recurve design came along, perhaps in Central Asia, around 1000 B.C. Persian archers had recurve bows by 500 B.C.

Today, archers can buy replicas of many bows that came before. Going online to Hunarchery.com is an education in itself. Csaba Grózer lives in a small village in Hungary where he builds custom bows in his well-equipped shop. His bows replicate the past: Mongol, Hunnish, Avar, Hungarian, Indo-Persian, Crimean Tartar, Assyrian, and other kinds of bows. From childhood, Grózer was enamored of all things outdoors as well as archery history, especially since Hungary was so rich in various bows that, for their era, were remarkable. And so an archer today can actually shoot a Mongol bow or a Syrian bow or a Tartar bow—or one of our own American Indian bows. Grózer's bows are showcased in this chapter.

THE ICE MAN'S BOW

The latest scientific dating on Otzi, the Ice Man, places this archer in the Stone Age about 5,000 years ago. His mummified body, found in a glacier in the Italian Alps, "reveals the secrets of the Stone Age," as one author put it. The recovery began as a routine removal of a body, since this occurs often in the Alps when modern-day hikers get lost. The result was considerable damage to a treasure of ancient equipment, not only Otzi's bow and archery tackle, but his many other pieces of equipment. The bow, which is our main interest here, was broken during recovery. Piecing it together again, we have a longbow 182 centimeters (71 inches) long, taller than its owner, who was only 160.5 centimeters (63 inches) tall (although that figure may well be less than his height in life).

The bow was protruding up out of the ice because it had been set against a boulder with care. Sadly, the part sticking out of the ice was snapped right off. The recovers did not know what it was. To them it appeared as a stick. When the broken part was removed from the ice to join the main piece, it proved to be a bow, but unlike other ancient bows that have been found, it was unfinished. Its owner was not granted the time to do that—evidence shows that he was probably murdered. The bow stave was made of yew, an absolutely suitable wood. Otzi's would-be bow had been carefully trimmed and the belly was evenly rounded. The stave was gracefully tapered to two trim ends. There were no bow nocks, which led to the belief that the string was just tied on. But we do not know that for sure; Otzi may well have planned to make the limb nocks later. The concluding fact is that the Ice Man's bow was a well-thought-out instrument of good potential.

While these very old bows are not nearly as ancient at the Ice Man's bow, they represent the same basic construction. They are self-bows, just like Otzi's, made only of wood, and plain in design, but very functional all the same.

THE ROMAN BOW

So how do we know what those ancients bows were like? Fortunately, archeologists have managed to find real examples, which the fantastic bowyers of our time (like Grozer) use to recreate these bows of long ago. In spite of real life examples, we don't know the exact nature of certain "bows that came before." Our knowledge of Roman bow manufacture in the 4th century A.D. may not be entirely complete, but it is good enough for our purposes. We know, for example, that the Roman bow was composite and very deadly in the field. The Roman legions may have lost a few battles, but not the war, with their military prowess under intelligent leaders and a senate that supported the troops.

The upper limb on many examples of Roman bows is longer than the lower limb and some experts believe this was a widespread trait. One recovered bow was assessed as having a draw weight of 60 to 80 pounds; it was impossible to pin it down closer due to condition of the example.

While the composite was the true Roman battle bow, evidence points to self-bows of wood as well, of a rather typical longbow design, probably used for training purposes. While bows are the main interest here, the arrows fired by Roman soldiers deserve a word or two. There were broadhead-tipped arrows designed to sever muscle and blood vessels, plus a narrower "bodkin" for penetrating body armor and shields. Grozer's replica of a Roman bow is 58$\frac{1}{2}$ inches long unstrung, 53 inches strung, with draw weight ranging from 30 to 60 pounds, a maximum draw length of 32 inches, and a fistmele of 6$\frac{1}{4}$ inches.

THE TURKISH BOW

When we think of the Turkish bow today, images of arrows flying very far come to mind. Flight shooting was definitely a pastime of the Turkish archer—and is once again today, after almost dying out. The Turkish bow is a recurve composite. The Turks had their own mounted cavalry and a short bow was perfect for battle from the back of a horse. The short length of the Turkish bow was ideal for a solider on horseback, but the bow was not hampered in arrow flight by its shortness. In fact, it proved ideal for sending a specialized arrow far.

Construction of the ancient Turkish bow followed the classic Asiatic design in composite form. It had a wooden core, often of strong maple; animal horn on the face of the bow; and sinew on the back. It was held together by animal glue, as was the Mongol bow—this could be a problem in wet weather. Unstrung, the Turkish bow takes an abrupt C-shape, with "bent forward limbs." Flight archery followed the decline of the bow in battle, and the Turks became best known for achieving great distances with their special

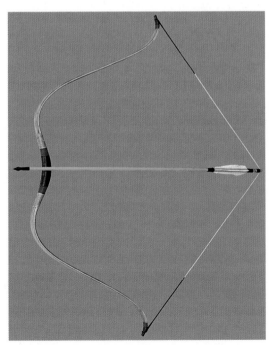

Another example of an ancient bow of advanced design for its era—or any era—a Scythian bow. Again, this is a Csaba Grózer replica. PHOTO
COURTESY OF HUNARCHERY.

flight arrows. History shows the art of Turkish bow making declined sharply in the late 1800s and almost perished altogether in the 1930s with the death of the "last" bowyer to continue the tradition—Necmeddin Okyay. But it made a comeback: today, you can buy a Grozer replica of an ancient Turkish bow. It is only 51$\frac{1}{2}$-inches long unstrung and when strung is a very short 44$\frac{1}{2}$-inches long. Choice of draw weight runs from 30 to 60 pounds with a maximum draw length of 32 inches and a brace height of eight inches.

MONGOL BOW

Another important historical bow, the Mongol bow was a "high-tech" instrument for its time. The Mongol archer was known for his horsemanship as well as archery skills. The Mongol hordes conquered and ruled the largest land mass empire in the history of the world. And it was the Mongol bow that played a major role in these victories. In most wars, the army with the best weapons wins, and the Mongol bow was up to the task. It was built around a wooden core with horn on the belly and some form of animal sinew on the back, all bound with glues. In effect, the bow was a laminate.

Highly recurved with super strength, the Mongol bow could wield a great deal of force from a very compact package. Historians credit some of these bows with a draw weight over 150 pounds, even up to 160 pounds. It is not beyond comprehension that a Mongol archer of high practice with built-up muscular power to pull such a strong bow could fire his arrow over 500 yards. And at closer range there can be no doubt that the Mongol bow would send an arrow through most protective body armor and shields. The

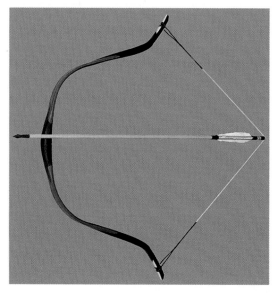

The Mongol bow was remarkable for its era-built with clear thinking and knowledge of mechanical principles. The reproduction is by Csaba Grózer of Hunarchery. PHOTO COURTESY OF HUNARCHERY.

Mongol archer-soldier did not avail himself of heavy armor, but rather relied on the speed of his horse to avoid being captured or killed. The horse-mounted Mongol was the light artillery of the day. The Grozer Mongol bow replica is $62^{1}/_{4}$ inches unstrung and $54^{3}/_{4}$ inches strung, with draw weights ranging from 30 to 75 pounds, a maximum draw length of 32 inches, and a brace height of $7^{5}/_{8}$ inches.

ESKIMO BOW

When I lived in Fairbanks, Alaska, I had a chance to see a few very old Eskimo bows. They were interesting mainly in the variance of design. Alaska's Digital Archives shows that all these bows were truly Eskimo; there was not just one particular type. One example is a sinew-backed (24 sinew strands wrapped around a central sinew cord) Eskimo bow made from spruce wood. Shell and horn complement the sinew of this bow. It is broad and flat, tapering to round knobs on the end. This bow is $52^{1}/_{2}$ inches long unstrung and 2 inches wide through the grip area. It is flat on one side, keeled from end to end, with a furrowed center on the other side. The Eskimo bow, in general, was short and composite in design, entirely suited for hunting from a kayak or traveling on a dog sled, where space was limited.

PENOBSCOT BOW

Of all the intriguing bows that came before, one of the most ingenious is the Penobscot. In my visits to Maine I made it a point to visit these gracious, intelligent, and handsome people, and I got to examine their traditional bow. This bow is perhaps the most difficult to describe in print. It has been called the Native American Double Bow and the Penobscot Coastal Native American Double Bow. Double is the operative word because this bow does have two sets of limbs, the main limb coupled with a shorter outer limb. The string goes from the main limb to a secondary shorter limb in front of the main limb.

In effect, though it is not entirely of a mechanical nature, this is a compound bow. It is hand-built, to be sure, and of wood, but the double limbs allow a change in draw weight by effectively changing the length of the back strings. Pete Ward reports that, "The back bow and strings help reduce string follow, adding to [arrow] speed." The writer continues, "This bow also sports lower hand shock as well as accuracy." Another feature cited was the adjustable draw weight, which helps match the arrow spine—the bow could be weight-tuned to better match a particular arrow. "To adjust the draw weight simply put the bow on a bench with each tip on a 1" block of wood. Now clamp the handle down to the bench bending the limb slightly backward. This will relieve string pressure. Take the old string off and twist it 2–3 times tighter." Primitive Archer online (http://primitivearcher.com) is a good source of information for bows like this.

ISHI'S BOW

Since the American Indian Ishi is one of our heroes in this book, a look at his bows through the eyes of Dr. Saxton Pope is in order. Pope wrote that "The workmanship of Ishi was by far the best of any Indian in America; compared to thousands of specimens in the museum, his arrows were the most carefully made; his bow was the best." Ishi, who never revealed his true name for religious reasons, called his bow *man-nee*. Pope relates that it was a "short, flat piece of mountain juniper backed with sinew. The length was forty-two inches, or, as he [Ishi] measured it, from the horizontally extended hand to the opposite hip." The bow was broadest at the center of each limb at about two-inch width.

The cross section of the bow was ovoid, or egg-shaped. This shape is important in describing Ishi's bow because it would have been found in every bow he made. It was not haphazardly chosen, but had operational significance. Pope says the wood for the bow was "obtained by splitting a limb from a tree and utilizing the outer layers, including the sap wood. By scraping and rubbing on sandstone, he shaped and finished it [the bow]." Ishi recurved the tips of the limbs by "bending the wood backward over a heated stone."

Ishi backed his bow with sinew. "First he made a glue from boiling salmon skin and applying it to the roughened back of the bow. When it was dry he laid on long strips of deer sinew obtained from the leg tendons. By chewing these tendons and separating the fibers, they became soft and adhesive. Carefully overlapping the ends of the numerous fibers he covered the entire back very thickly. At the nock ends he surrounded the wood completely and added a circular binding around the bow." Pope's account is fascinating because it shows that Ishi no doubt learned bow making from the teachings of someone else, who learned from another teacher, who got his information from yet another instructor, going back to the first inventor who realized that a sinew-backed bow would be stronger and have greater cast.

ALL-METAL BOWS

The late Val Forgett, a collector of rare and wonderful things, sent me a Persian all-metal bow. He did not know for sure exactly how old it was, but believed it was "very old." Of course, I did not try to shoot it. It came complete with a set of arrows. Metal bows were also manufactured in the United States following World War II, before the days of quality fiberglass. Mass production was the goal: good bows at a good price with a decent markup for profit. Several were made entirely of aluminum. At least one was constructed of

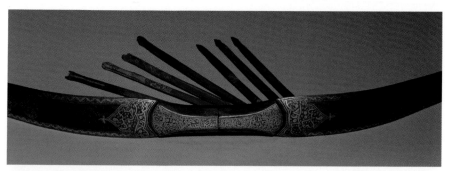

All-metal bows have been made for centuries; this one is from Ancient Persia.

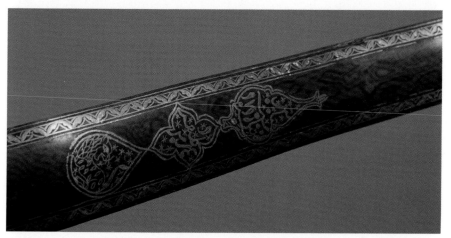

A close view of the Persian bow suggests that it was intended for art more than function. The details are clearly the work of an artisan.

The arrows that came with the Persian bow are also of fine workmanship and detail. The points resemble much later English arrowheads designed to penetrate armor— though these arrows may have only been ornamental.

magnesium, which immediately slaughtered anything like a good cheap price for the finished product. Seefab of Sweden made steel bows, both longbows and recurves, which were tubular in construction. These bows pulled apart in the handle, which was a steel tube covered in cork. A green-colored model, supposedly a British Commando bow, had a single pin sight. Metal bows had a good deal of hand shock and were subject to fatigue failure. The availability of good fiberglass put an end to the American metal bow, but Seefab continued to produce them for a while.

The Seefab takedown bow from Sweden was made entirely out of metal.

This is a Swedish all-metal takedown bow.

The bows that came before are important to those of us who appreciate the traditional bow today because each type represented a stepping stone in advancement while still retaining its rich history. All cultures that had a bow reveled in its uniqueness—the Apache, Egyptian, Chinese, Japanese, Korean—and all of these bows remained in power long after the musket was developed. A talented archer could send out numerous darts while the musket-shooter fiddled with powder, ball, and one of the different ignition systems from matchlock to flintlock and finally percussion. As for accuracy, the practiced archer had an edge over the blunderbuss shooter. In *Shogun* we see a Japanese archer cluster arrows far closer together than the Englishman could do with his firearm. That was a fictional story, but the shooting described in it is not fiction. The Japanese archer with his great (very) long bow could outshoot the muskets of the same feudal time.

While most of the manufacturing styles were abandoned as the modern traditional composite bow came to be, many of the principles remain in force. Laminated limbs, for example, do what sinew once did in producing strength and cast. The twentieth-century bowyer, and now the twenty-first-century artisan, learned much from the bows that came before.

We see, for example, the Wilson brothers, Bob, Jack, and Norman, refining idea after idea until the Black Widow recurve bow of the late 1940s became a reality. That bow was designed with wood core limbs between

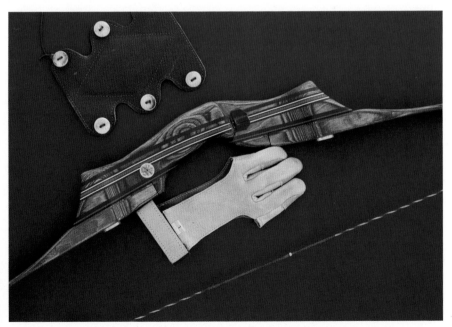

Today's Black Widow bow continues the Wilson brothers' legacy of excellence.

fiberglass laminations. The year 1957 saw the Black Widow bow on the market commercially. Black Widow left the scene around 1976, but was picked up again by the talented Ken Beck. This was the computer age now and Ken of course had the design formally studied through scientific methods. Very little change was required to make the current Black Widow bow shoot smoother or faster than the original. In the mid-1960s I wanted a Black Widow bow but I did not get one for a very long time to come.

Today, the march goes on to make the best possible bow *without* trampling on the legacy of the bow that continues to perform without mechanical enhancement (although perhaps the Penobscot bow mildly challenges this). At Pronghorn Custom Bows, as just one example of continued experimentation, the bowyer has come up with something "new." Actually, the bow is not new in thought but in success. The first all-glass limb bows were advertised as the best thing to come along since indoor plumbing, but in fact these early all-glass bows did not compete well in performance. By using modern technology and materials, an all-glass-limb bow was born that drew smoothly, shot a fast arrow, and would not delaminate readily in a warm environment. On the long trail into the hinterlands, this tough bow was a match for the terrain and the dozens of mishaps that can occur in the outback. It did not replace the fine composite limb bows of this particular bowyer, but the all-glass limb bow is another testament to the fact that the stickbow evolution is far from over.

5

Bow Geometry

Longbows and recurves differ tremendously in handling and shooting characteristics, and these differences are perceived differently by individual archers: "I can shoot a longbow a lot better than I can shoot a recurve." I've heard that more than once, as well as the exact opposite. The great Howard Hill claimed he was not "good enough" to shoot a recurve bow accurately. Of course, he *was* good enough. He simply preferred the longbow. Meanwhile, a number of archers go the other way.

Not only do bows vary from one type to another, individual bows vary. An archer may try several different longbows, finding that each one performs differently in his hand, and the same with recurves. That is why it is important for the archer to try different bows from various bowyers in order

Bows vary greatly in their design, and, as a result, their performance. A look at these limbs, recurve on top, longbow on bottom, demonstrates the point.

to determine which particular design is best suited for him or her. It's the geometry of the bow that defines its shooting characteristics, and that's where the individual differences come in. The word geometry is often used in the bowyer world to describe design particulars.

The great exhibition archer Bob Marquart shot arrows blindfolded into balloons resting on a lady's head—*with his recurve bow.* Most exhibition shooters, however, go with the longbow. One reason is pressure on the riser. The longbow riser is not affected much by the archer's grip, while grip on the recurve riser can alter arrow flight and placement to some degree. Also, the high-wrist design of some recurve bows, especially for target shooting, can be worthwhile. The deep throat of the grip causes the hand to angle downward at the wrist so the bow comes to rest naturally in the web of the hand, ensuring very little pressure on the riser itself. Otherwise, the straighter "broom handle" grip of the longbow provides excellent control.

An obvious difference between longbow and recurve characteristics is the limb tips. The string does not lie along the limb at all with a longbow, while it rests upon a few inches of the recurve's working limbs. If you torque the handle of a longbow, arrow flight will not be greatly altered. Meanwhile the same pressure directed to recurve limbs can affect the path of the arrow. The two types of limbs are appreciably different. The longbow limb is narrow with a thick core. The recurve limb is wider with a much thinner core. It is therefore

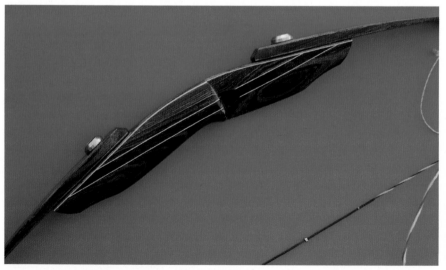

The very riser of the bow can alter how that bow performs. While the concept is not chiseled in concrete, the riser on a recurve bow, shown here, has a greater effect on arrow flight than the riser on a longbow. A medium, not super tight, grip is recommended for the recurve bow.

The recurve bow limb is normally much wider than the longbow limb, which contributes to its specific shooting characteristics.

easier to twist the limb of a recurve. In spite of that, thousands of modern archers do very well with recurves, preferring them to longbows. As long as the recurve riser is not held in a death grip, this bow style delivers the goods.

A number of bowyers returning to the scene when traditional tackle made its sweeping comeback scoffed at reflex-deflex geometry. One told me there was no such thing, that it was only a made-up term. Today, that same bowyer advertises reflex-deflex bows, where the limbs or riser bend inward toward the archer when the unstrung bow is held in hand as if ready to shoot. On a reflex-deflex recurve, the bases of the unstrung limbs bend inward; this can be seen in a side view of the bow. The upper parts of the limbs point outward, with the tips away or outward from the riser. A reflex-deflex longbow shows the same effect. While there are no curved limb tips to point away on the longbow, the limb tips still flow outward from the riser. Reflex-deflex design is popular today because it reduces hand shock and recoil. Hand shock is vibration felt in the hand. Recoil is forward-thrusting of the riser, as if the bow were "trying" to launch itself after the arrow.

The geometry of risers is especially interesting because bowyers hold so many varying beliefs about it. Some bowyers, as well as some archers, prefer a huge riser, believing that bulk at this point promotes stability. Other bowyers and archers believe heavy risers do nothing for stability in the field, although they may exhibit some value on the target range. I submit that if extremely heavy risers were more stable than slimmer handles, all target bows would have them, which they do not. Furthermore, the amazing performance of exhibition shooters like Byron Ferguson proves that slim risers are not a deterrent to great shooting.

One point in this bow geometry game is undeniable—the heavy riser lends mass to the bow. But is that always good? "I do not want to pack the weight of a mechanical bow in a traditional stick," one archer said, while another found the heft "stabilizing." Two recurve bows of very different geometry were weighed for comparison. A Herter's recurve from the mid

This Pronghorn Ferret recurve bow is of a modern design revered today for its arrow speed and its "good shooting manners."

twentieth century with handsome but hefty riser came in at a half ounce under four pounds. An all-glass-limb Pronghorn Custom Bows Ferret recurve weighed two pounds, four and a half ounces.

On the question of riser geometry, personal preference steps in. Traditionalists are prone to appreciate beauty in their bows. Therefore, some find big risers with deep throats lovely, while others think that risers "hewn from a section of telephone pole" are uglier than a truckload of hog noses.

Another aspect among the myriad geometric possibilities in the design of a bow is inboard limbs versus outboard limbs. Inboard limbs are behind the riser, while outboard limbs are in front of it. This is a difficult criterion for me because I don't always find theory verified by reality. In theory, inboard limbs are more stable than outboard limbs because the bow hand is in front of the limbs, resulting in less influence upon the bow. Also, inboard limbs can have a lower brace height than outboard limbs which in theory makes the bow *seem* easier to draw. Of course, a 60-pound bow is a 60-pound bow. And yet some bows "draw harder" than others of the same draw weight.

A bow that stacks, requiring more force at the end of the draw, certainly seems to "pull harder" than a smooth-drawing bow. One bowyer put it this way: stacking is "a case of more draw weight 'at the bottom' than at the top."

Length of limb (with respect to length of riser) is another significant feature in bow geometry (design). Longer limbs weigh more than shorter limbs and therefore require more energy to move them, so we may conclude that

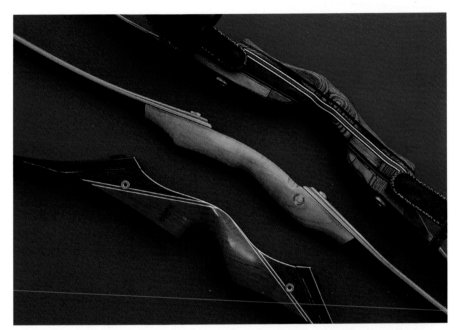

Here, we see three very different risers. The Black Widow recurve bow on the top was specially ordered with a "broom handle" riser with a shallow grip area. The Three-Piece Takedown Pronghorn longbow in the middle is typical of the longbow family—very shallow grip area. The Predator recurve on the bottom has a rather deep throat area.

Here is a prime example of a bow with a hefty riser section, highly appreciated by some archers who like a medium weight in a bow.

These are both recurve bows, but they vary greatly in geometry. The bow on the left has a shallow grip like a typical longbow grip, while the bow on the right has a much deeper throat for a handle. When shooting a recurve bow with a deep grip, like this one, do not choke down hard on the grip, as it can affect arrow flight.

shorter limbs fly a faster arrow. But longer limbs with a shorter riser can promote smoother draw, which is more important than a minor gain in arrow speed.

Bow geometry has a lot to do with arrow speed. However, anyone who chooses a bow based only on arrow speed may be cheating—cheating him or herself, because some fast bows have lousy "manners," stacking or producing a lot of recoil or hand shock. If an archer loves his straight-limb 90-pound bow that fires a hunting-weight arrow at 172 feet per second he should stay with it. If that arrow is heavy, it will penetrate well because of its momentum. One day, I witnessed a friendly bout between three bowhunters—compound versus modern recurve and English longbow. The longbow won for penetration into a stump with an arrow that, if memory serves, weighed around 700 grains. The compound won the day for casting the farthest arrow, a 400-grain dart. The recurve bow shooting a 500-grain arrow fell between the two. Nothing was really learned abut the bows because it was an apple versus orange show—except that each archer was happiest with his bow regardless of penetration or distance achieved. It was a matter of confidence. The longbow man had taken more game than either compound or recurve hunter—not because his bow was better but because he was a better woodsman.

There is no single bow design that pleases all archers regardless of the geometry. In testing a "flatbow" with its wide flat limbs, I found that it shot quite well in spite of geometry that suggested it might be a slow-boat. The last word in testing arrow speed is chronographing. The machine has no bias. It does not care what the archer likes, how much he spent on his bow, or even how well the bow handles—with little to no stacking, hand shock, or recoil. Shoot an arrow. The arrow flies through the screens and a velocity figure is revealed. The chronograph is discussed further in chapter 8, Bow Tests and Choosing Your Bow.

How a bow "works" becomes a significant factor in bow geometry. The best bowyers, I am convinced, have an excellent grasp of what makes "the little stick get away from the big stick real fast," which was how a hunter in Zimbabwe explained the bow to a companion as I looked on. (The bow had not yet been invented in that region of the country—spears and snares prevailed.) Well, in a way, the man was right. The little stick does get away from the big stick "real fast." The bow is a machine, a device that performs work. In physics, work is basically the transfer of energy from one physical system to another. It can be expressed in various units, including the foot-pound, which will be the most useful here.

The source of energy that makes the bow work is the archer. Fire a gun and it does all the work, except for holding it up and pulling the trigger. In archery, the archer provides initial energy by drawing the bow. The bow stores that energy and transfers a good deal of it to the arrow when the string is released. No machine transfers 100 percent of its energy from the initial source to another system. But good bows do quite well, which is why an arrow delivers so much force to a target. A bow that is drawn, but not fired, has *potential* energy (energy at rest). Potential energy becomes kinetic energy when the string is released. For our purposes, kinetic is the energy possessed in a body due to its motion (it is equal to one-half of its mass times velocity squared).

The important point is how much force the bow delivers. Again, I won't go into complicated science; this is only a basic glance at how the bow performs. Kinetic energy is expressed in foot-pounds. Keeping it simple, a foot-pound is the energy required to move one pound a foot—think of lifting a one-pound weight one foot off the ground. The formula for this is "scientific." I believe Sir Isaac Newton came up with it a long time ago. It's simple to work with a calculator doing the basic math gyrations. Square the velocity of the arrow, then divide by 7,000 to reduce to grains (there are 7,000 grains in one pound), and then divide the resulting figure by 64.32, which is a con-

This slim bow transfers a lot of energy through a good, efficient design. This bow is capable of shooting a 500-grain arrow at 200 feet per second, and yet it weighs well under two pounds.

stant for acceleration due to gravity (which we know thanks to Galileo and his experiments). After all of this, we have a nice little number. But that number is good for only one grain of weight. Multiply the weight in grains of the arrow, and you have the total kinetic energy of the arrow. By this formula, a 500-grain arrow at 200 feet per second delivers 44.42 foot-pounds of kinetic energy. Let's round up to 45 foot-pounds for easy comparison. A .22 rifle shooting Winchester high-velocity ammo, a 40-grain bullet at 1,300 feet per second, has 150 foot-pounds of kinetic energy, almost three times the "force" of the 500-grain arrow.

So would I rather hunt elk with a .22 rifle than a bow with a 500-grain arrow at 200 feet per second? Not at all! The opposite is true. That bow with its 500-grain arrow is a very powerful tool. But in a different form. The really important thing here is the momentum of the arrow. Momentum is a scientific concept. The trouble is, the scientific formula for momentum uses mass, which is difficult to work with in the English system of measurement. Some technically unscientific formulas try to show momentum using weight instead. Two from the shooting world are P-F (Pounds-Feet) from the late American gun writer Elmer Keith, and TKO—Taylor's Knock-Out—from the African elephant hunter of old. Keith's formula is bullet weight times velocity divided by 7,000. (Keith probably chose 7,000 because this is the number of grains in one pound, but in fact this step is just to make the long number simpler.)

Bows can deliver great power to arrows. An American bison or "buffalo" bull like this one can weight 2,000 pounds, with record weights as high as 3,000 pounds for a huge herd bull. Yet a single arrow from a bow brought these beasts down for the Plains Indians.

As a licensed professional hunter (PH) in Africa, I am not nearly as concerned with foot-pounds of energy derived from a scientific formula as I am momentum taken from a non-scientific formula. The wonderful .300 Weatherby Magnum, a big favorite in Africa, drives a 180-grain bullet at 3,200 feet per second to achieve over 4,000 foot-pounds of kinetic energy. My .45-70 PH rifle that fires a 500-grain bullet at 1,800 feet per second is worth only about 3,600 foot-pounds. But I trust the .45-70 over the .300 to stop a charging Cape buffalo. Using Keith's formula, the .300 has 82 P-F, while the 45-70 has 129 P-F.

Going back to the .22 Long Rifle and the 500-grain arrow, the .22 now has 7.4 P-F, while the 500-grain arrow has 14.3 P-F, twice what the gun has. It is momentum, by my calculation and belief, that equates to penetration in the bow. And it is the geometry of the bow that affords the stored energy to provide penetration.

C. J. Longman's archery writing, which has always interested me, contains many stories of the incredible feats achieved by traditional bows. Longman quotes "the Welsh historian, Giraldus Cambrensis, who was born 1147, [and who] tells some wonderful stories of the penetration attained by the

Left: The force that propels the arrow comes from the strength of the archer, entirely unlike the firearm, whose force comes from a powder charge. Because of this, the very style of shooting a bow contributes to its performance. Here is an example of good instinctive shooting form. Right: An efficient bow transfers considerable power to from the physical strength of the archer to the arrow. This old arrowhead was found in the woods, buried in a tree trunk.

Welsh archers in the wars of Henry II, tales which are quoted in most of the books on archery." One of these tales tells of two soldiers "flying towards a tower for refuge" when archers fire arrows at them. The arrows strike a gate made of holm oak (also known as Mediterranean evergreen, or Holly Oak), "penetrating right through it." Longman decides to test the potential penetration of a particular English longbow, "65-pound self-yew by Aldred." He finds a "stout gate" and sends an arrow crashing into it from seven yards. "This test corresponded pretty closely with that set to the archers of his guard by King Edward VI, and the result was pretty much the same," he reports. "The arrow on this occasion, having a less formidable target to deal with [than the big gate of the castle in the story], did not smash, but penetrated the gate right through." We don't know the thickness of the gate, but gates are built to last, so surely it was an inch or more. Longman was interested in further testing with a more formidable arrow, but writes, "I was,

Many modern archers enter huge country like this with nothing more than trust in their bows. That trust is the result of good bow design that transmits force to an arrow.

however, deterred by the reflection that it was not my gate, and that I had already made one hole in it." He concluded, "This hole can, no doubt, be cured by a piece of putty skillfully inserted, but the spear-head arrows would have made a more formidable wound."

Longman also correctly reasoned that the better the bow geometry, the greater the transfer of archer energy to bow energy to arrow energy. This would lead to a faster-flying arrow, and the faster the arrow, the greater the cast. He could not, however, with his bows and flight arrows (specially designed for distance) exceed 300 yards. Longman points out that in Shakespeare's play *Henry IV*, one of the characters alludes to a great archer who could make an arrow fly twelve score yards. Longman concludes that in Shakespeare's time to hit a clout at "twelve score" yards was considered a great feat. He concluded that a distance of 280 to 300 yards was about maximum for the medieval bow. (A Turkish flight arrow in freestyle shooting achieved 937.13 yards in 1959.)

The problem with distance shooting to determine a bow's worth is the fact that the test is seldom done with similar, let alone identical, tackle. This is all right as far as the bow goes, but watch out for the arrows. I have informally experimented with distance shooting and at least one factor comes to the fore. There are bows that simply perform better, draw for draw, than other bows. How much this means in practical terms is hard to say. So what? So Bow A shoots the same arrow farther than Bow B. So what? Perhaps Bow B is much easier to manage, delivering more arrows spot-on than Bow A. Regardless that these "tests" are faulty, they can reveal interesting data. One day I shot a 75-pound bow and a 57-pound bow, and found that the lighter one shot the same arrow the farthest. This test was totally unscientific, but it must say something about bow design, materials, and other factors.

It's a balancing act. The bowyer has to consider all dominant factors of design in order to arrive at a bow that behaves well in the hand, that is a pleasure to shoot many arrows from per session, and that still provides decent arrow speed for cast and penetration.

6

Draw Weight Sense

Chapter 7 goes into testing a bow to choose the right one for the individual archer. Draw weight, one of the most significant factors in deciding on a bow, is so important that I will address it separately here, before going on to chapter 7. Over the years, I have watched many excited archers coming to the longbow and recurve and then falling prey to that dragon known as draw weight. They do not, perhaps, understand that they must be able to fully master their new bow rather than the bow mastering them. If an archer cannot enjoy a pleasant rove or practice session that involves turning loose many darts because the bow tires him or her, then that is the wrong bow. Mastering the stick requires full control. If tugging back on the string requires more concentration than what you devote to proper stance, anchor point, release, and the other factors of archery, good shooting goes out the window. I fell into this pit myself when turning from the mechanical arrow-shooter back to the curved stick.

I see three "time periods" of bow draw weight popularity as archers took up the ancient game in modern times. The first saw the serious archer carrying a heavy-draw bow reminiscent of distant history—the times of Robin Hood. The Thompson brothers' "small game bows" were 40- to 50-pound draw, big game bows 60- to 70-pound pull, and their special "snakewood" was rated at 90-pounds. Pope and Young came along with their heavy-draw bows soon afterwards.

Howard Hill fits perfectly in this slot. For Hill, an 85-pound draw bow was a piece of cake. A photo of this fantastic archer reveals a man of obvious strength. Bob Swinehart, who followed Hill, and who hunted many parts of the globe, patterned himself after his mentor. Hill wrote of Swinehart (in the foreword to *Sagittarius,* Swinehart's autobiograpy), "for a man his size—weight 170 and height 5' 10"—his strength is prodigious. He can handle bows pulling 100 pounds!" Hill also pulled bows 100 pounds and heavier. Some today can do it too. A good friend, who would be embarrassed if I told his name,

Bill Wiesner demonstrates his full mastery of a strong bow as he takes aim at a tree squirrel for supper. The ease with which Bill handles his bow proves that the draw weight is right for him.

let me examine a bow from his collection that he used to use frequently, but in time retired because he found lighter, more efficient bows that shot even faster arrows. On the scale it drew over 100 pounds. He strung that bow without standing up.

Now for what I call the middle period, a period of lighter draw weights. It was a time of mostly recurves from numerous manufacturers—Wing, Herter's, Browning, and many more. Bowhunting seasons were popping up all over America; the cry was: "Be a Two-Season Hunter." That is, go with both bow and gun. Thousands heeded the call. Relying on what information they could find, many game departments set a minimum draw weight of 40-pounds pull for big game. Taking that as a benchmark, hunters bought bows in the 40- to 50-pound, or sometimes 55- to 60-pound draw weight. When I ordered a beautiful Browning, I went from a 75-pound longbow to 47-pound recurve. That was the trend.

The third period in traditional bow draw weight popularity, a period in which moderate draw weight prevailed, continues today. Fred Bear lived most of his life in a middle ground with a 65-pound recurve for everything. He proved that 65 pounds was sufficient to propel an arrow with plenty of "power" to do the job. Fred must have known something, because today's longbows and recurves are often ordered in the 55- to 65-pound range.

But there are many still, who, unfortunately, fall prey to the gremlin called Mr. Over-bow. Newcomers, whether one-time archers returning to the game or those just getting into archery, step into their new bows not always matching draw weight to personal physical limits, as well as to the task at hand (you don't need a 60-pound bow for rabbits or roving). I rank draw weight as the number one cause of failure for archers who devoutly wish to enjoy the interesting and rewarding stickbow game, but go away disap-

The recurve on the left exemplifies the bows of what I call the "middle era" in draw weight, at around fifty pounds. It's a Herter's bow, quite prominent in the days before the compound came along.

pointed. This is especially true for those coming from the compound domain. "Let's see," the bowhunter says, "I shoot a 70-pound compound, and my new traditional bow won't have a mechanical advantage. So I'd better go with at least 70-pound or heavier."

The bow is ordered. It arrives, a thing of beauty. But there's a problem. The bowman who could break over a 70-pound, even an 80-pound compound, cannot reach full draw and *hold* an anchor point with his new 70-pound longbow or recurve. The greatest force required to draw a compound occurs when the string is pulled back about one-half draw length, whereas the stickbow demands greatest force at full draw/anchor point. With a traditional bow, you need the muscle development not only to pull the string back, but also to maintain a solid anchor point until the arrow is away.

Heavy draw weights were developed in the distant past because it was the best way to achieve what was called "cast," a familiar topic in this work. One formula for longbow arrow speed that I do not personally use, but which certain longbow devotees believe in, involves the number 115: take the draw weight of the longbow, add 115, and that is the *range* of arrow speed *potential*. A 70-pound longbow would have a potential arrow speed of 185 feet per second, according to this formula. The formula is troublesome at best because it leaves out arrow choice and other factors. But it's okay as a rule of

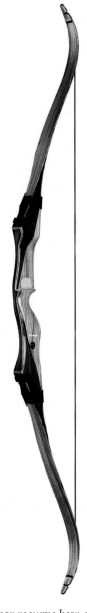

thumb and is applied by some longbow bowyers with a degree of satisfaction.

There were many great bows in the past. Most of them were built through trial and error with that master teacher, Experience, leading the way to success. Bow makers of old were not sitting around using computer models to find out how to gain the most efficiency from a design. Heavy bows were developed because they provided the thrust necessary to overcome some of the normal loss associated with any working system. Also, the way to "power" rested with a heavy arrow with great momentum, as discussed in chapter 5. But no machine, including a bow, transfers 100 percent of its stored energy.

Think of a car. The engine may have 300 horsepower, but you sure won't see 300 horsepower applied to the tires. Lots of ponies are sucked up between the engine and the wheel. The same goes for the bow. It may draw 70 pounds, but the arrow will not gain 70 pounds of thrust at the nock. Even compounds, with their mechanical advantage, cannot do that. Going back to the analogy, some cars transfer more of their engine's power to the wheel than others. Today's stickbow is more efficient than yesteryear's. Modern bowyers know more about working designs. They have better materials to work with as well. Proof of this rests in simple draw-weight-per-inch tests as well as chronograph runs. A modern recurve or longbow of 60-pound draw may shoot a faster arrow than a 75-pound bow of the past.

Before chronographs, a bowyer might come to believe that a certain limb material offered more efficiency potential than another. For example, a bowyer may have selected one core wood over another for his limbs. Proving it meant shooting, perhaps for distance—a reasonable test, but inferior to the solid facts pro-

This Bear recurve bow, very much like the bow Fred Bear carried all over the world in the pursuit of big and even dangerous game, has a draw weight of only 65 pounds.

Top: This custom bow was built with the customer in mind, not only with regard to choices of wood and bow length, but especially with regard to draw weight. The "power" is in the glass laminations, and the expert bowyer knows just how to choose those laminations to end up at a given draw weight. Bottom: This extremely heavy longbow was built to set a record for draw weight pulled by an archer—not for use on a daily basis. It registered 186 pounds on a bow scale. Note the massive riser and multiple laminations used to achieve this draw weight.

vided by the chronograph. Today, bowyers can build bows with different materials and, by keeping all other things equal, such as draw weight and the arrows used, they can definitively prove to themselves which material provides the best performance in their bows. As always, there may be serious trade-offs. Making a bow shoot a little faster while losing the advantage of smooth operation is one example.

The super light-draw bows of the past failed to drive hunting-weight arrows with decent velocity and energy to bring down big game. Super light-draw bows are still unwise for big jobs. However, looking at draw weight alone is no longer a valid means of choosing a bow on the basis of arrow velocity. That is because today's more efficient bows do not have to have quite so much poundage to get the job done. This isn't wishful thinking. It's a chronograph-proven fact. In my file there is a test for arrow speed with a 66-pound draw bow against a 57-pound draw bow. The two bows fired identical arrows at almost identical velocities. More recently, I ran a 75-pound bow

This custom bow under construction is already on the road to a final draw weight because the limbs are already prepared. The bowyer will do further work on the bow as it is finished, which will result in a final draw weight.

against the same 57-pound stick and the 57-pound bow shot the same arrow *faster* than the heavy bow, because it was more efficient.

This chapter is not intended to scare archers away from heavy-draw bows, regardless of their efficiency or lack thereof. There are too many happy archers out there enjoying bows that are not as efficient as others. Sometimes these archers revert back to the "old days" when success with a specific bow or rifle imbued it with special powers. A neighbor of mine during my high school days in Yuma, Arizona, believed that his uncle's .30-06 "hit harder" than his father's .30-06, although both rifles had the same barrel lengths and shot the same ammunition. I give credit to the archer who believes in his bow without ever having to know how fast it fires an arrow. All he knows, and all he needs to know, is that the bow works for him.

So this is not an attempt to dissuade an archer from abandoning a bow because it is not efficient. Nor is it an attempt to talk down heavy-draw bows in favor of light-draw bows. It is, however, a plea for archers to understand that draw weight by itself does not always indicate performance, and, more importantly, that trying to manage a too-heavy bow can heap defeat on the archer. It's an even stronger plea for the archer coming into the world of traditional bows to think hard before deciding on draw weight for that new bow. Additionally, it is reasonable for the prospective newcomer to the stickbow to take up a program designed, preferably by a professional trainer, to build the specific muscles required to manage a bow of reasonable draw weight. It's common to see smaller archers who shoot a lot able to draw a bow that much bigger people cannot manage.

Chester Stevenson, in his book *The Old Bowhunter,* wrote, "I found that I could shoot best with as strong a bow as I could pull." There's a river of logic running through that sentiment because a heavy draw bow, *as long as the archer can control it,* provides a smoother release than a light draw bow. The reason is obvious. Keeping the fingers on the string of a drawn heavy bow is much more difficult than holding a lightweight bow at full draw. So when the archer's fingers relax, the string, with all that tension on it, explodes forward. There is little tendency with the heavy bow to allow the fingers of the bow hand to curl around the string. However, you will eventually reach a breaking point, where the cleaner release isn't worth the effort and loss of control the greater weight causes. Plenty of super accurate target shooters have no trouble with string release with lighter-draw bows.

The heavy bows of yesteryear required a lot of physical training. In a section in his book called "Bar Bells

An archer who works up to full mastery of a given bow weight will usually carry that bow for all shooting, from target practice and roving to small and big game.

in the Bow Den," Stevenson reports that "many of the hunters had no trouble with the big bows because they trained a lot." It was also "no problem to shoot the comparatively light 70- and 80-pounders when we were training to pull one hundred." Training was not only with bows. "My own special training," Stevenson wrote, "was with a kettle ball in the weight lifting program."

He leaned forward against a chair, lifting the kettle ball by its handle straight up from the ground toward his chest. The kettle ball, a round weight with a handle, is still popular today. Chester used his properly, lifting the kettle ball straight up from the ground to his chest, to gain the strength needed to draw his bow without straining his back.

Another problem is the law of diminishing returns. If a bow always delivered a hundred percent of its stored energy to the nock of the arrow, then going heavier in draw weight would produce more arrow speed. But due to the law of diminishing returns, there is no perfect correlation between rising draw weight and arrow speed increase. Once again, to explain the point, a firearms comparison is appropriate. I have simplified this example, leaving many important factors out of the equation, but the basic principle is the same. A .300 Winchester Magnum achieves close to 3,000 feet per second for a 150-grain bullet and 50-grains weight of a certain powder. The same gun shooting exactly the same bullet can reach 3,300 feet per second with 77.0-grains of powder, according to the Lyman manual. A thirty-five percent gain in powder weight did not produce thirty-five percent more velocity, but rather around ten percent gain.

Likewise, going up X percent in bow draw weight will not always produce Y percent additional arrow speed. And that's all right, because the added bow draw weight may allow a heavier arrow to fly straight and true, thereby increasing momentum and penetration. In my own meager demonstrations with the chronograph I have come to believe that with modern top-of-the-line recurves and longbows being made in this century, a bow in the 50- to 65-pound range is a wise choice for big game. Small game joins the pot with just about any bow. I won't discuss very light bows much after this, except in chapter 20 on stickbows for kids. While going too heavy can be counterproductive, going too light is no way to pursue big game.

My 61-pound Ferret recurve drove an arrow through a mule deer at 25 paces, the arrow sticking in a dirt cliff behind the deer deeply enough to require a tug to pull it free. My 57-pound Black Widow put an arrow clear through a deer at 40 paces. A friend fired an arrow through the chest cavity of a bull elk at 15 paces. The arrow stuck in a tree behind the bull, burying the head two-thirds deep. His bow ran around 55-pounds draw. I know where I stand after years of pondering the issue. It's pretty simple, really. If I order a recurve or longbow tomorrow, I'm going to say, "Try for just under 60 pounds." If the bow turns out 55-pound draw, I'll smile like a kid with a chocolate ice cream cone.

Those who have the build to draw the heavy bow should run right out and order one. The rest of us have two choices. The first is to be happy with a stickbow in the 60-pound class. The second is to work up to a heavier draw if we feel a need for one or if we are pursuing extra large or dangerous animals. Working up can mean heading for the gym. In my town, we have a trainer who works with archers. He knows all about which muscles do what and how to make those muscles stronger. Of course, another way to work up to a heavier bow is to start light and build. Start at 50 or even 45; master that level. Then work up until you've reached your goal. Keep one thing in mind, though: you may have a physical limit which cannot be exceeded no matter how much effort you put in.

One of my acquaintances just got back from Africa, where he took a huge Cape buffalo with one arrow from a 95-pound longbow and heavy arrow. At the same time, the son of an African acquaintance recently got a Cape buffalo with a 50-pound bow and a medium-weight arrow. The best I can say about draw weight is this: as long as the archer is not over-bowed to the point where he or she cannot control the bow, heavy is fine. For me, though, I find that bows in the 55- to sub-60-pound draw weight are capable of doing anything I want to or need to do with the stick. If you have a hard-drawing heavyweight that fires a great big arrow, keep it. Use it. Enjoy it. But if your heavy-draw bow won't put the same arrow out faster than a lighter but more efficient bow, then you're pulling extra weight for exactly nothing! And that's that.

7

Bow Tests and Choosing Your Bow

"How fast does it shoot?" In the days of King Arthur, I doubt that question ever came up; a bow's *cast,* however, was considered very important. The same was true in Shakespeare's time, as we saw with the play *Henry IV,* in which one of the characters extolls the virtues of an archer who could cast an arrow far. But it comes down to the same thing. Going to guns again for a comparison, consider a 150-grain bullet moving at 2,000 feet per second and the same bullet at 3,000 feet per second. The faster bullet shoots the farthest. The laws of physics do not take a vacation when it comes to archery. Faster arrows travel farther than slower ones.

Arrow speed can be overrated in traditional archery, especially when the concern for velocity takes precedence over other highly important aspects of choosing a bow, such as stacking, hand shock, or recoil. Be that as it may, interest in how fast a bow shoots an arrow is often first on the list of criteria when an archer chooses a new longbow or recurve. Chronographs are prevalent today, not only in archery shops, but individually owned.

The chronograph calculates the speed of projectiles: bullets, arrows, pellets, or whatever else you are shooting, in a start and stop sequence. In the past, it was often called a "counter chronograph," because it counts time. The missile enters the domain of the first screen, starting the count, and then passes the final screen, stopping the count. The smaller the time lapse between start and stop, the faster the object was going.

The three main variables when chronographing a traditional bow for arrow speed are all related to draw length. They are draw itself, anchor point, and release. If draw varies, thrust upon the arrow varies, thereby altering arrow velocity. Is this a serious problem in the field? Only when the draw varies so dramatically that arrows fly at greatly different speeds, thereby altering trajectory. However, it can make a difference when testing arrow speed to the foot-per-second level. If the anchor point varies it has the same effect as varying draw length. Release is a third variable affecting arrow speed. If

This chronograph has a tape readout that gives five important pieces of information—the highest velocity in the string of shots fired, the lowest velocity, the extreme spread between the two, the average velocity, and the standard deviation from the average velocity.

the archer plucks the string for one shot and then allows the string to move forward for the next shot that is the same as varying draw length, and of course alters the reading provided by the chronograph.

While the gifted archer who has total control of his or her bow at full draw can get away with shooting bow by hand when testing for arrow speed, the rest of us must employ a device to eliminate varying draw length, varying anchor point, and varying release. We want truly sound results. Any device that holds the bow firmly in place so that it is drawn and released "mechanically" is acceptable. This may be as simple as a sawhorse with a padded cross-bar attached at the front end to secure the bow's handle. The bow is drawn by pulling the string back, using a release (trigger) to eliminate any chance of plucking the string or allowing the string to move forward before the arrow is released. In order to achieve exactly the same draw length for every shot, a simple line is drawn on the top of the sawhorse to indicate full draw. The bow is brought to its prescribed full draw point with the release, and the arrow is sent through the screens of the chronograph. Draw, anchor point, and release of the arrow are now fully controlled. Ideally, the same arrow is shot over and over, thus eliminating variation in the weight of one arrow over another, which of course would skew results.

Shooting just once will give a measurement of arrow velocity—for that shot—but to get a really accurate idea of how fast a bow shoots, you should shoot several times and average the velocities. A "string" of five shots is sufficient for testing arrow speed provided the bow is held in a rest. If a

Testing with the chronograph is valid because the machine itself is reliable as long as it is used properly.

mechanical rest is not used, the string, the number of shots counted as a single test should be at least ten. A twenty-shot string is better yet because the greater the sample tested, the more accurate the final results will be. The twenty-shot string also provides more numbers for high and low number elimination.

Lacking a mechanical device to control draw length, anchor point, and release, a longbow or recurve can be hand-held to give a sufficient idea of arrow speed with a twenty-shot string coupled with eliminating highs and lows. Eliminating especially high and low velocities in the string gives a more reliable average. Consider a twenty-shot string using the same 500-grain arrow for every shot (it's tedious to have to retrieve the arrow every time to shoot it over again, but worth it). Of the twenty shots, let's say that fifteen hover around 200 feet per second. Five vary from this speed, either appreciably faster than 200 feet per second or much slower than 200 feet per second. Both the high and low velocities are now removed from the string. Highs are removed because they most likely represent an over-draw of the bow past the bow's prescribed draw length. For example, if the bow is rated at 55-pounds pull at 28-inch draw and the archer pulls the string back around his or her ear to 31 inches, the thrust on the arrow is increased. We do not want this; we want to know the average velocity of the test bow *at its prescribed draw length*. If the string is not pulled back to full draw, thrust on the

When the chronograph is set up properly, as shown here, it reveals bow efficiency to a high degree of accuracy.

arrow neck is reduced from what it would be at the 28-inch draw, and an unusually low velocity will result. Taking out both high and low numbers provides a better idea of the test bow's arrow speed at its intended draw length.

Standard deviation is a rule of variance. Very basically, it can be thought of as a *reliability* figure. If, for example, a standard deviation reads only ten feet per second for an average arrow speed of 210 feet per second, the reliability of that set of figures is "good." If the standard deviation runs 30 feet per second from the average velocity, that's not as good. So the lower the standard deviation, the better. That is really all we need to know. The truly scientific minded have a cow when the rest of us just skim the surface to get a decent idea of what's happening with our bows, but personally, if traditional archery were scientific, I wouldn't be that interested in the game. I get enough high-tech in my daily life and I'll bet most readers do, too. The engineers in the crowd are invited to investigate force draw curves and static hysteresis.

But the extraneous variable belongs in our domain because the grassroots archer needs to be aware when he or she is presented with test data that does not add up. The extraneous variable is something at work in a test that ends up "lying" about the results. A super arrow speed might be the result of a chronograph glitch, such as a glint.

Testing bow speed without a chronograph is possible, but only a chronograph gives a truly reliable result. Pope once tested arrow speed with a stopwatch—not an entirely worthless instrument, but certainly not a chrono-graph. The easiest method relies on cast. In a vacant field under entirely safe conditions, the archer takes the bow he is interested in, aims about 45 degrees skyward with the point of the arrow, and lets fly. Best to shoot a dozen shafts for a better idea of arrow speed. Of course, shooting for cast will in no way give arrow speed itself. But faster arrows fly farther than slower ones, so in testing bows side by side with similar darts a comparison can be made. Shooting for cast may even teach us something about bow efficiency, as an efficient bow of lighter draw may cast an arrow farther than a heavier-draw but less efficient bow.

Learning about a bow through totally subjective testing is sometimes necessary, especially when an archer has a chance to try different ones, perhaps bows owned by friends. While bearing no resemblance to science, in this case, the subjective is valuable. You don't need to have actual foot-pounds of recoil force on paper to tell you that a .22-rimfire rifle "kicks" less than a .375 Magnum. Your shoulder will let you know. That's why we can get away with subjective longbow and recurve "testing" that isn't really testing. Archers vary widely simply in what they like or have become accustomed to.

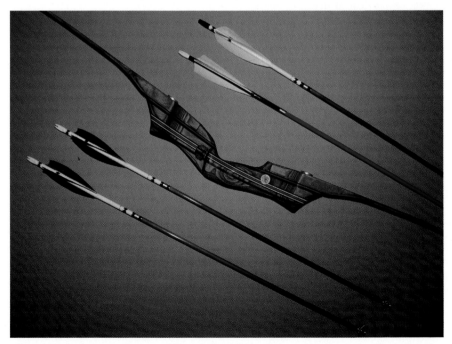

There is usually some degree of "hand shock" in a bow as the arrow is released and the limbs slam forward. However, a bow like the one shown here has so little hand shock that it is unnoticeable.

Along the lines of subjective discovery, there are recoil, hand shock, general bow handling, overall characteristics, stacking, noise, bow mass weight, and quality. Other considerations can include bow quiver adaptability, tuning, and, yes, beauty.

My partner and I used to shoot every day. Our bows at the time were far from efficient. They had bad manners and good bows would have put them in the shade. And yet we did well with them. It was personal. Sometimes I wonder if we spend too much time looking for a bow that fits us rather than fitting ourselves to a bow. We had fit ourselves to those not-so-good bows, learning to overcome their bad points.

Today's better bows just don't recoil. I suspect the reflex/deflex design may have something to do with this. But I'm only guessing. While recoil is a tangible condition, it is sill subjective and personal. One of my old bows, a stick of questionable design and overall quality, would leap forward every time I sent an arrow downrange. I got used to it. I adapted to it. I fit myself to that bow. In the end, I got rid of it, not passing it on to another archer because that would be no favor. I just threw it away.

Hand shock is not recoil. But both terms fly about in the breeze and there are plenty of fine traditional archers who will tell you there is no such thing as either one. They simply never paid attention to recoil or hand shock and I credit them for this. They adapted to their bows; they fit themselves to their bows rather than insisting that the bow fit them in every respect. Regardless, I have shot bows that truly did vibrate in my hand, and though this is not a sufficient black mark to condemn an otherwise good stick, hand shock is not a plus.

General bow handling is highly significant, even though personal demonstrations are far from any paradigm of testing I know of. Handling is probably the most difficult aspect of all the criteria. I know what it is. I feel what it is. But I cannot easily explain what it is. I have picked bows up that, just by holding them, I knew were not for me. They did not "handle" right, right being my subjective call. These bows simply did not *feel* friendly in my hands. Does that make sense? I think it does. Pick up just about any tool. It might be a hammer. Does it feel right? Would it be easy to work with? I rank this criterion high on the list, even though it is a phantom. I remember picking up one bow that I now shoot often. It felt right from the start. It had that elusive "general bow handling" hog-tied.

Overall characteristics is less a specter than general bow handling. Now we get into a basic choice between longbow and recurve. Their individual characteristics can be entirely different. Heavy risers, light risers. Deep throats and broom handles. Long risers, short risers. Tall bow, short bow, in-between bow length.

Top: When you are testing a bow, especially with the possibility of buying it or one like it, pay attention to "feel"—how the bow feels when you're shooting it. While this is almost entirely subjective (though a really bad bow will not feel good for any archer), it is a valid and important test. Bottom: An important part of testing a bow for "feel" is deciding between the "longbow grip" or "recurve grip." This longbow shows a very shallow grip area.

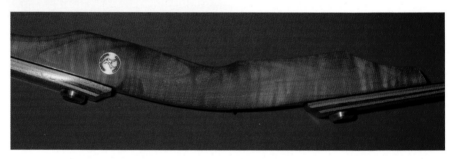

General bow characteristics are a matter of personal preference. Once, I was camping on the Wyoming/Montana border and of course had two bows and a batch of roving arrows. By happenstance an archer I knew spotted the camp and stopped for a fish fry. He asked if we might go into the woods and challenge a few stumps and pinecones. During the course of our roving session, he suggested we each try the other guy's bow. I didn't like his and he didn't like mine. Mine felt odd in is hand, his in my hand. We could have worked on adapting. But there was no point. He kept his bow and I kept mine.

While force versus draw curves can be revealing, showing how a bow builds and holds energy, the resulting figures, interesting to the technically-minded as they may be, are not all that useful for those of us who are solely interested in "testing" a bow at the grassroots level, subjectively. Related to

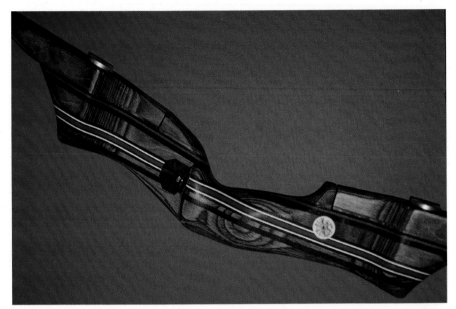

Bow stacking—force required to draw it increasing out of proportion toward the full draw point—is all but eliminated in the better composite bows like this Black Widow.

the force-draw idea is stacking—but a degree in physics is not required to find out if a certain bow stacks. A bow scale comes into play. The scale not only determines specific poundage at a specific draw length. It can also reveal how that poundage builds. The tale is told toward the end of the draw. Going to a sample I still have on file, one longbow drew 3.0 pounds for each inch up to twenty-six inches, but required 4.5 pounds of force to reach twenty-seven inches and the same to reach full draw at twenty-eight inches. So that bow stacked.

Now the big question—can the archer handle it? Does stacking cause a problem in shooting an accurate arrow? Maybe. Maybe not. It depends on the person pulling the bowstring. Those "bad bows" we carried in days gone by stacked. We learned to overcome it. Regardless, today's better-engineered longbows and recurves should draw smoothly from initial pull-back on the string to full draw. A scale is good for checking for stacking. But perhaps the best way to see if a bow stacks to shoot it. If drawing the last couple inches throws the archer off because of stacking, that's important. And if not, then just keep shooting those happy arrows downrange, whether the bow stacks or not.

A noisy bow can normally be quieted using the information presented in chapter 16, and therefore is seldom a serious problem. If the bow squeaks or groans when pulled, it's probably a takedown model. Check where limbs

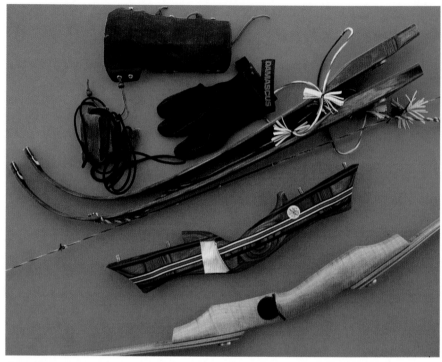

Choosing a bow includes deciding between a takedown or one-piece bow. The takedown bow has the advantage of collapsing to very manageable transportation size, plus the ability to use different limbs on the same riser.

connect to platform of riser; that's probably the culprit. Then apply the remedies discussed in chapter 16. They work.

Bow weight is a serious matter in choosing a bow, and also an important part of the subjective analysis of a particular bow. There are some bows, mostly recurves, that with a loaded bow quiver tip the scale not too far from a lightweight hunting rifle. If heft is important to an archer, he or she should settle for nothing less than a lighter stick. Target recurve bows I have shot, especially with the straight up and down stance, compound-like, often had heavy risers. They were fine, but for me I'd look for a lighter stick to carry in yonder hills.

Overall quality is not that hard to determine. Takedown bows that lack the skilled hand usually reveal that problem at the location of limb and platform. No gaps here, please. The takedown limb should hug the riser as if both were one piece. On any expensive bow from a custom shop, the fadeout should be absolutely beautiful. Fadeout is better "told" in a photo than in

While the takedown bow has its advantages, the graceful lines of a one-piece bow are undeniably attractive. This Pronghorn bow is a perfect example of one-piece beauty.

words. On a takedown limb, the heavier part near the riser fades into nothing going toward the tip of the limb. Still not very good. Close-up photos tell more, or a magnified view. Does it seem unfair to apply cameras and magnifying glasses if the unaided eye is satisfied with the fadeouts on a bow? Maybe so. But today a custom bow, except for used bargains, bites the wallet like a pit bull. And the buyer should expect fine workmanship along with good finish.

Test a bow that wears a bow quiver with the quiver on the bow. If the quiver holds several arrows, shoot the bow with the quiver full (you could be carrying a blunt by hand, which is safe). Now shoot with one arrow missing in the quiver, then two, and down to empty. Some archers are so sensitive to the bow quiver changing weight from full to empty that they are better off toting arrows in some other manner.

Today's sticks tune up without much trouble. The stick, once tuned, stays that way as long as the archer watches for string-stretch and other factors that can change the factors that were present when tuning the bow in the first place. A well-tuned "good" traditional bow, locked up in a bow shooting machine to eliminate human frailty, punches a group right along with the compound. The only reason tuning is mentioned in this chapter is as a reminder that no bow should be expected to perform without the simple tuning measures touched on in chapter 7.

Finally, evaluate the bow for beauty. Beauty is important, though not truly a part of bow "testing." Is it subjective? Of course. But a bow should please its owner visually, like an interesting painting.

8

The Custom Bow

I think the biggest mistake in ordering a custom bow is not going for the gold. I say this because too often the archer will not be satisfied with a bow that he or she compromised on. Price is always important, of course. The old saying "If you have to ask how much it costs, you can't afford it" is rubbish. In my line of work as a full-time outdoor sports writer I have met some very rich lads and lassies, and every one of them proved to be highly interested in the price of anything and everything, right down to stopping at the gas station that sold the fuel two cents a gallon cheaper than the competition. Everyone should be careful with their money. Having written this, I still say: buy right the first time. I know, because when I got back into the stickbow game I ordered my first custom bow based in part on economy. Big mistake.

Custom means more than quality. It also means class.

I didn't have that bow for six months before I sold it at considerable loss to an archer who liked it.

When traditional bows became popular again, there were literally no more recurves or longbows being built in the Bear Archery, Browning, Ben Pearson or other factories. But thousands of archers wanted to get back to the romance, thrills, and just plain fun of pulling the string on a bow without the help of wheels and pulleys. So where were they going to go for that new longbow or recurve? There had always been bowyers in the background building "sticks," even when selling their bows was unlikely. I met one of them at a gun show—I had essentially gotten out of archery at the time, having given my last compound to a cousin. As I walked by his table, not really interested at the time in a longbow, he said, "Aren't you Sam Fadala, and didn't you used to shoot longbows a lot?" I said yes to both. Then I took a look. "Darn it," I said. "That's what I used to do. I used to shoot longbows and recurves. And it was fun." The man at the gun show was Herb Meland of Pronghorn Custom Bows in Casper, Wyoming, and his one-piece Pronghorn longbow put me back on the stickbow track. Of course I chronographed arrows from that bow with its red elm laminations, and at first I was almost afraid to write up the results for fear I'd not be believed. Arrows flew at 190 feet per second for heavy arrows, and at 200 feet per second for darts running around 450-grains weight. The last compound I had shot faster. But 200 feet per second was fast enough to "get the job done." After all, most of my previous bows, including a favorite longbow in "green glass" from the Ben Pearson Company, averaged closer to 160 to 180 feet per second, depending on arrow weight. Those "slow" bows sent arrows completely through targets animate and inanimate, so how could I not be satisfied with 190 to 200 feet

A custom traditional bow shows high quality workmanship, right down to the perfect lacing on this grip.

Today, there are a large number of part- and full-time custom bowyers building the best traditional bows of any era. Herb Meland of Pronghorn Custom Bows is one of those fine craftsmen.

per second with proper-weight hunting arrows? How fast was the arrow Howard Hill used on an elephant?

About at that time a new magazine surfaced. On a trip, I stopped at a store to check the magazine rack, and there it was. Volume I Number 1: the first issue of *Traditional Bowhunter* magazine. As I read it cover to cover I learned that I was hardly the only one interested in going back to the longbow and recurve. So how could the demand be met? The tried and true archery companies of past years were making compounds. That's where the money was. If archers were going to have newly-made traditional bows (and tackle), the custom bowyers, many if not most of whom were working in one-room shops, would have to provide. They did and they still are.

A wise fellow by the name of Ken Beck quit his regular business and bought into the Black Widow Custom Bow Company. Black Widow was a high performer when the Wilson brothers ran it and Ken was out to see that the new Black Widow retained the reputation it had always enjoyed—and got even better. Were they custom or factory-made bows? The Black Widow struck a compromise in the fact that the bows were not produced in the one-room shop. But at the same time, they were made one at a time. Those last words are a pretty good definition of custom bows—bows made one at a

This unique Black Widow bow has a forward-set handle for shooting a very short arrow.

Ken Beck took over the Black Widow operation and today the Black Widow bow is available in many different models. This one has a special straight grip.

time. They may be made by hand, but a bowyer may also use the proper machinery to remove slow and tedious effort in sanding and shaping. Custom means personal, a bow built in a small to medium-sized shop instead of a factory, with considerable handwork and a multitude of options.

But be careful. The bows are truly custom, built for an individual archer in a particular draw weight or with a different handle shape, but the basic design of the bow will reveal the particular beliefs of the individual bowyer. Each custom bowyer has his or her own idea of what a custom bow should be: one bowyer may believe strongly in large risers while another prefers slimmer risers. That's why the first step in seeking a personal custom long-bow or recurve is studying the various designs offered by each bowyer. In perusing a recent (as this is written) copy of *Traditional Bowhunter* magazine, I encountered—well, too many custom bowyers to list here, each with their own designs. Great Plains Traditional Bow Company offers its B-Model One Piece Recurve with a forward-set handle, arched beam, and contoured grip. Is that what you like? Then go for it. But order it up just for you in length, draw weight, and other particulars. The Acadian Woods Custom Longbows & Recurves Company makes the Cajun Hunter, unique with reverse forward handle, positive grooved shelf, hand-sewn leather grip, and special overlays in 62-, 64-, and 66-inch lengths. The customer chooses the wood he or she prefers. Tim Mullins, a Louisiana bowyer, has been at the game full-time now for eighteen years, an example of where the custom traditional bow game has gone. Demand has all but forced bowyer Herb Meland to concentrate on his Three-Piece Takedown Longbow because the word got out that it was fast-shooting, feather-light in the hand, and offered in a wide range of wood choices, draw lengths, and poundage. The point is this: step one in looking for a custom bow is considering the particular style that winds your watch.

For a custom bow, choose a custom bowyer, a person recognized for his talent and expertise. Most custom bowyers advertise in archery publications.

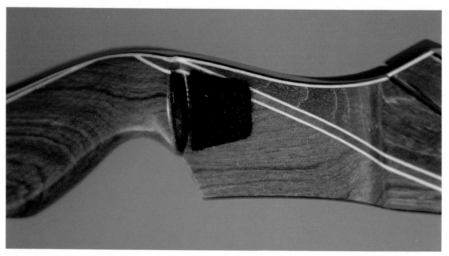

Styles of custom bows vary tremendously with the ideas and particular preferences of each bowyer. While bowyers have their own ideas concerning the "best" custom bow, every professional bow maker is capable of altering that design to some degree to suit the archer. This bow, for example, exhibits a rather deep throat in the grip section.

But there are a few great ones that don't shout about their wares because they can't even keep up with the demand as it is without calling for more work. Ideally, learn as much as you can about the bowyer before ordering. Today, there are numerous traditional clubs. The last time I looked I counted over sixty, and those were only the ones advertised. Look up the nearest club. Join. You'll find a group of archers willing to give advice (most of them *more* than willing) about custom bows and bowyers. Personal preferences will prevail, but it's still a good way to start shopping.

You will have to make many decisions. Recurve or longbow is the first. Check out the chapter on that subject. Longbows are light, graceful, fast-shooting (these days), and dependable. Recurves are easier to manage for some archers and due to more stored energy often produce slightly superior ballistics. But don't choose a bow based on arrow speed alone. You may be sorry, especially if the bow has "bad manners," such as hand shock or stacking. And bad manners can be found in both types of bows.

Some of the members of the traditional archery clubs may not be excited about having a custom bow shopper trying his or her bow. But most will be happy to allow a few arrows flung downrange. It doesn't take long to decide if a particular custom bow is "your cup of tea" or not. This applies to much more than the choice between longbow and recurve. Each bow will have its own particular "feel" in the hand. Two custom bows may deliver exactly the same arrow speed, yet handle very differently in draw or other aspects. Usually, it is not a matter of one bow necessarily being better than another, only different.

You should also consider overall bow length. In the past, it was easy to determine bow length based on arrow draw. Short bows were best suited to shorter draws and vice versa. Also, shorter traditional bows often suffered poor cast. I owned one super short bow: it was handy as sliced bread, but it stacked like hay in a winter barn and arrow speed was more like that of a tortoise than a hare. Today, however, there are some short bows that enjoy smooth draw and good arrow speed. This has occurred as bowers studied the geometry of bows and experimented with many different materials, especially limb laminations. So it is no longer feasible to lay down a solid rule that short bows are going to stack, pinch the fingers like a vice, or fire slow arrows. Nonetheless, the custom bow seeker must be careful when he or she shops for a very short bow, making certain that it has been designed properly, with the right materials, to prevent the problems associated with short bows of the past.

If you're coming from the world of the compound, remember that even long-armed archers seldom need more than a 28-inch draw, not if they go with the proper compressed, crook-elbow form typical of Howard Hill and

Bowyers vary tremendously in the design of their creations. This gives the archer a wide choice styles.

other instinctive shooters. I went from a 31-inch compound draw to a 28-inch stickbow draw. That's due to a different stance. The traditional bow is managed as part of the archer, rather than as a mechanical tool separate from the bow shooter's body. As outlined in the chapter on instinctive shooting, the traditional archer is fluid, not rigid. Elbow is cocked not locked. Knees are bent. All of this contributes to a shorter draw than with the mechanical bow, which is held straight up and down at the perpendicular.

Order draw weight based on your ability to hold an anchor point for at least a few seconds. I agree with other archers as well as bowyers that after 60 to 65 pounds, the law of diminishing returns steps in and arrow speed does not increase enough to be worth the extra tugging. And I promise that 60 to 65 pounds is sufficient to down any North American big game. It was certainly enough in the hands of Fred Bear, who took everything from moose to polar bear with his 65-pound recurve. One afternoon after playing tag with a buck antelope on the high plains of Wyoming, I finally got my oppor-

This all-glass-limb bow from Pronghorn Custom Bows has proved itself under all shooting conditions, here providing a sage grouse.

tunity as the old-timer doubled back on his trail toward where I was waiting. The angle was upward. I let fly with a bow that drew well under 60-pound pull. I missed. The buck reversed course, giving me a second chance. I missed again. Then the pronghorn dropped in his tracks. Both arrows had sailed right through him. I never saw either arrow again, though I looked.

There are many choices to make about the grip: high-wrist, low-wrist, leather-wrapped, uncovered wood, large, small, locator, no locator, three fingers under, and so on. And of course, don't forget left-hand versus right-hand options. I believe that the deep throat grip is better suited to the recurve than the longbow. But that's a personal preference. I prefer straight-wrist shooting over shooting with your hand down and a sharp bend at wrist, which many target shooters go for with their recurve bows. Try some different styles and decide for yourself.

Another choice is between a one-piece bow and a takedown. I have heard that takedowns lose efficiency. If so, my chronographs never showed

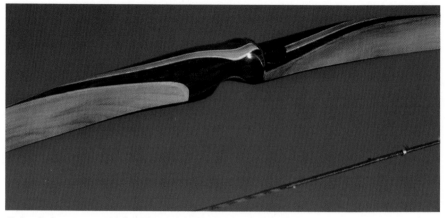

Grip choices vary widely. This is a rather deep throat, but there are grips with much deeper throats as well.

that to be true. If you travel by plane, or for some other reason have a need for compactness, then a takedown is the only way to go. Or if you want one riser with extra sets of limbs so you can change the draw weight on a single bow, a takedown is again the answer. One-piece bows are of course just as good as takedowns, but today the reverse is equally true. The longbow I shoot most today is a Pronghorn Three-Piece Takedown. And yes it does have two sets of limbs, a lighter set for longer practice sessions and small game, and a heavier one to propel a heavier arrow for bigger work. If you want an extra set of limbs for your takedown bow, for a perfect match consider ordering them with the bow rather than afterwards.

Lamination choices run wild: maple, Osage, bamboo, red elm, yew, glass—the list is longer than a trip across Texas. Fancy lams require clear glass over them to show off grain and color. Talk to the bowyer for his opinion on which materials he likes best for his bows and why he chooses them. Wood for risers also run the gamut from simple rock hard maple to almost any wood strong enough to serve the purpose. I have one bow with an English walnut riser. I also have a beautiful bow with a cocobolo riser that contrasts with the Osage lams.

Decide up front about having inserts installed for a bow quiver on that recurve or leaving them out, carrying arrows instead in one of the many different types of arrow-carriers now on the market, including daypacks.

Decide whether you want a fancy or simple bow. While the compound bow is a "machine" and looks the part, the traditional bow is in line with what I call "working art." I would not settle for one that is beautiful but shoots a slow arrow. However, I know of no traditional bowyer who is unconcerned with eye appeal. Furthermore, even hardworking plain traditional bows exude grace through their very lines. Ask the bowyer about finish. There are

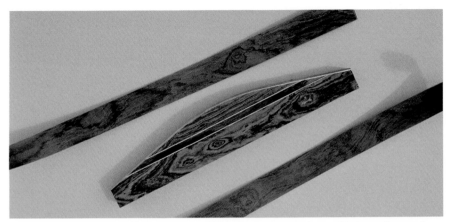

Here is the beginning of a three-piece takedown longbow of very high grade wood.

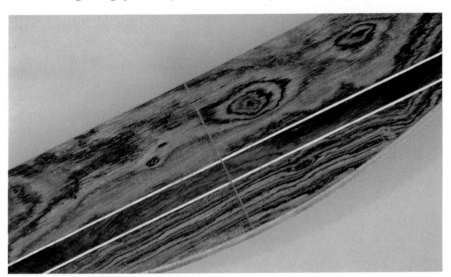

Fancy or plain is another archer choice in a custom bow. A fancy bow begins with exotic wood like this.

many options, such as snakeskin limb coverings and hand carving, overlays, or other artwork—even wood-burning. You can also get a hand-rubbed oil finish or a bright, dull, or crinkled polyurethane finish—you name it.

Good custom recurves and longbows come with a reasonable warranty. No one can expect the bowyer to replace limbs that delaminated in the hot trunk of a car. On the other hand, a bowyer will replace the bow in the unlikely event of a failure in bow due to some unforseen event, such as a glue failure.

After considering all these options, go ahead and order that custom stick—even if it's the only one you will ever buy. Chances are you'll love it.

9

Bow Setup and Tuning

The Ben Pearson Company led the entire archery industry for quite some time; his company was the largest in the world by 1950. T. J. Conrads reports that the Pearson plant was turning out twelve thousand arrows a day with a total workforce of three hundred employees. In 1956, Pearson Archery brought out its trademark bow, the Laminated Takedown Recurve. Being a takedown bow was a huge factor for its success because archers could break the bow down small enough to carry just about anywhere and reassemble it for duty in seconds. Ben took the bow to Alaska to hunt polar and brown bears—called brown bears until common sense was trumped by taxonomy; now everything is a grizzly. His takedown Bushmaster bow accounted for the world records of the time for both polar and brown bears. That was in 1956. By 1962, the company had increased to over five hundred employees.

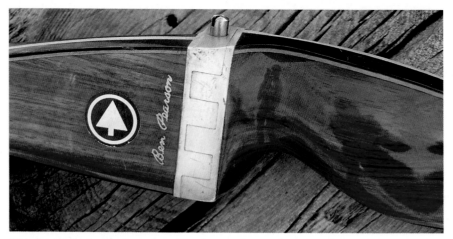

This is a Pearson takedown bow like the one that made a radical impact on the world of archery. Pearson's bow is an example of the era that put assembly-line bows in the hands of thousands of archers.

The Ben Pearson takedown, with its unique design, could be purchased by any archer in the land. These photos show how this bow came apart with a coin.

Ben also made archery films. I recall two—one in which he took ducks out of the air with uncanny regularity, and another where he got a javelina at a measured 130 yards.

Ben's bows were good. He spearheaded assembly line production without losing quality. Conrads calls Ben the Henry Ford of the archery industry, the first to build precision machinery to assemble good production bows. I know the bows were worthy because I ended up with a couple of them that I bought used after the company more or less "disappeared." Ben retired from bowmaking in 1967. He died at age 72 in 1971. The company was sold and resold but without the great archer at the helm, it just sort of dwindled away.

These introductory remarks to bow setup set the stage for this important chapter because Ben's takedown caused a big stir. Because of its design—and those of many more takedowns to come, of course—thoughts of setup and tuning began to prevail in "our camp" of bow shooters. Personally, I simply strung my sticks without regard for careful setup or tuning because they were extremely simple bows, mostly self-bows, not sophisticated enough to gain much advantage from careful tuning. I might have concern for fistmele and may have tinkered a bit with the nockset point, but that would be it. Ben's bow, followed by Fred Bear's, brought new setup demands. The bows were worth "tinkering with" for better performance, especially Fred Bear's, with its "multidirectional fiberglass." And so I precede setup with a note or two on the deserving Ben Pearson and Fred Bear because what they did with bows some time ago has dictated many of the setup and tuning practices we use today.

Aren't these just little things? There are no little things in setting up and tuning traditional tackle. Even the almost weightless strike plate and arrow rest count. The goal is simple, yet profound: to prepare the bow, along with its attending tackle, to perform as closely to its intended design, manufacture, and potential as possible.

I once watched on television in our then small town as a local archer set out to "prove" that a 50-pound bow was "deadlier" than a .30-06 rifle. The screen went blank as a shooter fired the rifle in the small studio. When the picture came back, the archer stepped forward, drew his bow, and proved beyond any doubt that indeed a 50-pound recurve bow in the Ben Pearson/Fred Bear style was deadlier than the .30-06-provided you are shooting a bucket of sand. The bullet died quickly in the sand, just as it would in water, but the arrow with broadhead pierced the bucket "clean through," protruding well beyond the side of the pail.

As a high schooler, I was impressed. Shortly after that demonstration, I attended an archery show of sorts—more an introduction to the better bows of the day than an exhibition. The first thing the teacher said—I remember the idea if not the exact words—was "If you want your bow to perform, you have to set it up right." The first thing he did was step through the bow between string and limb, bending the limbs to get the string loop attached to the string nock. When I got my first recurve bow (fortunately, an inexpensive one in used condition) I bravely stepped through between string and limbs and neatly torqued the upper limb into a permanent twist. I still shot the bow, but it eventually found a home in the dump. The upper part of the string never aligned again with the limb groove. I was catching on that the bow is, after all, a machine and, like any machine, demands a certain respect in handling, including setup and tuning.

There are three major parts of setting up the bow. These are *brace height, nocking point,* and *the arrow.* Having written those words, I hastily add that the other "more incidental" factors can bring a bow to smooth, accurate, enjoyable shooting or make it as reliable as the weather. The bow maker will (or at least should) provide instructions with the bow, especially brace height and nock set location, so that the archer has a starting point to work with. However, it is not possible for the bow maker to know an individual archer's particular shooting style and idiosyncrasies, or, for that matter, the archer's unique physical ability. And so setting up the bow and consequent tuning falls entirely upon the shoulders of the bow owner.

SETTING UP THE RECURVE BOW

Step one in setting up and tuning a recurve bow is using a bowstringer. Never do the step-through to attach the loop of the string to the string nock. The wide limb of the recurve bow can twist and take a set, and the string will never lie along the string groove again. Bowstringer designs vary, but the basic idea is the same—a cord with loops or pockets at the ends to hold the bow tips. Full instructions for using a stringer can be found in chapter 23, Bow Safety—and, of course, will come with any stringer you purchase.

SETTING UP THE LONGBOW

As with the recurve bow, the first step in the important setup and tuning of the longbow is using a stringer. Never do the step-through to attach the loop of the string onto the string nock. The narrow limb of the longbow, with its

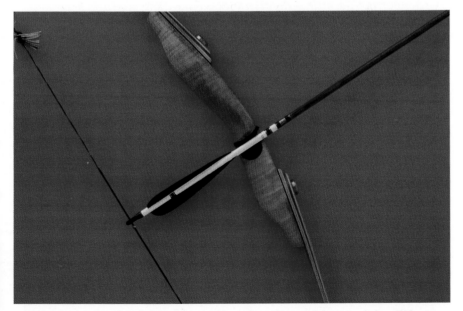

Although most longbows, like the one shown here, have thick cores, it is still best to use a stringer.

Limb bolts must be secure, but overtightening can cause a crack in the surface of the bow.

thick core, stands up far better to the step-through or push-pull method of stringing the bow, where you set the bottom limb tip against your foot, pull the bow toward your body, and slip the string onto the upper string nock with the other hand. The bowyers I know use step-through and push-pull. I've done it, but the stringer is safer for both bow and archer.

SETTING UP THE TAKEDOWN BOW

In setting up the takedown bow, the initial step is securing the limbs to the riser "good and snug" and not so tight as to fracture the glass or finish on the bow limb. The second step is ensuring that there is no squeak when the bow is drawn. If the bow squeaks, the problem is at the joint between the limb and the riser. Lubricate lightly at this point with anything that will not attack wood or finish to "retune" the bow to quiet. Another solution is to install a very thin buffer. See chapter 17 for more on this subject.

ASSESSING DRAW LENGTH

To assess your draw length, start by ripping off the topmost part of a paper match pack, resulting in a square about 1.5 by 1.5 inches. Now take a *full-length* arrow shaft, with or without fletching, tipped with a target point. Push the target point through the center of the paper square. Now the paper will slide up and down the shaft. Nock the arrow and slide the piece of paper down the shaft until it is within a short distance from the riser; the exact distance is not important, just get it close. Now draw the arrow fluidly, as you would normally shoot from your preferred stance. As you draw the arrow, the paper square will slide against the riser.

The paper square will have been moved down the shaft to the exact front of the riser. Measure from the inside of the arrow nock to the point where the paper square stopped sliding on the arrow. That is your exact draw length with that arrow. I like to add 0.5 inch to the exact spot that the paper square ended up touching the riser. If it stopped at 28 inches, I cut my arrows off so that the length from the inside of the nock to where back of the broadhead or any other type of point will end up at 28.5 inches. Others will prefer a full extra inch in length to ensure zero contact between the drawn broadhead arrow and the bow hand.

When I was shooting a compound bow, my arrow length was 31.5 inches, plus the half-inch safety zone which brought total arrow length to 32 inches. I had to go with a slightly stiffer arrow than I would with a shorter draw because the longer the arrow, the more likely it is to "whip," being more flexible. When I sent away for my first longbow after not shooting one regularly for a time I ended up with a reverse handle by John Schultz, a fine bow and fast-shooter. I wanted to shoot at the draw length of my compound bow. I soon found that this was a stiff and upright stance that did not work well with the stick. With no effort at all, I went from 31.5-inch draw to 28-inch draw by flowing into the bow, bending a little at the knees, and tilting the bow (see chapter 10).

SETTING UP ARROW SPINE

Setting up not be quite the right term here—"selecting" an arrow of a given spine may be more appropriate—but in keeping with the theme of this chapter, let's allow it. The point is to find a stiffness (spine) of arrow that matches the bow. Since spine is associated with bow draw weight and draw length, it makes sense to start with an arrow that matches the draw length and poundage within 5 pounds or so. With a wood arrow and a bow of 55 pounds at 28-inch draw, a 60-pound spine arrow would be a prudent start. At some archery shops, you can buy two arrows of different spine instead of having to buy a whole set that may, in the end, not work with a specific bow setup. The best way to test for arrow spine in a particular bow is to observe the flight of the arrow. Unfortunately, the archer must be prepared to work on all three major setup criteria simultaneously.

There is no other way to arrive at the correct arrow of proper spine with the right nocking point plus the best brace height. It's a matter of adjusting all three as many times as is necessary to find that sweet spot where everything is synchronized. A starting point could be brace height or nock set location. I like to begin with an arrow that *should* perform properly in the bow

Arrow spine should be selected to correspond to the draw length and draw weight of the bow. The arrows shown here are spined for a 60-pound bow at 28-inch draw.

according to the draw length and weight. Every arrow made is given a particular spine value, even when the term "spine" is not used. For example, an aluminum shaft may be "2017." This four-digit number breaks down to two numbers—20 and 17. The 20 in this instance stands for outside diameter of the shaft in $1/64$-inches. The 17 stands for wall thickness of the shaft measured in thousandths of an inch. So a 2017 shaft is $20/64$-inch outside diameter with a wall thickness of .017 inch. A 2219 aluminum shaft would be $22/64$-inch outside diameter with a .019-inch wall thickness (nineteen one-thousandths of one inch).

I did not devote an entire chapter to aluminum, carbon, or any other arrow material because traditional archers these days are inclined toward wood. However, this is not an omission based on prejudice. When I got my first Black Widow bow I shot aluminum arrows and carbons right along with wood. Aluminum arrows are today better than ever, and they were already excellent when they hit the market in the middle 1950s. Today, there are so many different choices in aluminum shafts that I urge you to check out those that fit your personal bow best. The carbon shaft is also better than ever, as proved by current examples such as the Easton St Epic N-Fused, boasted as being 182 times stronger than steel and 18 times stronger than Kevlar. Beman, Carbon Tech, PSE, and other companies also make fine carbon arrows.

Spine recommendations from shaft-making companies are worthwhile as starting points. But the archer will find that there is often a wide range of stiffnesses that function very well with a single bow. As an example, I have

A bow square is used to determine the length of the fistmele (brace height), the distance from the string to the throat of the grip.

had four or more different aluminum arrows shoot just fine from one bow. Buy aluminum or carbon shafts in very small quantities and shoot them from your bow for flight characteristics. A good starting point is the exact spine called for in the chart put out by the arrow company, plus one spine level higher (stiffer), though sometimes you will have to experiment with two or even three higher spines.

You also have to juggle trying out a different arrow with the same fistmele and nocking point on the string, the same arrows with different brace height and nock set locations, and so forth, until the melody is perfect. Tuning then means ensuring that these variables *remain constant*. And remember that in some instances, the spine of the arrow may have to be much heavier than normal for good arrow flight. An example, and a rather rare one, of a heavier spine demand is a 60-pound draw weight bow that belonged to a friend of mine. That bow demanded wood arrows of 85/90 spine for proper arrow flight.

SETTING UP FISTMELE

The bowyer will have recommended a specific brace height (distance from the string to the throat of the riser). But it is a near certainty that the new bow owner will adjust that distance to his or her personal shooting habits, posture, physical ability, stance, and other factors. Begin by twisting or untwisting the strands of the bowstring to shorten or lengthen it. This will affect the distance from nock to riser. If the bower calls for a brace height of 8.75 inches, for example, then lengthen or shorten the string, using a bow square tool, until that distance is achieved.

Now shoot the test arrow. Don't be overly concerned about a fishtail wag or a porpoise roll at this point. Pay much more attention to how the bow handles. Listen for noise. A very low fistmele on a recurve bow can create a racket with string-slap, the string smacking down on the string groove cut into the limbs. A somewhat higher-than-called-for brace height may quiet the bow to some degree, and may even provide a smoother draw, albeit with a probable slight loss of arrow speed.

SETTING UP NOCK SET LOCATION ON STRING

Start with the recommendation of the bowyer, who provides a nock set location starting point. I like to start only $1/8$ inch above the horizontal so that, in effect, the arrow is slightly "looking down" at the arrow rest. I have, on occasion, had good luck with the arrow at the horizontal—parallel, as it were, with the arrow rest—but a nock located to point the arrow downward toward the arrow rest is preferred by far. If $1/8$ inch does not send a clean arrow away, go up, perhaps to $7/16$ inch, and even to $1/2$ inch. Use the bow square all the while to determine where to move the nock set. The only nock set I will recommend is the little brass job with the plastic insert. Using nockset pliers, you can move this nockset up and down the string quickly and secure it perfectly in place. The cost is minimal and the lifetime is just about forever. The nockset can be located so that nock of the arrow rests on top of the it or under it. It does not really matter.

The first step in setting up a proper nocking point on the string is using a bow square to determine a particular starting point.

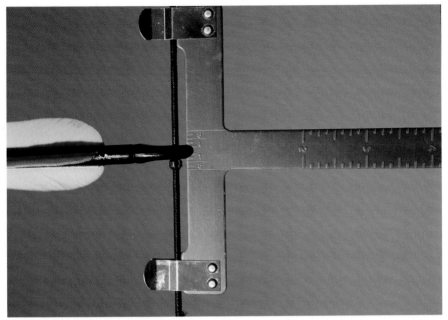

The arrow is placed on the string. The throat of the nock is centered on a point on the bow square.

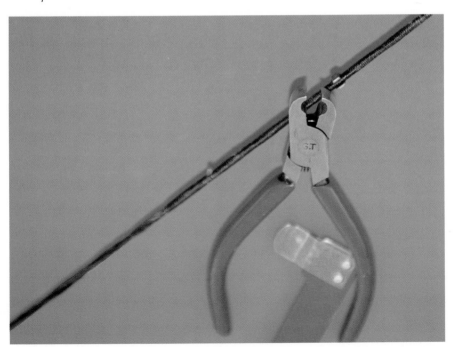

Nocking pliers are used to secure the nockset to the string.

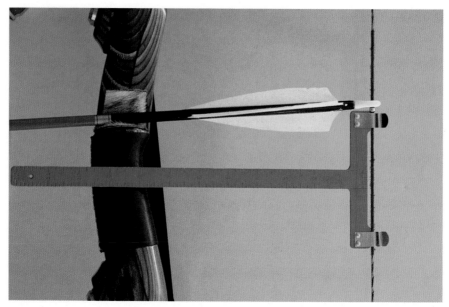

Here, we see that the nock is elevated above the horizontal line of the bow square. This is normal. However, the amount of elevation is determined by actually shooting of the arrow to check for stable arrow flight.

SETTING UP STRING SILENCERS

Refer to chapter 16 for a discussion of silencers and how to attach them. Silencers quell the *boo-wang!* of the bow and are an important part of bow setup tactics.

SETTING UP ARROW FLETCHING

Sometimes, due to the archer, the bow, or both, the arrow must be dressed in large fletching, even helical (twist), in order to gain stable arrow flight. I recall a particular bow belonging to a friend of mine that absolutely demanded high-profile fletching (large helical feathers) for good arrow flight. It was a longbow in the 80-pound draw class and fletching with less surface area resulted in a wig-wag of the arrow.

SETTING UP ARROW REST AND STRIKE PLATE

Material choices run wild. Enough has been said about shooting through the gap, where the arrow rest and plate separate to make a trough for a hen feather to fly through. I do that with some bows. But the three-piece longbow I shoot often these days has no such gap. The strike plate and the arrow rest meet and arrow flight is perfect. An archer can elect for an elevated arrow rest, the type more associated these days with the compound bow. However,

If a single string silencer is used, experimentation is required to find the ideal setting on the string. Here, a single silencer is located approximately halfway in between the lower bow limb and the throat of the bow. Measurement to the inch or less is seldom required.

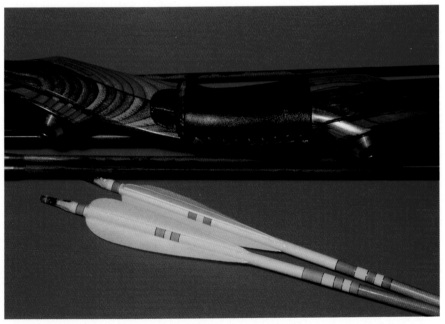

Setting up fletching is vital for the obvious factor of stable arrow flight, but also for quiet flight. The fletching here is straight offset fletching.

This is but one of many ways to set up an arrow rest. A dot of epoxy is located on the strike plate and another dot on the arrow rest. This provides a small gap between the strike plate and arrow rest.

I have found no advantage with this type of rest with traditional bows. Shooting off the shelf leaves nothing to be desired.

BROADHEAD SETUP
Broadhead selection is more choice than setup. Today's fine, well-balanced broadheads fly like target points. Broadheads can be mounted vertically, parallel to the riser, or horizontally, parallel to the ground. I go vertical with a two-blade head (really one blade with two sides), such as the Grizzly. If the archer wants to try mounting the single-blade broadhead horizontally it will work. For multiple blade heads, such as the Coyote II, simply mount them on the arrow. Tuning with broadhead means trying different ones to determine which ones give you the best arrow flight.

QUIVER SETUP
The bow shooter should be able to comfortably pull a shaft free from its moorings, slipping it on the string with facility—quickly and quietly when need be. My recurve bows, being (with one exception) beautiful one-piece bows I will not drill for insert, wear bow quivers. Longbows may also wear bow quivers. My friend Tracy Villwok, a great archer and bow collector, has a two-arrow quiver on his favorie longbow. For roving and small game with a longbow, I like a loaded backquiver. My favorite is the Chewiwi of Isleta, New Mexico, which is beautiful and serviceable.

Even the almost weightless strike plate can have an effect on total bow performance. Here a template is being made out of paper. The template will be used to cut out a strike plate that fits exactly.

The template is laid up against the bow to ensure that when the strike plate material is cut, it will be fit correctly.

Contact cement is used to attach the strike plate to the riser.

BARE SHAFT AND PAPER TUNING

Bare shaft (no fletching) and paper tuning are okay, but I see no need for either because my single goal is a properly fletched arrow flying hot, straight, and normally. The theory is, if a bare shaft flies fairly well at close range, once fletching is attached it will be just wonderful. Paper tuning is shooting bare shafts into a big sheet of paper. If the hole made in the paper is round, the arrow must have been flying point-on. If the hole is elongated, the arrow must have hit sideways. The round hole is what you want.

Are these little things? Some particulars of setting up a bow and keeping it shooting great by occasional tuning are small, such as that tiny nockset. But in setting up and tuning, it's the little things that can make a big difference.

A bow quiver must be secure. Anything less can cause rattling and unwanted vibration in the bow hand.

10

Archer Control

There's a good deal of psychology in bow shooting. This fact is perhaps more evident in the traditional bow than in the wheel-and-pulley mechanical job. Archers who can put an arrow into a pine knot at thirty paces when shooting without witnesses can't hit a straw bale at half that distance with an audience. They get "psyched out." This chapter is for all who want to upgrade their control of the bow, making the bow do what they want rather than the bow mastering them. When the archer has gained full control over the bow, he or she has confidence, and confidence is required in any sport to do well. Imagine the pole vault athlete who is not confident that he can rise on that whippy stick and make it over the bar. He's done before taking his first step off the line.

FITNESS FIRST

Consider yourself an athlete. You don't have to be that tall. You don't have to be that powerful. But if you shoot a longbow or recurve with resolve, you are an athlete. Your job is to rise to the level of your born ability. I have mentioned my friend before, the powerful fellow who strings a hundred-pound-pull longbow while remaining seated in his easy chair in the living room. I was not granted the physique to ever do that, no matter how many weights I lift or how many hours of training in the gym I put in. Most of us will never be up to that sort of physical prowess. But we can draw *our* bows—bows that are within our physical ability. And more importantly, we can *improve*, coming closer and closer to our potential by answering a desire to "get stronger."

This may involve a regimen under the eye of a professional coach. Or a plan okayed by a personal physician who has issued a clean bill of health for a workout program following a physical examination. Or it may require shooting our bows several times a week for an hour or so each session. I have concluded that a bow over sixty-five pounds pull is not going to provide enough edge to beat a bow closer to fifty-five pounds draw weight. But even fifty-five pounds means building those specific muscles that do the job. So shoot that bow within the range of your ability until drawing it to full anchor point is no more difficult than opening a can of pork and beans. Physical mastery of the bow becomes the first step in psychological management of the bow.

CONCENTRATION PRACTICE
Mastering bow shooting means learning to concentrate. Without concentration, the arrow is an unguided missile. This is triply true for the shooters of longbows and recurves who go by the instinctive or reflexive method of shooting. There are no sights on that bow. If there were, your eye could rivet on a mechanical sight to ensure that the aiming point remains optically pasted on the target until the arrow gets away. Without sights, your eye has to be like Superman's, able to burn a hole right through that target. Think of a magnifying glass in the sun, its hot little spot concentrated on a piece of paper. Soon the paper smokes and a hole has been burned right through it. Your eye is that hot little spot of fire. Burn a hole in the bull's eye and let your natural hand-eye coordination do the rest.

NIGHT CANDLE CONCENTRATION
My five-acre backyard away from the city, with its large backstop to capture arrows, is a safe place for night candle concentration practice. In semi-

Concentration practice is enhanced by specific targets, such as this 3D turkey behind brush; the archer has to thread an arrow through that brush to hit the mark.

darkness (it's never pitch black when I shoot) I set up candles and light them on a windless night. The small flames are perfect for heavy-duty concentration, which in turn promotes archer control. I set up six or more candles in a row because I am not Byron Ferguson who flicks out the flame with the point of his arrow. I am more likely to snuff my candles with the breeze from the feathers. Another trick is using a flashlight beam concentrated on a nighttime target. It works because the beam automatically focuses attention on the aiming point.

BODY CONTROL

I suppose if I were more dedicated I would take yoga lessons three days a week, but I prefer shooting a bow instead. People who do yoga with any semblance of seriousness can promote their own bodily controls to significant levels. My mother would not tolerate wimpy behavior. If we got scraped from a bike fall she dabbed on the iodine (not a recommended practice today), wrapped a strip torn from a clean sheet around the wound, and said, "Now get back out and play." We learned that physical pain could be almost ignored with concentrated control. Meditation would be a helpful practice. But for me just plain taking to the outdoors with bow in hand and a resolve to loose "clean arrows" is my meditation.

If body control were single-faceted, it would be easy for the archer to "get it right" every time. But it's hardly that way. Body control is many-faceted. Every little detail must be attended to. Moreover, all the details of body control must be in play *simultaneously*. It does no good to have great control of knee-bend while the bow arm elbow is rigid as a piece of drift wood. It does no good to have great bow arm control while your knees are locked like a vault at Fort Knox. All aspects of body control must act together-foot placement, the nonrigid body (bow-shooter's crouch), uncocked bow-arm elbow, relaxed knees, stable anchor point to the same spot always, that clean arrow release—it all works together.

TARGET PANIC

Old-timers called it *hunter's ague.* Later, it was called *buck fever.* It was the condition of panic upon sighting game, the hunter sometimes racking the cartridges from his lever-action rifle right onto the ground without firing a shot. Target panic for archers sometimes manifests itself as the inability to turn the arrow loose, fingers sort of locked on the string; more often it is the opposite—the short draw. A good remedy is using a very light-draw bow, bringing the arrow to full anchor, and then forcing yourself to hold for the count of ten before loosing the shaft. Do it over and over until letting the arrow fly becomes a part of your routine and style. Try staring at the target for

Body control means at all times, not only when standing in front of a target, ready to cast an arrow. Body control includes being constantly aware of one's surroundings, even when hiking.

a while without turning an arrow loose. Just look at the spot you want to hit. Let an arrow go only when you have mastered your breathing and heartbeat.

TRANSFER PRACTICE FOR ARCHER CONTROL

The more closely a practice session simulates whatever the archer wishes to perform, whether hunting, target shooting, or even roving or informal straw bale fun, the better the transfer value. Practicing with 3D targets, for example, can help the archer learn to control his or her bow in the field better than practicing on a big round target with multiple circles, while practicing on that big round target with multiple circles is just right for transfer value to target shooting. Even a form of practice completely unrelated to the kind of shooting you want to improve at is better than no practice when trying to build archer control. But remember that haphazard practice may be worse than leaving your bow on the rack.

PRACTICE DOES NOT MAKE PERFECT

Practice does not make prefect. Only perfect practice makes perfect. Flinging arrows haphazardly may in fact take you further away from your goal of improving your control. One archery coach put it this way, "I'd rather see my students shoot one arrow with correct form and concentration than fifty

Coming upon any game that might end up in the pot can result in a minor temporary panic once called "hunter's ague," now more familiar as buck fever. This panic can throw an archer off balance.

A 3D field of targets is good for "practical practice."

arrows sprayed down the field." Part of the problem is that we often have such a great time shooting traditional bows that we may become lulled into putting more importance on the flight of the arrow than on placing that arrow exactly on the target, be it a grouse for campfire supper or a knot on a tree stump. Bowhunting is an act of precision physical and mental coordination. Sometimes that is forgotten and when it is, archer control goes out the window.

Only perfect practice makes perfect. One way to make practice more perfect is shooting from a position that comes as close as possible to "the real thing." This archer practices from a stand because he wants to get good at shooting from a stand.

ROVING FOR ARCHER CONTROL

As part of practice transfer (from practice to a specific shooting goal) roving is about as close as an archer can come to simulating arrow-shooting under field conditions, because (painfully obvious) all of the shooting takes place in the field. The target is always changing, not only in substance, but in distance. But mostly, the rove works so well because while it's fun to march around pinning pieces of refuse to the ground, missing is boring. And so concentration on every shot is the rule, even though the mark is only a bit of litter or a left-behind beverage can.

Roving can be good practice for instinctive shooting. The compound bow-shooter with a rangefinder has an advantage. And yet the traditional archer shooting instinctively can shoot very accurately as well. The rangefinder is ideal for figuring out the precise distance from arrow to target for the compound bow archer. Once the distance is known, the sights are set to match and if the bow is controlled, a hit is likely. Meanwhile, the instinctive archer has fired a dart using his computer (the human brain) and very

Roving is a practical and superior means of gaining archer control in the field. It results in the best brand of instinctive shooting at targets at all different practical distances. Checking the distance of a shot with a rangefinder after the shot is okay. But not before.

often with uncanny accuracy. While I do not use a rangefinder to relate distance to shot, I often employ my Leupold RX-1000 TBR to tell me how far a shot was *after the fact.* Or I like to "scope out" distance simply to see how close I came at guessing how far it is across that canyon or to where that buck antelope stands on the prairie.

SURVIVAL HUNT ARCHER CONTROL

The survival hunt with a bow: I talk about it too much, but there is a strong element in a situation where missing the mark is also missing supper. The survival hunt puts an entirely new dimension on archer control. It's not that the bow-shooter will starve if game is missed; it's hardly that grave. But there's a big difference between bringing that cottontail, quail, grouse, partridge, or other edible to camp, and reaching into the pack for crackers. The elements of the rove are also present in the survival hunt, but sharpened to the keen edge of a flint broadhead. In roving, there is always the friendly, "I bet you can't hit that stick" as it lays half buried at the base of tree fifty-plus yards away. So you try. So you miss. So what? Coming close is in most cases sufficient reward. The same reward rarely attends a miss on a prime edible. You came close, missed, and the rabbit went away to furnish a coyote his supper.

Going on a survival hunt tones the archer greatly, not only in the physical game, but also in the mental game of shooting instinctively. Here, the author pauses for a rest stop on a survival hunt.

There is a whole new element of "positioning" on the survival hunt. It's a precursor to going for that prize deer or elk. Stomp down the hill on a rove, joking with your partner, scaring every sensible creature within earshot into its hiding place—no problem. Stomp down the same hill making a racket and the game you frighten into its lair could have been a good and rightful harvest. So you take on a whole new attitude on the archery survival hunt. You have to have archer control—fully.

"GET A GOOD READY" FOR ARCHER CONTROL

George Washington Sears remains one of my heroes from the world of woodsmanship. He was known as Nessmuk to his readers, a short, slight fellow and the first person I know of who invented lightweight backpacking. His book, *Woodcraft*, remains inspiring, even though our high-tech gear today eclipses the nineteenth-century technology he used. What Nessmuk would have given for my Coleman Cloudcroft sleeping bag! The grand old hunter, on one of his many-day survival hunts with nothing but a small-caliber muzzleloader in hand, ran into an immense wild boar. Although the consummate outdoorsman, Nessmuk found himself "so badly 'rattled' that I could hardly handle my rifle."

"At first I was provoked at myself for not getting a good ready," Nessmuk wrote, "and shooting him in the head; but it was better to let him live." "Getting a good ready," to Nessmuk, meant quickly and efficiently learning to control all of your emotions, from joy to fear; only then is your body relaxed and prepared to do whatever is necessary under the situation, such as defending yourself against a huge wild boar if the animal decides to attack instead of flee. Getting a good ready—learning through practice to gain full mental *and* physical control swiftly— is extremely important to archer control. There is plenty of time to get "rattled" after the shot.

IMAGINATION AND ARCHER CONTROL

One of the best forms of archer control is to imagine the shot before taking the shot. On the movie screen of your mind, there flies the arrow, straight, hot, and normal, right to the mark. In still-hunting, which is not staying still, but rather coursing through the habitat with knowledge of both wildlife and "lay of the land," imagining the shot before it ever comes to pass is highly important. You come to a thicket. You imagine that something you wish to harvest is in that thicket. You imagine where it might be lying, and which way it will go if it runs out of the thicket. Most of the time, the imagined shot never happens, but when it does, you will have, to echo Nessmuk, gotten "a good ready."

ARCHER CONTROL IN CARRYING THE BOW

It may seem simplistic, but a lack of archer control in carrying a stickbow through black timber or thicket jungle can put the bow-shooter off balance during the entire time in the field. It is important to procure a bow that "carries well" for you. It's a personal thing. When getting back into the simpler string-gun, I made the mistake of buying a recurve bow with a riser that felt like a two-by-four in my hand. It was a heavy bow, heavier than necessary to my way of thinking, and longer than I liked. But the archer who got it after me found none of the faults in that bow that I told him about. That bow just "carried bad" for me. So point one is: get into a bow that feels good in *your* hand, that you can manage in the field fluidly and without feeling that it's a burden.

Don't expect a bow to conform to you. You conform to the bow. My mentor in the writing game, Jack O'Connor, used to say that he wanted a rifle that carried with the weight of a wristwatch while hiking, but turned into ten pounds when it came time to shoot. Since there is no bow that carries like a wristwatch, magically becoming full-size just before the shot, then it's up to

Part of archer control is managing the bow in the field, which sometimes means finding a temporary resting place for it.

A bow that feels good in the hand carries well for the archer. I took this brace of sage hens with what I call my "deadly stick," a Pronghorn Custom Bows Three-Piece Takedown Longbow that is light and easy to carry but shoots a strong arrow.

us as archers to get used to packing the strung stick, practicing different methods, if necessary, to master the bow in the field.

ARCHER CONTROL IN CARRYING ARROWS

Part of bow management in the field is how we end up carrying arrows. Today, there are a variety of options.

Side quivers and back quivers go so far back in time that as usual we have no idea when either came along. Otzi, the Ice Man, had a back quiver. Konrad Spindler, the author of *Man in the Ice,* tells us that Otzi's quiver "consists of a longish rectangular fur sack, narrowing a little toward the bottom." This is very similar to my favorite quiver. Otzi's quiver was made from "the hide of a stag-like animal such as red deer or roe deer." Otzi's quiver is so complex in design and construction that the description of it in Spindler's book fills several pages.

The problem with a back quiver for those of us who enjoy an overnight in the great outdoors is that it takes the place of the backpack. While the back quiver is by far my favorite way to manage arrows on a rove or during practice sessions, now that I have learned to control arrow removal as an "automatic" response, I don't take it on the long treks. A bow quiver on the recurve bow works ideally—arrow management is convenient and fast. On what I call "deadly slivers," those sweet little longbows, a full-size quiver

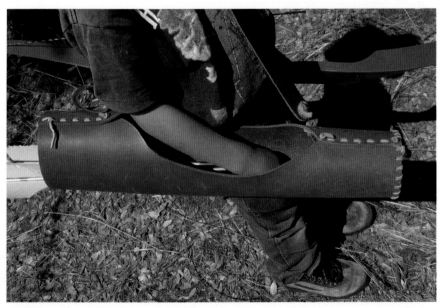

Archer control of arrows comes in many forms, including the side quiver shown here.

Back quivers have been used for so long that it's impossible to determine when they were invented. The ancient Ice Man himself had a back quiver to manage his arrows in the field. This is a modern-day custom high-capacity back quiver.

may be out of place. The Great Northern Longbow Quiver can be ideal, though. It holds five arrows and is easy-on, easy-off, and shock absorbing.

The 3D Quiver Pack is large enough at a capacity of 1,100 cubic inches to contain all of the important equipment for a full day in the woods, especially fire starter and lifeboat matches. The 3D holds up to two dozen arrows, depending on their size and points, the arrows riding fletching-upward. It's seventeen by eleven by sixteen inches in the main compartment. The 3D Quiver Pack works like a back quiver for either right-handed or left-handed archers—reach back, grab a shaft, lift and pull the arrow forward to nock on the string of the bow. I'm a big fan of the Rancho Safari Catquiver family as well. The upshot of all this quiver talk is that arrow management in the field is very much a part of archer control, and it is up to the individual bow-shooter find a way to carry arrows that promotes control.

SMALL GAME ARCHER CONTROL TRANSFER

Hunting small game and birds on its own or as part of big game trip keeps the eye sharp. This aspect of archer control hinges into many others—especially the survival hunt and rove. I find that as I still-hunt for small game

Sometimes a bow quiver is the best way for the archer to control arrows in the field, especially (but not only) if he or she is also carrying a pack.

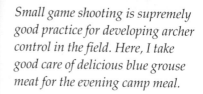

Small game shooting is supremely good practice for developing archer control in the field. Here, I take good care of delicious blue grouse meat for the evening camp meal.

and birds with a bow my concentration is boosted a notch higher than when I'm intent only on seeking bigger critters. And something else—since the bow is so quiet it is perfectly all right to keep muscles warmed up by firing a JUDO point arrow now and then into that sand bank or other softer landing spot. It is helpful to pack a little hot-melt cement to reinstall JUDOs that come loose.

Archery control is total orchestration of each separate part of shooting the bow. When it is achieved, the result is vastly increased enjoyment as well as high-end success, whether your arrows are cast at pinecones or at a winter's supply of venison.

They Call It Instinctive

11

The old wooden corral was rotting away, but there remained sufficient downed boards to house a veritable colony of cottontail rabbits. We were backpacking into the area, living mainly "off the land" with only our bows, and a protein supper sounded good. We didn't find a rabbit under the boards we moved aside but, "There's one right under that bush," my partner announced. I suggested he nock an arrow and provide for us. He did latch an arrow onto the string of his compound bow, but try as he might, he could not align the pin sight on target, which required a vertical bow. I walked over, bent down, tilted my longbow to the horizontal, and that night we had fried

One wonderful advantage of instinctive bow-shooting is the ability to shoot from different positions, including kneeling. By canting the bow, this archer will be able to deliver an arrow to the target without standing up or having to align sights.

rabbit in our skillet. It's something like throwing a baseball. While only a few special people can pitch a 90-mile-an-hour screamer over the plate, the majority of us can toss that ball with fair accuracy, even though it has no sights.

This is not to say that longbow or recurve is more certain in directing arrow to target than compound. Considering sights, releases, relaxation factors, and other mechanical advantages of the compound, the opposite is true under most, but not all, circumstances. A friend of mine hunts the elusive Coues whitetail of the Southwest with his bow—a compound. He considers a fifty-yard shot a bargain, and has taken bucks out at a full hundred yards. Finding his game first with binoculars, he "beds the buck down" and then in stocking feet (ouch!) gets as close as he can before launching an arrow. In that rather open habitat his compound is superior to my longbow for delivering arrows uncannily at long distances (although when my brother and I were shooting longbows every day we could hit a cardboard box [orange or apple size] at one hundred yards with surprising regularity).

In tangled thicket or black timber where a still-hunter earns his chance at close range, however, the instinctive archer is not at disadvantage. I have seen Vern Butler and Bob Taylor thread arrows through small openings in the brush to strike right on target. Bob, at an archery show in Wisconsin, created

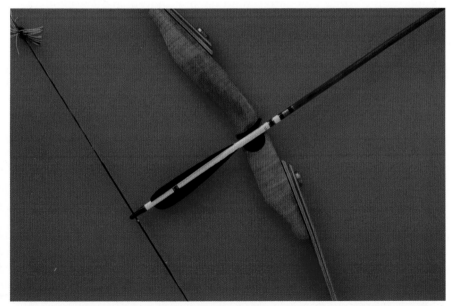

The bow type does have something to do with instinctive shooting, although any bow, including the compound, can be shot without sights. However, a bow such as this longbow is ideal for instinctive shooting—it is light in the hand and highly maneuverable.

groups at twenty yards that rivaled compound clusters, proving that a practiced archer using his instincts can make a fine record of strikes at closer ranges. And how about the great Howard Hill driving a cork on the end of his arrow back into the barrel bung? Or Reverend Stacy Groscup powdering an aspirin out of the air at eighty-two years of age on his first try with a bow he'd never shot before? Or Byron Furguson snuffing a candle, not with a brush-by of feathers, but with the point of the arrow? These talented archers performed these feats with longbows, not compounds.

I have witnessed compound bow shooters suddenly reverting to the more "natural" method of firing arrows. One afternoon on the high badlands of Wyoming, my partner and I were about to cross a fence when we caught sight of something on the ground—a shed antler, only a two-point buck (western count), but super heavy and downright interesting. "Must have come from an old-timer on his way down," we agreed. We tucked the antler into a fanny pack and moved on. No more than two hours later we glassed up four bucks traveling together. "Look at that!" we whispered in unison. In the group was the very buck that had shed the antler, one of those coincidences that defy fiction. Consequently, my partner stalked the bachelor herd while I waited on a trail that might bring action my way after his shot, because there was a four-by-four in the group I wouldn't mind having (didn't happen). He made a great stalk and got within range, but before he could line up the sights on his compound bow, a sharp eye detected him as he edged around a big boulder.

Instinctive shooting is highly useful in any territory where opportunities may arise in heavy foliage.

There was only a second to act. He canted his compound just as I would my longbow, reverting completely to instinct. The arrow was on its way, hot, straight, and true. The buck didn't make forty paces.

The bowman who uses sights can cluster arrows in a tighter group than the instinctive archer can. I believe that. But I also know that there are situations where the natural archer will torpedo a shaft on target before the sight-shooter gets his bow perpendicular for aiming. I am reminded of two miners I used to run into on my way up the mountain for Coues deer some years ago. They were .30-30 fans, each shooting a Winchester 94 carbine. I could shoot circles around them with my scope-sighted bolt-action .270 at long range, that rifle no doubt the better tool for those tricky desert whitetails. But in the thick of it, where both miners liked to hunt, their all-but-instinctive style of snap-shooting was absolutely deadly. A buck jumped at fifty paces was venison.

Howard Hill said he used what he called "the split vision" or "secondary aim" method, more or less using the tip of the arrow as a "sight." Hill's discussion of this method can be found in chapter 5 of his book *Hunting the Hard Way.* I wonder if the "computer" between our ears is actually using something the eyes sees "unconsciously"; maybe instinctive shooting is actually a process of deciphering angles and combining that information with prior knowledge of trajectory. I suppose it doesn't matter how we do it as long as we can do it—draw the bow, stare at a specific spot on the target like trying

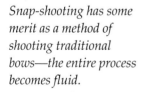

Snap-shooting has some merit as a method of shooting traditional bows—the entire process becomes fluid.

to burn a leaf with a magnifying glass in the sun, hold steady, release smoothly—and zap! The arrow hits the mark. The vast majority of stickbow archers don't feel handicapped without sights. Meanwhile, compound people can go instinctive if they want to, and some do.

Back to those snap-shooting miners for a moment. They declared that they never saw the sights on their carbines. I very much doubt that Howard Hill in his prime ever concentrated on the tip of that arrow either. And yet, bullets from those .30-30s could only go where the sights were aiming. It's possible that Hill's split vision shooting was not so very different. There was no conscious concentration on the tip of his arrow any more than the miners "worked" at lining up the sights on their carbines; yet both arrow point and sights were definitely directed with great purpose in order for bullet or arrow to strike the mark.

Maybe the word itself is a problem. Are we born with the ability to shoot bows? I really don't know. But I've seen a two-year-old toss a ball pretty straight, and I recall the day Dean Barrett, a brilliant engineer at the Hodgdon Powder Company at the time, was visiting my home and I put on a demonstration for him, shooting targets at the archery range in my back yard. "I'd like to try that," Dean said. Had he ever shot a bow? Not that he could recall. He didn't feel comfortable trying to anchor in the normal fashion, so he pulled to his chest, anchored, and let go. The arrow zipped into a straw bale twenty yards away. He did it again. And again. Maybe the word "reflexive" makes more sense than instinctive, but we use the latter and probably always will.

The first step in learning to shoot a bow instinctively—and there I've done it, stepping away from the idea that we're born knowing how to do this—is a good bow handle grip. I think that the bow-hand has more to do with arrow direction with recurves than with longbows. I have no idea what role it plays with compounds, although I suspect that a death grip on the handle is detrimental with any bow. What I do know is that strangling the grip of the bow brings inconsistency and loss of control, while a firm grip, but not super forceful, ensures uniformity from one shot to the next. As a swordsman said in an old movie, you have to hold the sword like a bird: If you hold it too tight, you'll kill it; too loose, and it will fly away. Likewise if you hold the bow too tight, the handle torques; too loose, and the bow tries to head downrange with the arrow.

The second step in becoming a proficient instinctive shooter rests in the angle of the held bow. Hill said he canted the bow to reduce the angle of arrow to target. Some traditional archers, on the other hand, hold a bow perpendicular to the ground, so that it is straight up and down. But most of us manage to shoot sitting, kneeling, and even lying flat on the ground by cant-

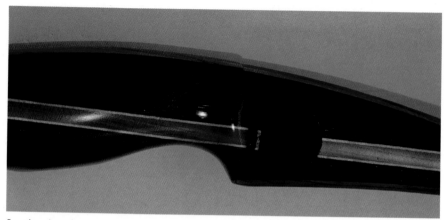

Instinctive shooting is affected by many aspects of the bow, including the very riser and grip of the bow. The archer who chokes hard on the grip of the bow may find his or her arrows going astray.

ing the bow, tilting the top bow tip to the right for a right-handed shooter, or to the left for lefties. The tilted bow forms a V shape where arrow rest and strike plate join, making a valley for the arrow to rest in. Canting also puts the eye more in line with the arrow. There are no sights on the vast majority of longbows and recurves, and yet the eye, a computer called the brain, and an anchor point that acts something like a back sight work together to deliver an arrow on target. Eyes lined up over the arrow do mean something.

The third step is developing a good stance, vital because the bow becomes part of the human machine with instinctive shooting. Being off balance is just as problematic in instinctive shooting as it is in any other sport. So is having a rigid body, which prevents fluid motion. Unlock those knees. Put your left foot a bit forward for a right-handed shooter; turn your body slightly to the left; crouch a bit (some excellent shooters crouch a lot!). Lean forward a little. Tilt your head (right for the right-handed shooter) so the eye is looking somewhat down the arrow, the arrow resting, as just mentioned, in the V shape created when the bow was canted to make a valley. By far, most shooting will be from a standing position. But at close range, many instinctive archers can direct arrows into the target even from more restrictive postures. Instinctive shooting can be done from a kneeling position (with right-handers planting the left knee on the ground). This way, the bow can be swung in a wide arc. Test this on the living room floor—not a bad place to practice with an "unloaded" bow.

The fourth aspect of instinctive shooting is the anchor point, essential for consistent instinctive shooting. If the string-hand comes to a rest at a different parts of the anatomy shot after shot, or stays out in space with a short-

Every archer will have a personal style of shooting a bow instinctively. This archer shows a fluid form in a comfortable crouch, with his elbow drawn straight back and the angle of his bow forming a V for the arrow to rest in.

draw, you will generally have poor arrow grouping. An exception is the few archers who do not bring the bow hand to rest, yet maintain the same spot out in front of their faces. While this can work, it's not recommended. I used to believe that my anchor point was with the second finger of bow-hand at right corner of mouth, but realized one day that this wasn't the case. The second finger of my right hand did touch the right corner of my mouth. But what I was really going for was having the third joint of my pointing finger tucked against the tip of my right cheekbone. A floating anchor point, incidentally, is sometimes acceptable. At very close range I may raise my nocking point to just beneath my right eye.

The fifth aspect is release—how the arrow "gets away" from the bow. Done right, it's an escape, the fingers of the bow hand letting it loose and the arrow taking off almost on its own, sort of like good trigger squeeze on a rifle or handgun, where the shooter is almost surprised when the firearm "goes off." Two general release methods exist along with many variations. Let's call these the flower petal and pull-through. Both work; which you should use depends entirely on which you are comfortable with. The first is like a flower suddenly blooming, all of its petals shooting outward at the same time. Only it's the archer's fingers that relax, uncurling to turn the arrow loose. When this release is done right, the bow hand remains on the anchor point. Pull-through, which is my style, begins with a slight relaxation

Byron Ferguson, one of the world's best archers, demonstrates his impeccable instinctive shooting form as he shoots in an exhibition that includes snuffing a candle flame with the point—not the feathers—of an arrow. Note especially the absolutely solid anchor point and the firm bow arm.

of the bow-hand grip, and the fingers come back, usually ending up an inch or more behind the original anchor point-hence, pull-through.

Step six is following through. All aspects of traditional form must be working for best results, so it's impossible to rank one as more important than another. Release, for example, is just as vital to good shooting as anchor point. But if I were forced to rank each aspect of good traditional shooting, follow-through would be at or near the top. Ideally, the body remains close to the same posture after the arrow is away, especially the archer's head, which should not bounce forward as the arrow leaves the bow. Also a big problem is bow-arm drop. I think there is an almost natural tendency to re-lax the bow arm as soon as the arrow is away, which would be okay if the ar-row were truly gone—but often that's not the case. In fact, the arm may be on the way down just as the arrow is turned loose, which leads to a miss. Just like in bowling, golf, and football, follow-through is important in instinctive bow-shooting.

Another key aspect of instinctive shooting is draw. There are different ways to pull that string back: two main styles are push-pull and straight pull-back. Push-pull is just that: the bow is pushed out with the bow arm as the string is pulled back with the bow hand. In the second method, the bow arm is extended with the elbow bent and it remains in the same position after the arrow is gone. Which is best? Since there are superior instinctive archers who

One excellent practice for the traditional archer is to set up a straw bale without any mark on it whatsoever and shoot arrows to absolutely specific points on the bale. This was recommended a long time ago by Maurice Thompson.

use the push-pull method, who am I to level a negative about it? But I personally prefer the straight pull-back method, where the bow arm remains stable as the bow is pulled to full draw. A variation of bow-drawing is double-clutching. Rather than one continuous pull, the string is drawn back almost to anchor; stopping a couple inches short, then the draw is finished with one quick motion. I can't recommend double-clutching. But I have a friend who uses it. He's a very good shot.

Arguably, the most important aspect of instinctive shooting lies between the ears, not in the arms and hands of the archer. Mental control is required to master this shooting method and the psychology is not necessarily easy to describe. I've "psyched" myself out and missed shots many times just because people were watching. I get somewhat self-conscious about that and lose concentration. I was going through a bout of, for me, super good shooting in a camp. Then other members of the group began watching rather intently. It didn't bother me at first, but I soon became self-conscious and my arrows began flying errant. One day in my own backyard archery range, and with only one person looking on, I began flinging arrows around the bale, missing the center.

Another killer in instinctive shooting is self-questioning. It reminds of the millipede story. When asked how in the world he kept all those legs synchronized, the millipede "fell prostrate into a ditch, not knowing which leg came after which." When we start asking, "How did I do that?" we're headed for big trouble. Shooting instinctively is like playing ping-pong. The body goes into motion while the mind freewheels. The brain is working, all right, because as I said earlier, it's the computer that makes instinctive shooting possible. But once we begin questioning how we were able to direct that arrow into a pine knot at twenty-five yards with a bow with no sights, trouble is on the way. We're likely to fall into that ditch, not knowing which arrow came after which. Instinctive shooting is a game of natural human activity, with the body in control while direct conscious thought is temporarily ignored. If an archer can turn off his mental machine, allowing his eye to "burn a hole" in the target, he's on his way to a hit.

Confidence is part of the brain game as well. It comes with success, reaching that point where arrow after arrow sings its way to the target. Practice has a lot to do with it. I like to rove or "stump-shoot," which is roaming around the countryside (I hike, but also ride my mountain bike) looking for inanimate targets: bits of paper, hunks of wood, twigs, discarded beverage cans, and so on. Roving is good practice and a good way to pick up litter. The Zwickey Judo point is ideal for this kind of shooting because it grabs grass and such, stopping the arrow so it doesn't go skipping off into hard-to-find places. Practice from a tree stand is also important for those who climb into one every hunting season.

Another great trick is shooting in the dark, where safe. A flashlight beam is concentrated on the target. That is the only available light. The archer cannot see the arrow or anything else. I know, I said the eye should be centered

The reward of learning to shoot the traditional bow instinctively is being able to go into the field with great confidence.

over the arrow by canting the bow, and that's true, but shooting in the dark comes after the archer has reached instinctive proficiency and the method is internalized. Now the eye *is* over the arrow, even though the archer cannot see the arrow, and the target itself is the concentration point. It's amazing how closely arrows can be clustered into a lighted bull's eye in otherwise total darkness.

We can talk about all kinds of equipment ideal for instinctive shooting. But I'm not so sure it makes sense. A good bow is a good bow. Matched arrows are matched arrows. Glove or tab? Doesn't matter. Both work fine. One point I can make with confidence is do not allow yourself to be over-bowed. When the archer has to concentrate on how in the world he or she is going to tug that string back on a bow that is too strong, instinctive shooting goes downhill. I don't want to see us back in the fifties and sixties, where light-draw bows were the rule. But I know that today's best-ever stickbows can sink a heavy arrow deeply into a bale of straw at fifty to sixty-five pounds pull. I think the law of diminishing returns sets in at about sixty-five pounds. Bless those powerful arms that can draw an eighty-five-pound bow with ease. But the archer with a too-heavy bow tends to lose that natural ability to nock an arrow, draw, anchor, and release in an almost unconscious effort.

This chapter closes with a suggestion: Read G. Fred Asbell's book, *Instinctive Shooting*, Volumes 1 and 2, which takes the information in this chapter into book length.

12

The Wood Arrow

The arrow is to the bow what the bullet is to the gun. It is the arrow, or "dart," that makes contact with target, be it a pinecone under a tree during a happy roving session, or a broadside of freezer-bound protein. The range of materials useful for traditional arrows is not limited to wood. When fiberglass came along, archers learned that it was viable for arrows. Aluminum shafts were always successful in longbows and recurves; the Easton Company is renowned for high-quality aluminum arrows. There were even arrows of steel. And of course, there are synthetics of various manufacture. Carbon is well-regarded, used in Traditional Only Carbon Arrows, Beman carbons, and others. Before the telephone and motorcar, archers were employing different products for arrows. But all in all, wood remains in high esteem by traditional archers of the twenty-first century, and is still the most-used material for making arrows for traditional bows.

The Ice Man's arrows, made five thousand years ago, reveal what arrows from the distant past were like. His arrows were quite remarkable, one having a composite two-piece shaft. If the forepart broke an entire arrow would not be lost. He also had in his quiver a tapered arrow—the forepart was thicker and therefore heavier than the back of the arrow. Weight up front aided stability. Did Otzi know that? Or did he taper his arrow "just because?" The shafts of the Ice Man's arrows were crafted from laburnum, an Old World tree yielding a dark, hard wood. Interestingly, this tree also produced a poisonous alkali that may have been employed by the ancients in some manner, possibly as a medicine.

As a kid, before the days of video games, I spent hours hiking around with a homemade bow, shooting arrows constructed of reeds and chicken feathers. Later, I purchased darts four for a buck. They broke easily. So it was back to making my own. I discovered ramin wood, which is nothing more than hardware store doweling. Ramin is last on my list of arrow woods today, although some archers like it because it builds into "logs," a term for

The Ice Man lived as long as 5,000 years ago, yet his arrows were very much like ours—or rather, ours are like his. The arrow in the center is an example of a kind of fletching that goes "way back" in time.

"very heavy arrow." Unfortunately, even from the heaviest-draw traditional bows of today, including those 85-plus pound longbow demons, ramin arrows fly as pretty as a lead kite. Even for shooters who limit their outside range to thirty yards, these heavyweights dive like a bald eagle going for a fish. Heavy is great. Too heavy is—well, just too heavy.

Going from just about last on my list of woods to my first choice, there is Port Orford cedar, so named because much of it comes from the Oregon coast. It's really Lawson cypress and it also grows in other places, such as Formosa. Air-dried cedar cures ideally, making a straight shaft. And if that shaft does not behave, taking on a bend, it readily returns to straight with nothing more than burnishing, (rubbing vigorously with a coarse rag to warm the wood) after which it is simply hand-bent "by eye" right back to straight. Tapered compressed cedars add another dimension to the cedar shaft. These are compressed (squeezed down), but also the nock end is reduced in diameter, usually from 11/32nds to 5/16ths for about the last nine inches of the arrow. Compressed tapered cedar shafts are an excellent choice because they seem to remain straight forever, at least in areas of low humidity. I have lost compressed cedar arrows in my Wyoming back yard in winter snow, only to recover them in springtime, still straight and shootable, albeit

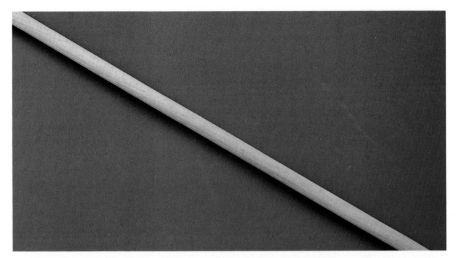

Arrows of reasonable flight quality can be built from many different woods, even hardware store doweling like this (ramin wood). However, there is a vast difference between just okay wood and ideal wood for arrows.

in need of new feathers. While regular arrows made of cedar or other suitable woods may winter well, the compressed arrow shaft, due to its density, thwarts moisture better than noncompressed shafts.

Cedar is not only capable of turning into a straight arrow, it is also strong, taking a pretty good whack without splintering. It turns into a medium-weight arrow of stiff spine. Spine is a supremely important element in managing the archer's paradox as the arrow literally bends around the riser. I don't agree with the notion that 90/95-pound shafts must be selected for 60-pound-pull recurves and longbows, not even when those bows have risers cut to center (so the arrow is almost in line with the center of the limb). Proper cedar arrows of reasonable spine fly hot, straight, and true. For example, my 60-pound-draw bows get cedars spined to a stiffness of 60/65. This may not work for every archer, but this is what works for me.

While cedar is king, there are many princes in the world of wooden arrow materials. One that has found its way into traditional archers' tackle boxes is Sitka spruce. This wood is much like cedar in behavior, although it does lack that alluring aroma of cut cedar. As a test of uniformity, I sorted one hundred Sitka spruce shafts for weight, which is the only fair way to study a wood for its ability to turn into arrows. The best dozen from the hundred Sitka bare shafts cut to the exact same length weighed 360, 360, 360, 360, 360, 361, 361, 361, 361, 361, 362, and 362 grains. Remember that a grain is 1/7,000 of one pound (437.5 grains making one ounce). So that is sterling uniformity.

Without doubt, Port Orford cedar remains the king of wood for today's traditional archery arrows. These beautiful arrows built by Rusty Izatt are made from parallel Port Orford cedar shafts.

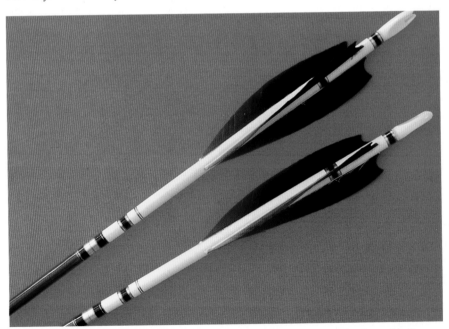

These fine handmade arrows are made of Sitka spruce with goose feathers. I believe that Sitka spruce is essentially on par with Port Orford cedar for strength, arrow flight, and other important factors.

While this represented the best of the hundred Sitka spruce shafts, matched weight capability proved excellent and the resulting fletched finished arrows performed perfectly. Torture tests also verified the toughness of this arrow wood. I found them capable of slamming into oak stumps without undue suffering, perhaps even a bit tougher than cedar—and it was a fair assessment since the Sitka spruce arrows were compressed and tapered just like the cedar arrows they vied with for strength. Conclusion: Sitka spruce gets an A+ for consistency and strength, a wood that is capable of producing a fine finished arrow. However, it never overtook cedar and it's safe to say it never will in traditional bow shooting.

Slow-growth pine is another wood for arrow-making. The batch of test shafts came from North Central British Columbia where harsh winters retard growth—hence "slow-growth pine"—producing a much tighter grain pattern than in the same trees found farther south. These dense shafts weigh more per inch than cedar or Sitka. But they don't turn into ramin logs. My test lot of full-length slow-growth pine $^{23}/_{64}$-inch diameter shafts averaged 450 grains in weight as opposed to 360 grains in weight for $^{23}/_{64}$-inch diameter Sitka shafts, both in uncut full length (32 inches).

I tested the batch of slow-growth pine shafts further. The shafts had arrived tightly bundled to prevent warpage. I removed them from the bundle

In the Far North, pine grows very slowly due to climatic conditions. Because of this growth pattern, the resulting wood is dense and can be used to make fine arrows, though they often weigh more than cedar shafts.

and wiped down thoroughly with a trace of paint thinner on a cloth to get rid of pitch. Then the hundred shafts were rebundled and allowed to cure for two months. After that they were subjected to forty-eight hours in a closet with a humidifier running. Each shaft was hand-straightened before being turned into an arrow. There was minor warping, but well within the limits of normal tolerance.

Chundoo is another arrow wood. It has good elasticity, meaning it tends to bend on impact rather than splintering. It turns into a straight shaft with a little handwork and it finishes just as smooth as cedar or Sitka spruce. It becomes a respectable arrow that takes finishes well, and it can be crested just like other woods. While not a popular wood, chundoo deserves honorable mention in this chapter. There has long been controversy about chundoo, some saying it's no more than an Indian word for lodgepole pine. Perhaps so, but lodgepole pine is noted as *Pinus contorta,* while I find chundoo listed as *Pinus sylvestris.* Regardless, tested chundoo shafts had reasonable durability, stayed straight, and were easy to restraighten when required.

Douglas fir also can be made into arrows. It's a tough wood and it has the enviable quality of very straight grain *in some selections*—but at the same time other lots may show considerable wavy grain—not good for arrows. The batch of Douglas fir shafts I tested were the same price as noncompressed, nontapered cedar shafts from the same source. It's important to clarify that these Douglas fir shafts were not "run of the mill." They were hand-selected premium grade shafts, top of the line. Had the shafts been of "regular" quality, the verdict may have been different. When finished, the batch of Douglas fir arrows proved straight and remained straight after considerable shooting. However, those that did take a bend were not as easy to straighten as cedar. A set of Douglas fir arrows prepared for use in rocky terrain suffered less catastrophic damage than cedar arrows in the same setting, shot for shot.

The wood of the larch is another possible choice. The tamarack tree, a kind of larch, makes a strong, durable arrow. The wood grows in colder regions of the Northern Hemisphere such as the boreal (North Temperate Zone) forests of Russia and Canada. It comes in numerous species, over ten. One of the larch's attributes is that it is waterproof. That is why larch is good for building yachts and smaller boats. It is also tough and durable—tough meaning it takes a whack without splintering, and durable meaning long-lasting under duress. It comes quite knot-free, which is important when making wood into arrow shafts. My tests with a few larch arrows verified toughness of the wood, but it did not perform as well as cedar or Sitka spruce.

Ash arrows are straight and tough. Ash is, after all, noted for its strength as a wood. It is very dense. One thing noticed with the small number of ash arrows available for testing was the elastic or flexible nature of the finished

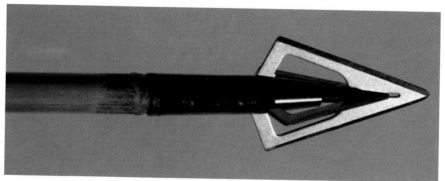

So many different woods have been used for arrow making that a complete list becomes very long. This arrow was built with a wood not normally considered ideal for arrows, yet it proved worthy in flight and strength, though not on par with cedar or spruce.

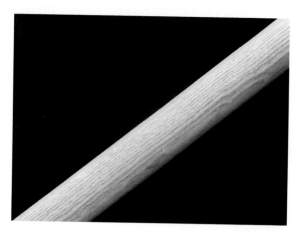

This is ash, a tough wood that can be used for arrow making. The arrows generally turn out quite straight and capable of lasting a long time in the field, especially on roves where arrows may be shot at hard objects.

arrow. This should come as no surprise because ash has been used for making bows, and bows certainly demand flexibility to store energy and then release that energy to the arrow as the wood returns to its original shape. The ash arrows did seem to survive blows that would have proved fatal to some other arrow woods. As with many other woods, ash has never competed favorably against cedar and part of the reason could be that the finished arrows are very heavy. The ash arrows tested were well behind similar cedars in velocity. Allegheny offers ash arrows for heavy-draw bows up to 150-pound pull.

Maple is well-known for its strength as a wood used in gunstocks (especially curly or tiger-stripe maple in fine muzzleloaders) and many other applications. Maple is common and highly regarded in bow making. As for an arrow, the maple lot tested averaged considerably heavier than cedar shafts of the same size. The set of arrows constructed from maple by a professional ranked from pretty to beautiful, although the fletcher said that finish was a problem, the wood resisting staining. The finished arrows were not, in the shooting that was done, as tough as the aforementioned ash arrows. But they were better suited to the 60- to 65-pound test bows than ash.

Aspen, a tree in the *Populus* genus, has been and still is used by coopers (makers of wood barrels, tubs, and so forth) and pack saddle craftsmen. The French used it to make sabots. The sabot was originally a wooden shoe, but in this context it is a "carrier" for a projectile. The sabot allows the use of a smaller-than-bore-size projectile. Today, plastic sabots (mispronounced sah-bats by most, actually sah-bows) are found in muzzleloader shooting. For the present purpose, since aspen was used in medieval archery, replica aspen arrows are available in medieval style, finished, and beautiful. They cost about 140 dollars for a dozen. As far as making modern traditional arrows from aspen, it can be done, and is being done. I did not test aspen arrows; however, I have seen a few at archery conventions and they were good-looking arrows.

Poplar must be included because finished arrows made of this wood are available. But I do not recommend them highly. There are various types of poplar and the wood has been used in products from guitars to cheap plywood, matches, and paper—especially paper. Being high in tannic acid, poplar has been employed in leather tanning. A favored use in archery today is the "kid's arrow." Finished arrows come in spines up to abut 35 pounds. The particular lot of poplar arrows that I tried in a 40-pound bow proved too "whippy" for consistency, the spine (stiffness) being too light. As this is written a dozen finished poplar arrows in $5/16$-inch diameter can be purchased for forty bucks with $2^{1}/4$-inch three-feather fletching. You can also get 30 arrows for 50 dollars, or 144 for 460 dollars. Interestingly, while the only poplar arrows widely available are in the 35-pound draw weight zone, Allegheny currently offers $3/8$-inch poplar arrows with 7-inch feathers "for bows less than 100 pounds."

Hickory proved disappointing. However, those who love logs will find arrows made of this wood much to their liking. A set of barreled (tapered on both ends) shafts purchased for testing were more costly than cedars. Lest hickory receive an unwarranted bad rap, I will point out that the hickory arrows were definitely strong, even to the point of rattling off of rocks at times without breaking. They were also smooth and straight. The hickory shaft, especially barreled (tapered at both ends), could find great favor with longbow enthusiasts who draw those 85-pound and even stouter bows. But out of bows in the 55- to 65-pound range, they died like ramins.

The range of possible woods for arrows is as wide as the ocean. Cherry wood, for example, tested well in one sample, arrows coming out lighter in weight, spine for spine, than cedar. They took a pretty good beating without

Aspen is not as ideal as cedar, but "good enough" arrows can be made from it for bows in lighter draw weights.

Proof that hickory is tough is exemplified in the fact that many thousands of baseball bats have been from this wood. However, the weight of hickory often results arrows that are like "logs," being heavier than desirable.

cracking and accepted stain relatively well. Bamboo can be heat-treated and turned into beautiful arrows and it also makes excellent laminations for bow limbs. It's an amazing plant. Actually one of about 1,500 species in the grass family, bamboo is the fastest-growing woody plant in the world. It's even edible, as bamboo shoots. A bow with Tonkin bamboo laminations can be a fine performer not only in arrow speed, but in smooth draw. As an arrow material, specially-treated shafts are worthwhile, but bamboo is leagues behind cedar in popularity.

It's important for the traditional archer to know something about arrow woods for two major reasons: application and availability. What type of wood is best for a specific job, and can that wood be located? For example, those who thrive on super heavy-draw bows may prefer a heavier arrow, such as hickory, while the rest of us match less dense woods to our bows ranging in the 60-pound draw class. As for availability, traditional archers used to have nightmares about cedar running out. But not anymore. And Sitka spruce is so good that if cedar did fall into short supply, archers could turn to that wood for arrows. Slow-growth pine, fir, and many other woods also turn into good darts for the traditional archer. But for now, cedar remains *numero uno* with traditionalists, even though it is not the only proper wood for arrows.

Remember that wood is a natural substance and cannot be controlled like a man-made product, such as aluminum or any of the synthetics. It is sort of like the human being in that no two people on the globe are exactly alike—even identical twins are not one hundred percent identical. Because woods vary it is impossible to accurately classify each type with every trait. All we can do is lay out general facts, as put down in this chapter. And so it may happen that a "heavy" wood and a "medium weight" wood turn out arrows of very similar heft due to the specific characteristics of the woods used for that particular batch of arrows.

Also, it is supremely vital that wood shafts be carefully sorted by weight when a batch of one hundred is purchased. The goal is creating sets. Each set is within a range of weight from the first to the twelfth arrow. A range of plus or minus ten grains may be considered for competitive shooting. But in the field, variations in a set of twelve ranging as high as plus or minus twenty to thirty grains is more than acceptable; most of us cannot under "real life" outdoor conditions shoot so well that an arrow weighing thirty grains more or less than the previous one will cause a wide miss. This individual nature of woods is the reason why we have some poplar arrows that are too light in spine to be consistent for true flight from a 40-pound bow, while there are other poplar arrows, ³⁄₈-inch in diameter, suited to 90-pound-pull bows.

Proof that wood arrows can be built as sets with minor variation in weight is shown in these sawed-off shaft ends with the weight of each shaft noted in ink. This matched set was made by first weighing the shafts and then using the Ace spine tester to sort them into groups.

13

The Broadhead

Love of traditional archery usually centers on the great bows and arrows. But there is so much more. It is the arrow that forms the bow's "ammunition," and the tip of that arrow that made the bow a tool of harvest and survival.

The broadhead is only one type of arrow point. There is also the target point, which comes in many different variations, including the improvised "blunt" that so many of us make with a drop of hot-melt cement in a spent .38 Special cartridge case. The case fits perfectly over an $^{11}/_{32}$-inch wood shaft. Useful for small game, but also for roving and practice, this "free" head has many admirers. The Bullet Nose Brass Point, made of solid brass, is still with us as well. So is the large blunt head—a fat rubber tip. There are metal blunt points that glue onto the wooden shaft or screw into aluminum and other insert-type arrows. The Ace Classic Point, reminiscent of medieval times, is good for roving and small game, and though target-oriented, remains formi-

Stone heads were made in many configurations, just as modern heads are to this day. Here is just one example.

The world of archery has seen hundreds of designs since the first stone head was prepared. Not all, by far, are broadheads. The various heads shown here are all useful to the traditional archer, including the Judo, with its wiry arms, an "unlosable head" ideal for roving.

dable with its super-sharp point. Parallel Points fit over the untapered shafts like those empty .38 Special cases, and are glued or crimped in place. They are very light, weighing only 20 grains. Snaro Bird Point has been around for as long as I can remember but I can still buy one. Rather than for target practice, this head is meant for the small game field. It is specifically designed for putting quail, grouse, or any other game bird (not wild turkey!) into the pot. On and on the list goes, with the great Judo point from Zwickey, claimed to be "the ultimate in stump shooting" points—and it is. It has what's called an unloseable head, with springlike wings that snare brush, grass, twigs, and other impediments to end the arrow's flight. There are also many different bowfishing heads for use with special arrows made to penetrate the water deeply.

Then comes the broadhead, which dates so far into the past that we do not know even the century of its inception. Archaeologists believe it was invented during the Stone Age. The Ice Man's arrows were tipped with points of stone. Stone (usually flint) arrowheads, while not as sturdy as modern steel broadheads, were capable of extreme sharpness—seven hundred times sharper than a modern single-edged razor blade, according to one assessment. Tiny shards of flint have been used in delicate eye surgery, being far

Another example of a stone head with a beautiful shape, a shape that in essence has not changed from distant past to this day.

keener than the best scalpel. The broadheads on the Ice Man's arrows are shaped just as we would expect-sort of like a diamond, the points of which begin to separate whatever they strikes while the widening parts of the heads increase the separation. Cutting instruments like broadheads are wedges. The edge of a knife, for example, is also a wedge. Think of the wedge used to split a piece of firewood. It begins its work with the narrow tip and then separates the wood more and more as it is driven inward. The knife or broadhead separates whatever it hits more and more as it penetrates it. Otzi's broadhead was made of "whitish-gray flint." We know that flint heads can

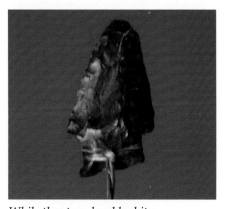

While the stone head had its disadvantages, including fragility, it also had the advantage of being extremely sharp. Stone arrowheads, as well as chips of obsidian and similar rocks, can be sharper than the modern scalpel.

be very sharp. The Ice Man had a small tool in his possession that the experts decided was a device for making or sharpening flint tools and arrow points.

Hundreds of broadhead designs have come along over the many years that archery has flourished—maybe thousands, especially if stone heads are included. As I think back on some of these, I chuckle. The inventors of some of these unique heads had fertile imaginations. There was a broadhead with circular (twist) blade engineered to "core out" a channel in whatever it hit.

These heads represent only a very few of the hundreds of designs that have come down through time. All are metal, but of different styles, with the exception of one major trait—each of these heads is a "cutting wedge."

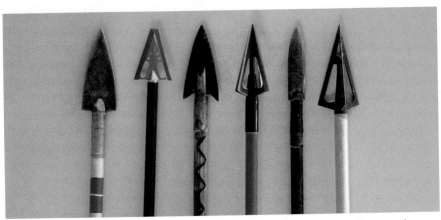

Three vintage heads with three contemporary heads—from left to right: one, three, and five are old style; two, four, and six are modern. The second head from the right could penetrate armor.

The ad showed an apple with a nice big hole in it. The only problem was that nobody was using them on apples. On more substantial media these heads, with their tremendous drag, stopped short after minimal penetration. I recall a wicked-looking head with a streamlined shape and super sharp point that

Heads of great imagination came forth over the years, many of them abject failures due to massive friction, wind planing, failure to penetrate, and other deficiencies.

might have been serviceable if it did not have fins. The fins added drag, reducing the penetration of this head. Once again, an idea meant to improve the broadhead actually detracted from the simple shape. This broadhead was advertised as having "more shocking power," probably meaning kinetic energy. Shocking power in arrows is a minor consideration, as discussed in chapter 5. Penetration of the arrow is the goal. Goofy-looking arrowheads, however, have always been around, created by the insomniacs of every age, perhaps.

Broadheads are so diverse and so interesting that an entire organization, the American Broadhead Collector's Club, thrives on locating and preserving them, from the mundane to the bizarre. These broadheads are normally those that were available for any consumer to buy, trade for, or find discarded, at one time or another. A particularly interesting head is the Pioneer Game Tamer, also known as the Pizza Cutter because it had circular blades that looked like the wheels used to slice through pizzas. Some broadheads have historical value as well as dollar worth. An example is the Peck & Snyder broadhead of 1878, believed to be the first broadhead manufactured for sporting use.

The Red Bow Star Point is a mechanical broadhead from 1953. It failed. The idea was that the mechanical head would fly like a target point, the blades opening on contact. Not only did it not work, it was unnecessary: all of the tried and tested broadheads we have today of nonmechanical design are extremely accurate, and the blade does not have to open on contact because it is already in place ready to go to work.

While new heads appear more often than changes in automobile styles, several remain in play, as they have for decades. One is the Zwickey. It comes in several different designs but the most famous is the double or two-edge style, something on the order of a dagger which cuts on both sides of the blade. The Zwickey Eskimo 2-blade is in that camp. It's made of high carbon steel with a heavy tip and it flies with good accuracy. Zwickey came along in 1938. Why is it still on the market? Because it continues to perform.

Another two-edge broadhead is the Steel Force, touted as a cut-on-contact two-blade single-bevel broadhead that delivers "awesome penetration and superb flight without resorting to mechanical gimmickry." Made of knife-grade stainless steel, the Steel Force two-blade is a heavy head for serious applications. The Magnus is another broadhead that has been around for quite some time. The Magnus II is two-blade weighing 100 or 125 grains, in contrast to the Magnus I two-blade, which comes in 135- or 160-grain weights. The Ace Broadhead dates back to the 1930s. Spot welded and copper brazed with interlocking ferrule, it's another good flyer in 125- or 160-grain weights. The Stos Broadhead is a two-blade head sharpened on both sides instead of the single bevel.

There are also multiple-blade heads. Multiple-blade heads are as diverse as snowflakes. The original Bear Razorhead could be converted from a two-blade to a multiple blade head with an insert. The Steel Force Hellfire Broadhead begins as a two-blade but adds an extra blade. The main blade is 2^1/$_2$ inches long, 1 inch wide. The additional blade is 1 inch long and replacements are sold separately. This head weighs 150 grains. The "snuffer" type

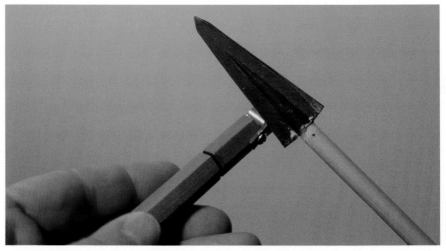

The simple Grizzly two-blade broadhead flies as true as a target point when properly mounted and fired from a well-tuned longbow or recurve.

broadhead, now found as the Magnus Snuffer, is one of many three-blade heads, with edges equidistant on a single ferrule. This broadhead is simple to sharpen—place it on a whetstone and let it gently glide as two edges sharpen at the same time.

The Woodsman is a three-blade head with the three-to-one ratio that Howard Hill recommended—it is three times longer than its width. This head flies just like a target point, with excellent penetration. The advantage of the three blades, aside from the obvious extra cutting edge, is that the head creates a "hole" rather than a "slice." The Woodsman is offered in different configurations with solid or vented blades. Another 3:1 broadhead, the Original Howard Hill, is back in tempered steel with chromium ferrule and riveted for strength. It comes in two weights: 160 grains for $^{11}/_{32}$ shafts and 145 grains for $^{5}/_{16}$ shafts.

A whole book could be written on the broadheads that remain "online" along with the hundreds that have gracefully died along the way. Today, the traditional archer is faced with dozens of choices. And it is totally impossible for anyone else to dictate which head an archer should choose. That's because most bowbenders have "a favorite," never-failing, deep-penetrating, reliable head that cannot be bettered. The reason these archers cling to a particular head is success—simple as that. We find successful bowhunters standing by many different types of broadheads because there are many good heads, not just one or two.

There are several factors to consider in choosing a broadhead "just right" for the individual archer. The first is accuracy. Accuracy is determined "by the bow," not the head. I doubt that there is even one of the "high class" broadheads on the market today that is inaccurate in and of itself. But different heads will fly differently from different bows—and when shot by different archers as well. For example, I was warned by one archer that a particular broadhead "wind planed," that is, it was steered by the wind. The odd thing about this warning is that the head accused of wind planning happened to shoot just like a target point out of my bows. But they did not perform the same from that archer's bows.

In order for a broadhead to fly correctly, it must be mounted on a straight shaft. Attaching a broadhead to a crooked or bent, in the case of aluminum, shaft may well give the false impression that there is something inherently wrong with the broadhead itself, when in fact if that head were attached to a good straight arrow, it would prove to be excellent. Showing that a shaft is crooked is simple: just spin the arrow on a flat surface and watch for the wobble. Another factor that can produce poor arrow flight with a given broadhead is the stability of the arrow *with that particular broadhead*. Stick a 160-grain head on an arrow that is under spined to begin with and it will corkscrew through the air. And what about fletching? Does the arrow have sufficient back-end drag to overcome the weight of the broadhead? I am not a fan of big banana fletching, but if an archer is sold on a particular broadhead that demands plenty of fletching surface area, big feathers may be required for that arrow to fly straight with that particular head.

The archer may be the cause of an arrow flying cockeyed, especially due to poor release of the string. There are very good archers who do pluck the string, who do not get as clean an arrow getaway as possible, and so blame may be placed upon a very good broadhead when in fact going to increased feather surface would improve the arrow flight. Because I so strongly believe that the top-of-the-line broadheads sold today are inherently accurate due to near-perfect alignment of the blade on the ferrule, I look to other reasons for poor flight. You purchase a fine broadhead, but the arrow flies lousy with it. First check whether the arrow flies perfectly with a target point. If so, don't blame that well-balanced broadhead.

The big question is whether the bow has been retuned to match the arrowhead. Some archers shy away from this—after paying perhaps thirty dollars for only three Phantom Broadheads, the archer may be unwilling to shoot one of those heads at a target and risk damaging it. Better do it—it's necessary and just part of the game. The head may be so superior in the mind of the archer that going away from it to another is not an option; in reality, however,

A head that steers the arrow may require helical fletching (top), while another head may do very well with straight offset fletching (bottom).

it may be a good option, since no matter how wonderful that broadhead is, it just may not be a match for a particular bow shooting specific arrows. So tuning is in order. The fistmele may require a change in order to direct an arrow point-on, hot, straight, and normal. The nockset may have to be adjusted. And yes, the fletching may require a change.

I have arrows in my collection of different spine and fletching, not all of them even the styles I prefer. More than once these different arrows, some with fletching surface areas I truly do not prefer, being strong helical or big banana, have proved that if I wanted to go with a particular broadhead, I would have to go away from my favorite arrow. When that happens, I look to another broadhead because my "standard" arrow flies just the way I want it to; I won't forsake it so that I can use a new broadhead that my arrow "does not like," for whatever reason. I know from experience that there are many fine broadheads that do fly on my arrows without going to more feather surface.

It is sometimes difficult for an archer to conclude that the broadhead that not only looks great but has been proved to be wonderful in the hands of others is simply not

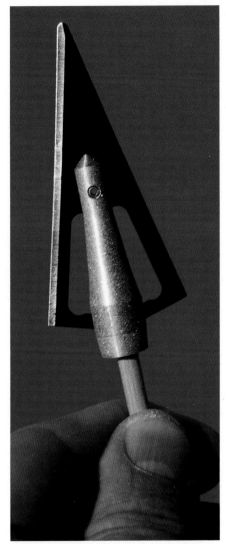

This is a two-blade vented broadhead. The idea is to reduce the surface of the blades to reduce wind planing.

gong to work out of a particular bow without going to changes that archer does not really want to make. A perfect example comes to mind: I had a bow that was shooting ideally with matched arrows. I saw a very heavy broadhead that I wanted to try. It carried a fine reputation and I just had to mount a set on my arrows. But it did not work for me or my bows and arrows, even though it proved superior in other archers' bows and arrows. Head weight

While these three heads do not share exactly the same characteristics, each one is a cutting wedge.

alone, then, can dictate the success or failure of a broadhead with a particular bow and its arrows.

Also very hard to rationalize at times is that after finding that wonder head and proving that it flies true on a test arrow, the entire set of arrows with that head in place will have to be shot before taking them to the field. There they go downrange, smacking into the target. Each time one flies in anything like a perilous direction, the archer sees images of dollar bills floating in the air. Yes, there is some risk in shooting every arrow in the set before going into the woods, but it has to be done. The alternative is much worse even than having one of those expensive heads make a really bad landing and become little more than a piece of defunct metal: the alternative is failure in the field because the one arrow not fired to prove its flight pattern turned out to be the one that didn't fly true.

Sharpness is not simply desirable. It is essential. Rather than trying to give a seminar on "how to sharpen a broadhead," I think that simply looking at the tools that get this job done is all the instruction necessary. The simple whetstone is a good starting point. When using one, just be sure to maintain the angle of the edge to be sharpened. And go lightly. Overpressure on the head is counterproductive to getting it sharp. Use a little honing oil on the stone. The stone is ideal for the snuffer-type head in that you can sharpen two edges at the same time by simply keeping the head flat on the stone. A diamond stone, such as the JewelStik, is a good one to mount on a work-

Sharpness and penetration are the two most important traits of a head designed for putting meat on the table. Here, a head is being sharpened to a razor edge.

bench. It works just like any other stone with its flat surface, but is actually made with diamonds, so it will function wet or dry.

The Diamond Hone is a sharpening tool made specifically for broadheads. It is hinged for adjustment of angles and therefore works with two-blade, three-blade, and four-blade heads. The Lil' Shaver is for sharpening two-blade heads, such as Zwickey, Grizzly, and Howard Hill broadheads. Then there are simply "sticks," some set with diamonds. These "go to the broadhead" instead of the "broadhead going to them": the stick is handheld and applied against the head, rather than, as with the JewelStik, the sharpening instrument remaining immobile. The list goes on and on, with all manner of different sharpening tools. And don't leave out the ordinary file. Get a bastard file of high quality; a single-cut file will leave a smoother surface after the job is done. F. L. Grobet is a trusted brand for files for use in broadhead sharpening.

There are so many good broadheads today that it is impossible to single out one, two, or ten for recommendation. Experimentation is necessary, along with a few basic rules: the first is to select a broadhead weight that matches the draw weight of the bow. A huge, heavy head may not fly from a lighter-draw bow (but of course it might). You just have to try it to find out. Don't try to build a set of broadhead arrows without at the least tuning the bow to match those heads. I have often been lucky in choosing broadheads that fly true with the same arrows and bow tuning that worked for target points. But this is certainly not always the case.

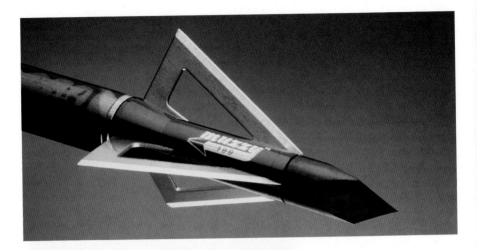

Top: It's not all old-time heads in traditional archery. This Muzzy head is perfectly at home on a traditional wood arrow. Bottom: The Coyote II broadheads flanking the center head are made with ferrule designed for a tapered arrow and are perfectly suited to the traditional arrow even though they are of a modern design with replaceable blades.

Finally, I must point out that while I adhere to traditional-style heads for traditional bows, I've had some fine experiences with broadheads normally considered "right" for compounds. The example that leaps to mind is a set of Muzzy broadheads that I took to Africa. One of those broadheads ended up taking a large old female Cape buffalo with one shot. The old dame didn't make a hundred yards before simply "going to sleep." The hunter who got the cow was surprised, and I must say I was, too. Not surprised that a perfect "boiler room" strike took this heavy animal out, but that it did it so quickly and from a bow that pulled only fifty pounds!

14

The Amazing Feather

If nature didn't provide them, we'd have to invent the feather, because it's the best traditional arrow fletching in the world. That's a bold statement, and with science coming forth with synthetic this and that rivaling the best products of the natural world, a better "feather" may come along any day. But it hasn't so far. Feathers donated by the avian world continue to work "just fine" and a lot more than just fine.

Feathers are forgiving. That simple statement just about says it all. Feathers "get out of the way," returning to their original shape after flattening out against the shelf and strike plate of the stickbow or a blade of grass or other not-too-formidable obstruction en route to the target. Feathers are so forgiving that I challenge the archer to try a simple experiment. Reverse the arrow on the shelf of the bow so that the cock feather, which normally faces outward, is now up against the riser in full contact. Shoot three arrows this way and then with hen feathers in normal placement against the shelf and strike plate of the bow. Now look at the cluster of arrows. All six arrows will be in the same group That's because the cock feather collapsed so perfectly against the strike plate/shelf that it did not deflect the shaft; it immediately returned to its appointed task of guiding the arrow. It "folded out of the way" and then went right back to its original form.

Feathers serve to guide arrows and stabilize flight. The feathers shown here are glued to the shaft in the helical twist configuration.

Feathers are forgiving. Smashing this feather down firmly will not ruin it. The feather will spring back to its normal shape.

Another feature of the amazing feather is its ability to continue serving to maintain arrow-on-course flight even with rather extensive damage. Before I returned to longbow and recurve, I spent a good deal of time with compounds, especially the Jennings Arrowstar, which was, for its day, a state-of-the-art instrument. In keeping with compound bow mentality, I chose plastic vanes over feathers, believing they would stand up better to the thrust applied to the arrow by the mechanical arrow-shooter. I soon learned that once a plastic vane suffered a tear or split, it failed to properly guide the arrow in flight. Plastic vanes had an advantage in wet weather, but that was it. I went back to the feather on compounds and never looked back. At a Bear Archery Company gathering in Alabama I was somewhat surprised to see several expert compound bowmen firing arrows graced with feathers, not plastic. These archers had learned that a split plastic vane compromised arrow flight, while feathers, even when visibly damaged, with missing sections, continued to keep arrows flying true, finding the bull's eye uncannily. In short, feathers make a superb guidance system, supplying sufficient back-end drag to keep the arrow flying point-forward. Having said all of this, it's important to throw in the fact that traditionally-oriented archers who wish to use vanes can do so. Shooting off the shelf is impossible, of course, as the plastic vane will "bounce" away as it hits the strike plate. But if you use an elevated arrow rest, vanes function with the longbow and recurve as they do with the mechanical bow.

Feathers are necessary to stabilize arrow flight. Theoretically, a perfect featherless shaft would fly true—that is, if it really were perfect. It's something like the round lead ball in a muzzleloader. If the ball were perfect it would fly rather straight through the air. But it never is, so rifling is used to rotate the lead sphere so that imperfections are evened out by rotating them on a common axis. Feathers stabilize an arrow in two ways: drag and rota-

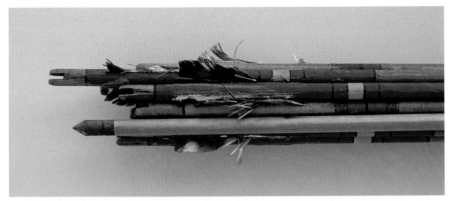

The feathers on these very old arrows are no doubt damaged to the point of no return, some being completely lost from the shaft. However, even extensive damage to a feather will not totally destroy its ability to guide an arrow.

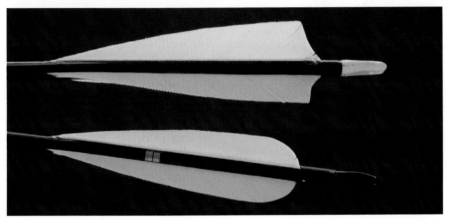

Feathers work in part due to drag on the rearward portions of the arrows. Feathers mounted parallel on the shaft are not usually recommended, but even parallel fletching will provide some degree of arrow guidance.

tion. Mounted parallel on the shaft, feathers continue to work surprisingly well due to the restraining effect of the atmosphere, which can be more powerful than gravity. Toss a sock and it quickly flutters to the ground. Put a little sand in the toe and the sock travels much truer along a somewhat parabolic line of flight with its kitelike "tail." That is tail drag at work.

However, parallel feathers offer zero rotational value, while mounting feathers offset on the shaft or with helical twist promotes a degree of rotation, not entirely unlike that of a bullet fired from a rifled barrel, but much less pronounced. My arrows fly true with straight offset feathers and that is what I prefer, in a $5^1/_2$-inch-long, low-profile design. However, helical twist is not

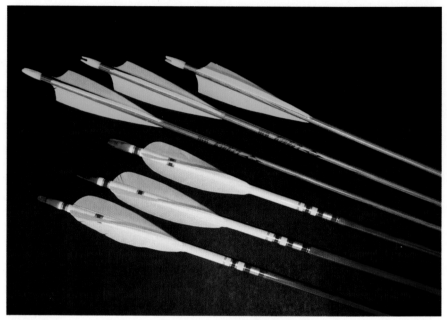

Better than mounting feathers parallel on the shaft are the straight offset style (top), where the feather is not twisted, but is mounted on the shaft at an angle, and the helical design (bottom), where the feather is twisted to provide more drag and a degree of rotation.

only acceptable, but decidedly superior when an arrow is not as straight as it could be, or the archer's release is slightly less than smooth.

The size of the feather, of course, dictates total surface area, and the more surface area, the greater the effect of the atmosphere on that feather. Ideally, total feather surface will be sufficient to stabilize the arrow in flight while at the same time not imposing so much drag that the arrow's forward motion is impeded. But when that surface area is greater than necessary to keep the arrow point-forward, the superfluous area results in unnecessary drag, slowing the arrow's forward progress. Furthermore, excessive fletching surface means greater in-flight noise. That's why I am not a fan of the banana-style feather unless it is necessary to stabilize an arrow that is perhaps not properly spined to the bow. The helical shape (with a great deal of twist, which causes a lot of drag) is also preferred when the arrow, for whatever reason, such as having a very heavy broadhead, requires faster straightening out after being subjected to the archer's paradox. Today's better broadheads are so perfectly engineered that they do not tend to "steer" the arrow. However, it is true that a very heavy broadhead may demand more feather surface to deter possible broadhead steering.

The feather second from the left is a flu-flu, ideal for when you want to shoot slow arrows to avoid losing them. It is, however, noisier than arrows with ordinary fletching.

The exception to the rule of "just enough and not too much" feather surface is when you want to purposely create super drag so that the arrow falls to the earth within a short distance of the bow. That is the flu-flu, which is ideal when the desired range is short. Flu-flu arrows also get lost less than arrows designed for longer shooting. Arrows with minimal drag can zip off a hard spot of ground and disappear into the outback. I believe a few of mine are still orbiting in outer space, because after looking intently for a long while, I never could find those lost darts.

An additional factor any type of proper fletching adds to an arrow is greater flight distance. An unstabilized arrow, sort of like the sock without sand in the tow, wobbles to earth much sooner than a well-stabilized properly fletched arrow.

Bare shaft tuning is big with certain traditional archers. They believe that if an arrow without feathers flies fairly well at close range, say twenty yards and under, then it must fly perfectly when feathers are added. That is true, but also a waste of time. I have never owned a bow that failed to shoot a *properly spined,* straight arrow perfectly when those shafts were fletched. Therefore, I buy my shafts, prepare them fully, including feathers, and shoot away. It works every time.

Feathers also function on any shaft material: aluminum, steel, carbon, fiberglass, and of course wood. The only trick is ensuring a proper match between glue and shaft finish, as addressed in the chapter on assembling arrows for traditional bows.

As I admitted earlier, the only negative feature of feathers is suffering in damp weather. When feathers are attached to the bird, natural oils are always working into them, but fitted to arrows, they can get soggy in snow and rain. A plastic food bag over the exposed feathers works to keep them dry. Commercial fleece covers, one hundred percent waterproof, are even better. There are also quivers designed to protect fletching from the elements. The Catquiver, at the time of this writing, is offered in several different styles, all protecting fletching fully from dampness. The Dawgware Quiver safeguards fletching totally as well, as do the TIMO quiver and the Safari Tuff Side Quiver sold by 3 Rivers Archery Company.

So what is the anatomy of the feather that makes it so special and useful to the traditional archer? According to the *Standard College Dictionary,* Harcourt, Brace, and World edition, a feather is "One of the horny, elongated structures that form the plumage of birds, consisting essentially of a hollow tubular quill attached to the body and prolonged in a slender shaft supporting a web or vane of closely spaced barbs interlocking with barbules and bar-

As tough as feathers are, and though they will usually snap back from a drenching, it is unwise to allow them to get soaked. Plus, a wet feather is not ideal for arrow guidance. One simple method of keeping feathers dry is covering them with a plastic food bag, as shown here.

bicels." Horny means tough and feathers are, for their scant weight, quite strong. Elongated, yes, so we can cut to length and shape desired for our arrow. The hollow tubular quill is split lengthwise to form an ideal platform for gluing the "half-feather" to the shaft. The hollow feature, plus molecular makeup, makes the feather extremely light in weight, providing surface drag without creating tail-heaviness. The closely spaced barbs interlocking with barbules and barbicels is the key to the feather folding flat and then returning to its original shape. Rub a feather "the wrong way" and the barbs separate, while a single finger-stroke smoothes them right back into place.

As with so many historical questions, we have no idea when feathers were first used in archery. Feathers may have first appeared on atlatl darts, although some historians believe that the bow and the "throwing stick" occupied the same time frame; if so, it's impossible to say which had feathers first, the stick or the arrow. I'm inclined to believe that the atlatl came first, but whether the flying stick wore feathers first or not is lost in the shadows of centuries past. Certain ancient African hunters attached feathers to their arrows, though others used tough leaves. The Ice Man, uncovered from a glacier in the Italian Alps 5,000 years after his passing, had arrows fletched with feathers, three per shaft, offset, just like mine. Or should I say mine are just like his? The American Indian archer used feathers for his arrows. Ishi used feathers from eagles, hawks, buzzards, and flickers; he seldom glued them in place, securing them to the shaft with thin sinew instead.

In fourteenth-century England, bowyers were not allowed to craft longbows after dark, lest they prepare a bad one that might let a soldier down in war. However, fletchers could work around the clock. Records reveal a 1369

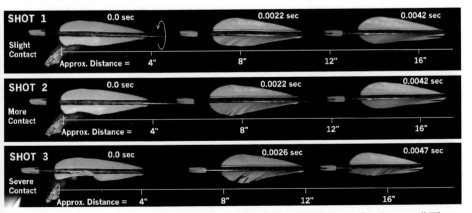

Trueflight ran extensive tests on feathers to determine "fold-down forgiveness." The results were remarkable. Feathers subjected to severe contact continued to function perfectly in arrow guidance. PHOTO COURTESY OF TRUEFLIGHT MANUFACTURING COMPANY.

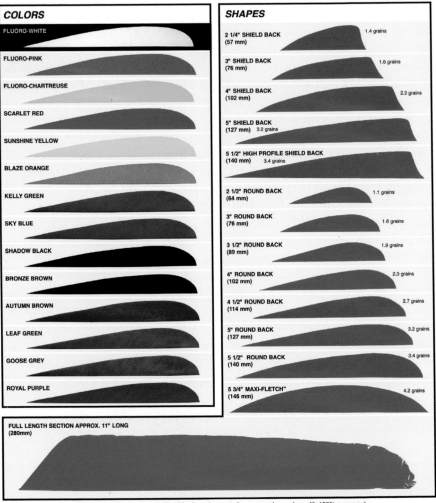

COLORS

FLUORO-WHITE
FLUORO-PINK
FLUORO-CHARTREUSE
SCARLET RED
SUNSHINE YELLOW
BLAZE ORANGE
KELLY GREEN
SKY BLUE
SHADOW BLACK
BRONZE BROWN
AUTUMN BROWN
LEAF GREEN
GOOSE GREY
ROYAL PURPLE

SHAPES

2 1/4" SHIELD BACK (57 mm) — 1.4 grains
3" SHIELD BACK (76 mm) — 1.6 grains
4" SHIELD BACK (102 mm) — 2.3 grains
5" SHIELD BACK (127 mm) — 3.2 grains
5 1/2" HIGH PROFILE SHIELD BACK (140 mm) — 3.4 grains
2 1/2" ROUND BACK (64 mm) — 1.1 grains
3" ROUND BACK (76 mm) — 1.6 grains
3 1/2" ROUND BACK (89 mm) — 1.9 grains
4" ROUND BACK (102 mm) — 2.3 grains
4 1/2" ROUND BACK (114 mm) — 2.7 grains
5" ROUND BACK (127 mm) — 3.2 grains
5 1/2" ROUND BACK (140 mm) — 3.4 grains
5 3/4" MAXI-FLETCH™ (146 mm) — 4.2 grains

FULL LENGTH SECTION APPROX. 11" LONG (280mm)

(Note: The printing process used for this sheet does not always reproduce colors with 100% accuracy.)

Trueflight Manufacturing Company has been providing feathers for archers for many years in numerous styles and sizes, including full length feathers that can be burned or chopped to shape by the archer. PHOTO COURTESY OF TRUEFLIGHT MANUFACTURING COMPANY.

Royal Command for 850,000 arrows to be delivered to the Tower of London. That order represented 2,550,000 feathers for three-feather shafts. In 1418 the English government demanded 1,190,000 goose feathers—and got them! Today, the demand for feather fletching has again skyrocketed, with the returning high interest and popularity of traditional bows. Arrows with vanes will fly from elevated arrow rests, as already noted, but every longbow/recurve shooter I know shoots off the shelf, which demands feathers.

Feather shapes are as numerous as leaves on a tree-well, a small tree. The two basic styles are parabolic (round back) and shield (square back). But the banana, the Pope & Young (a particularly pretty shape), and many other shapes abound. Roger Ascham, back in the sixteenth century, listed the triangular, square-shorn, round, swine-backed, and saddle-backed shapes. The triangular, true to its name, was shaped like a triangle. Cut a rectangle in half from upper left-hand corner to lower right-hand corner and you have the triangular feather. The square-shorn was a long, low rectangle, not really square. Round was very short, about a half-inch long, while swine-backed, for lack of a better description, is what we call parabolic today. The saddle-backed feather sloped concavely from high rear to low front, like the sway in a riding saddle. In the book *Arab Archery*, Nabih Amin Faris lists the martin's wing and Persian trim as traditional Arab feather shapes. I have seen many American Indian feathers at the Buffalo Bill Historical Society museum in Cody, Wyoming. A parallelogram shape describes some, but hardly all.

The number of feathers on a shaft varies. Some archers like four so they don't have to worry about mounting an arrow on the shelf with cock feather outward. I prefer three, and if an arrow is placed on the shelf cock feather inward, I don't care. That arrow will still fly true enough for all practical purposes. It's a matter of total surface anyway, not number of feathers. Three 5-inch shield-style feathers ½ inch high at the back, tapering to zero inches up front, amount to about 3.75 square inches of surface area, while four 4-inch

Feathers can be cut into many different shapes and dyed in a multitude of colors.

This Little Chopper Feather Die Cutter can be used to easily cut feathers to shape.

similarly-shaped feathers have around 4 square inches of surface—not much difference. Many American Indian arrows have only two feathers, indicating that drag was their main occupation rather than spin. The Vikings seemed to prefer four feathers. Ishi got along with three, just like the Ice Man more than five centuries ago. I like low profile feathers because they are quieter out of my bows than high profile ones, while still providing stability. But I know very successful archers who live by the high profile design.

Roger Ascham (born 1515), author of the classic archery book *Toxophilus*, wrote that "there is no feather but onlye of a goose that hath all commodities in it." In spite of Roger's advice, feathers from pheasants, peacocks, swans, vultures, blue herons, hawks, and many seabirds have also found their way onto arrows. Still, the domestic turkey provides, by far, the bulk of feathers for arrow fletching today, and all in all, it's the best choice. I have tried feathers experimentally from a variety of donors and to date nothing beats Ben's Bird.

The "gray goose shaft" of Robin Hood lore makes a beautiful arrow. But I found these historically exciting feathers somewhat soft, tattering quicker than Mr. Gobble-Gobble's, although the higher oil line on the goose feather does makes it slightly more moisture resistant. I bought a batch of goose feathers to test (no doubt surrendered by the Canada honker and not the gray bird of Merrie Olde England). They were advertised as the best goose

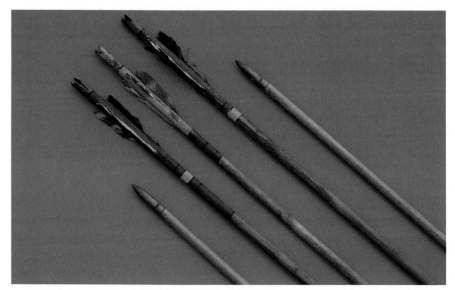

These very old arrows show a straight or parallel fletch, typical of Native American arrows.

feather since Friar Tuck gnawed a mutton joint, and they made my wallet groan. They also worked quite well and I ended up buying more goose feathers to assemble arrows for art as well as shooting. But for day-to-day use, the common turkey feather is a better choice.

Feather colors are chosen entirely based on personal preference. White feathers dyed in numerous hues prevail simply because turkey farmers have turned mainly to birds with white plumage—not because of color of the bird, of course, but because a variety that grows quickly, with a succulent, bold breast of white meat, just happens to sport white feathers. Natural barred feathers, provided by our great American gobbler, are pretty just because they are natural, I suppose—though you can purchase white feathers dyed in a barred pattern that cost a lot less than naturals. Natural barred feathers are said to be a little tougher than white ones, but I have discovered no such difference. In my own meager experiments with "wild" versus "domestic" turkey feathers, I have found both equal in strength and certainly in arrow-guiding potential. And the brighter the feather, the easier it is to find the lost arrow.

Another unimportant distinction, in my opinion, is the left-wing, right-wing controversy. Supposedly, right-handed shooters should use right-wing fletching, and vice versa. It is simply not true. Anyone can quickly prove this by shooting arrows of both types. I've tested this with a shooting machine. Left wing and right wing arrows flew to the same point of impact. Today,

When I tried the famous "gray goose shaft," I found it beautiful and serviceable, but not as tough as the ordinary turkey feather.

feathers from the left wing of a turkey are easier to come by, I am told, because right wings are clipped to prevent flying. If this is true, turkey raisers should figure out that feathers from both wings have sale value. I order left-wing feathers, although I am right-handed, because there are usually more left-wing feathers in stock. For the curious, here is how to discerning left-wing from right-wing feathers: Hold your hands up in front of your face. Cup them. The left hand represents the "bend" of the left-wing feather, while the right hand copies the right-wing feather's bend.

One thing I know is that I simply cannot walk past a fallen feather without picking it up for a quick look, and I've seen many others do the same. We humans seem to have an affinity for them. The next time you pick up a feather lying on the ground, examine it for a full minute or two before tossing it away. It truly is an amazing gift of nature to the traditional archer.

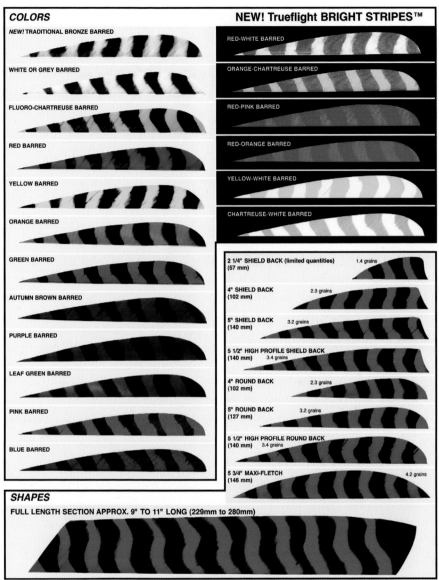

(Patterns will vary)

Feathers are mostly chosen on personal preference because all shapes and colors work well. Trueflight barred feathers come in numerous sizes, shapes, and colors, including Bright Stripes that help the archer find arrows after shooting them. PHOTO COURTESY OF TRUEFLIGHT MANUFACTURING COMPANY.

15

Assembling Your Own Arrows

I call it assembling, not making from scratch, which is what the devotee of primitive archery might do—making an arrow from a basic piece of wood. The traditionalist is far more likely, perhaps in the 99.9-percent range, to buy ready-made shafts to assemble into arrows, rather than building them from a chunk of raw wood. Why handcraft your own arrows when there are so many professionally made available just for the buying? I do it because assembling high-grade arrows that shoot perfectly in my longbows and recurves is one of the pleasures of traditional archery, a relaxing hobby in its own right (and money-saving). Arrows for compound bows are usually superbly made and shoot wonderfully, but seldom have charm, only utility.

Hand-assembled arrows can be plain. I have made many for roving that were simply clear-dipped. But the traditional archer will find that hand-

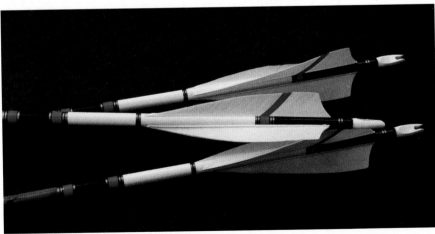

These beautiful handmade arrows have the special touch of an off-color stripe blended into the fletching. Note the fine cresting lines. Most of us will not get into cresting at a high level, but cresting tools are available for the amateur arrowsmith.

Arrow crafters mainly use wooden shafts, but a fiberglass shaft like this one can be fletched and crested just like a wood shaft.

assembled arrows for their bows can be mini works of art. Before delving into the how-to of arrow assembly, a word of caution—we "average" crafters will not achieve the arrows of the professionals who build darts so beautiful that we hate to shoot them (but I shoot them anyway). There are contests to see which artist can make the most perfect and handsome arrows; mine could never compete. But that's all right. One thing is certain—the average "homemade" arrow can be handsome if not beautiful. And it will shoot right along with the finest in the land.

The art of arrow-crafting is easy to learn, enjoyable, and inexpensive compared to professionally made arrows that will probably be more beautiful, but shoot no better. A "store-bought" dozen can run from seventy to a hundred dollars and much more. Products for arrow making abound. Dozens of different woods are available, including our beloved cedar, as discussed in chapter 11. And it's not only wood. Arrows can be assembled from any material that is offered in unfinished shaft form. This can be aluminum (I have assembled many aluminum arrows, mainly for recurve bows), steel tubing (which I have not seen for some time), fiberglass, carbon, or multi-material shafts. But in keeping with the trend, I will concentrate here on the wood arrow. The many tools for the craft can easily be found in archery stores and catalogs. A wealth of nocks, feathers, and all manner of finishes are as near as an archery catalog.

BUY YOUR SHAFTS

You will need wood shafts to make into arrows. See the information in chapter 11 to decide on which wood is right for a given bow and application. Buy a hundred shafts at a time. It hits the wallet harder to begin with, but the blow is softened when the arrows are finished in ten sets of ten or in runs of a dozen.

How to Order Shafts

I buy my shafts through mail order because where I live there never has been an archery store. We don't even have a real gas station in town, let alone a sporting goods shop. I have never been disappointed, however, with mail order. If you're not sure about the spine/weight of shaft you want, a good bet is the 3 Rivers Hunter Arrow Test Kits A, B, and C. Test kit A includes two arrows each of 35/40, 40/45, and 50/55 spine; B includes two each of 50/55, 60/65, and 65/70; and set C has two each of 65/70, 70/75, and 80+ spine. Or you can order by a spine chart. Going a little heavy is okay. Rely on the chart and add 5 pounds spine for Fast Flight bowstrings. Some of this "stuff" gets so technical that you wonder if you're not back in the compound world!

Sort the Shafts

When I have purchased good shafts I have not thrown any away. On occasion, I have run across "bargains" of a hundred shafts at a great price. These purchases are worthwhile, but you may end up tossing a few out (they smell good burning in the fireplace if they are Port Orford cedar). Supposedly, you're purchasing by spine and weight. In fact, you are not. For example, I ordered a hundred Sitka spruce shafts. No weight was given, only the spine, diameter, and length (in this case, 55/60, $^{11}/_{32}$ inches, and 31 inches, respectively).

No one can expect the arrow shaft company to take the time to weigh every shaft in a group. They'd go broke. So the first step is sorting your shafts by weight in grains. This particular set fell into three major weight groups. Although I weigh my shafts at first, I will have to sort finished arrows again by weight due to variations that occur during the finishing process. The same company offered $^{21}/_{64}$-inch diameter shafts *both* spined and sorted by weight plus or minus 20 grains. Next, examine for grain structure. This is done by sight. The ideal shaft has a very straight grain when viewed from the side. A slightly wavy grain is acceptable if you make sure to use the best portions of the shaft. The only shafts I would surrender to the fire would be the ones with wavy grains, as they might break.

Examine both ends of the shaft to see the reed of the shaft. The reed is direction of the grain as seen from the end of the shaft and shows which direction will have the greatest strength in bending. In doing your own spine testing, the reed should be straight up and down so you are testing the strongest aspect of the shaft. If I were entering an important competition, I might be more stringent in sorting shafts. But for all applications with my bows, finished arrows in a 60-grain range are more than good enough.

Here is a shaft with a cut taper. The tapering tool is as simple to use as a handheld pencil sharpener.

I have always liked tapered shafts for serious shooting, but in the field untapered shafts are just fine. Before going further with arrow assembly, it's important to say that prefinished shafting is available, and for not a lot more than unfinished shafts. Finished shafts are stained, sealed, and crested. The nock ends are tapered and the shafts are hand-spined. For the archer interested in assembling arrows simply by cutting them to length, fletching them, tapering the tip, and adding a point, these are a good buy.

BUY YOUR FEATHERS
Feathers come pre-cut and ready to mount or full-length. The advantage of the first is they're ready to go. The advantage of the second is you can shape them as desired. I have had a Little Chopper Feather Die Cutter for—I really don't know how long. One of my favorite styles is the Pope

Feathers come in a huge range of colors and shapes. These arrows were made with gray hen feathers and a barred red cock feather.

& Young. There are currently fifteen different shapes that can be cut by simply placing the full-length feather appropriately and giving the top a smack with a plastic-head hammer (not a carpenter's steel-head hammer). The sharp blade cuts a perfect feather. Another way to shape a feather is burning, as with the Young Feather Trimmer, a time-tested product.

MAKING THE WOOD ARROW
Gather Your Tools
- Pliers (small)—necessary for holding any type of point, including a broadhead, as it is being attached to the arrow with hot melt cement.
- Alcohol burner—to melt hot melt cement to attach points.
- Tapering tool—to trim nock end and point of arrow for attaching nocks and points.
- Scale—to weigh arrow shafts and finished arrows in grains (1 ounce equals 437.5 grains).
- Fletching jig—to mount feathers on the shaft perfectly every time.
- Small sharp knife—for incidental use.
- Hobby saw—for cutting wood shafts to length.
- Spine tester—tool to discover the spine of arrow shafts.
- Feather burner or chopper—for shaping feathers purchased full-length. Feathers may also be purchased ready to glue onto the shaft.
- Dipper—for dipping arrow shafts to coat them. Some are just simple tubes; there are also special dippers such as the Big Dipper (35-inch) for full coverage and Little Dipper (15-inch) for cap-dipping, with large enough reservoirs to dip a dozen shafts before refilling.
- Dipper cap (a gasket with holes that screws onto the dipper top)—does a perfect job of applying just the right amount of coating to a shaft.
- Arrow dipping rack—an essential item; holds dippers perfectly so shafts can be dipped quickly. Comes usually as a simple kit.
- Arrow boxes—after a fine set of arrows is constructed, these boxes prevent damage; they're self-locking with foam dividers to keep feathers from rubbing against each other.
- Crester—optional but worth the effort to produce high-class finished arrows. These little machines aren't cheap, but many have earned their keep when an archer found he or she had the skill to make a saleable finished arrow with beautiful cresting.
- Cresting brushes—special design for the application of very fine lines.

Gather Your Supplies
- Glue—Duco cement, Arrow Mate, Fletch-Tite, Barge Cement, and many similar products from numerous companies are used. Check to be sure the glue is compatible with the materials you are using (usually noted in catalogs or with instruction sheets) when choosing a glue.

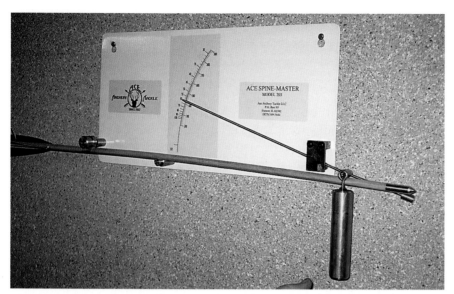

The Ace Spine Master is a spine-testing tool that has been around since 1927. The reason for its longevity is simple: it is easy to use and infallible in sorting shafts according to stiffness differences. Here, the Ace Spine Master is shown in action.

- Feather fletching tape—requires only a drop of glue fore and aft on the feather.
- Hot melt cement—perfect for attaching points.
- Gasket lacquer—ideal for sealing the wood shaft to thwart moisture; dries almost instantly. More choices are also viable such as Thunderbird Sealer, which applies like a lacquer but dries to polyurethane. Other sealers abound.
- Cresting paints—specially formulated for arrow cresting.

The tremendous comeback of traditional archery has brought with it a massive increase in both tools and supplies. The listing here is just

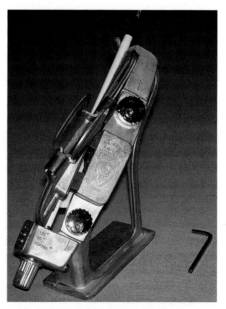

I have owned a Bitzenburger jig since the time I started making arrows. It is a precise instrument capable of producing professional-quality fletched arrows.

to get you started. You must obtain a good archery catalog to realize what is available. For example, there are now Cap-Wraps that can be rolled onto the shaft to create an instant cap in numerous colors.

Ready the Shafts

The full-length shaft can be dyed now, if you choose. I use Tandy dye, a leather dye that works well. Put a little stain on a clean cloth and rub the stain into the unfinished shafts smoothly. Be sure to wear plastic or rubber gloves so the stain does not stain you. Let the shafts dry for thirty minutes or so. Next, seal the shafts with an approved product. I use gasket lacquer applied in three coats for utility arrows, nine to twelve for fancier sets. By the time shaft number twelve is dipped, the first shaft is dry.

It's called gasket lacqueur, I suppose, because it is applied with a dip tube, with a gasket on top of the tube with a hole in it that works like a squeegee. I can dip a dozen arrows with multiple coatings of gasket lacquer in no time. Pour lacquer into the cup on top of the dipper, put the gasket cap on, and push the shaft through the small hole in the gasket, all the way down the tube to coat it; it will emerge with a thin coating of lacquer that will dry quickly when the shaft is positioned in the drying rack.

Cap Dip

You can color the nock end of the arrow by dipping the shaft into the shorter tank already described. The cap dip may run around ten to twelve inches in

The arrow in the center is plain with only a gasket lacquer seal, while the flanking arrows have been dyed red.

Left: Using gasket lacquer with a dip tube is a simple as inserting the shaft and then pulling it back out. Right: The cap dip is applied with a shorter dip tube.

length. White and red cap dips help in locating lost arrows and they also aid in flight visibility. There are few things prettier to watch than an arrow in flight.

Time for Feathers
You can cut the colored (stained or dyed) shaft to length now or later, sawing off one or both ends that may be slightly chipped or twisted. Using the tapering tool, give the nock end an 11.5-degree taper, and the point end, now or later, a 5-degree taper. "Screw" the nock in place so that when it is glued later the grain of the shaft will run horizontal to the strike plate. (Don't forget later that the nock has not yet been glued in place.)

Select feathers for the arrows. Choose the clamp for the kind of fletching you want. My Bitzenburger fletching jig comes with various clamps. I am most likely to choose the straight clamp for straight-offset mounting of feathers, but there are other clamps, such as left-wing helical and right-wing helical.

The Bitzenburger jig has settings for three or four feather arrows. Most of my arrows wear three-mounted with the straight clamp, but as noted, pitched offset. Arrows for very short range shooting may work with straight fletching, with no pitch at all, but straight offset or helical is preferred. Set the desired fletching pitch; say 120 degrees, whereby three feathers will end up

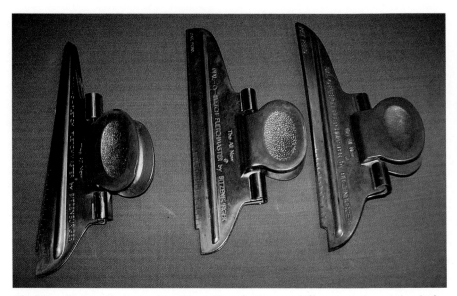

The Bitzenburger jig is capable of installing feathers at different angles on the shaft, using different clamps, shown here off the jig.

equidistant from each other on the shaft. Position each feather's back end to align with one of the index lines on the clamp.

Mark that index line with a soft lead (graphite) pencil for reference to remind you where the back of the feather must rest in the clamp. This will ensure that every feather's back end (facing the nock) is located in the same spot. Leave enough room from back of feather to accommodate the nock, about a quarter inch. Place the clamp on the jig now. The clamp on the Bitzenburger jig is held in place magnetically. Adjust the jig so that the feather lies properly along the arrow shaft for full contact. If not, when the feather is glued onto the shaft, parts of it will be "hanging in the breeze."

To ensure that the full base of the feather is in contact with the shaft, use an Allen wrench to loosen and then turn the two adjusting wheels on the jig, which allows the clamp to move. Tighten the adjusting wheels with the Allen wrench to reset them once the feather base is in full contact with the shaft. To gain a clear view of how well the base of the feather aligns with the shaft, hold the jig up with the unglued feather in place. Now it is easy to see from underneath whether the full base of the feather is in contact with the shaft. Helicals are less a problem because the twist is in the feather itself and so the base of the feather runs more parallel along the shaft. With straight offset, a feather might hang off fore or aft.

At this point, the feather, held in the clamp, is aligned with the shaft and ready for gluing in place. Scratch the base of the feather lightly with a fingernail to slightly "roughen it up." Apply an extremely thin bead of glue all along the base of the feather. A little excess glue will be squeezed out as the feather is laid along the shaft. Since fletching cement dries clear, a tiny line of glue on each side of the feather base is not unsightly. If glue "squirts out" along the base because too much was used, run a finger along the edge of the base to remove excess, like smoothing caulk in the corner of a wall.

Glues that come with a full seal across the mouth of the tube should be punctured with a paper clip to make a small hole, better controlling the glue line. Using needle-nose pliers, pinch the end of the tube for those cements that are not sealed for a narrow flow suitable for the narrow base of the feather. Gently, starting from the back, roll the clamp forward onto the shaft so that the base of the feather makes full contact. Do not press down, as this may eject too much glue. Instead, rest the clamp with the feather on the shaft. It may be necessary to use a straight pin or pencil point to press down a small section of feather (often in the front) that stubbornly resists full contact.

Let the feather dry for thirty minutes for a good bond. If the clamp sticks upon removal, this suggests too much glue was applied to the feather base. A trace of bowstring wax along the edge of the clamp helps in preventing

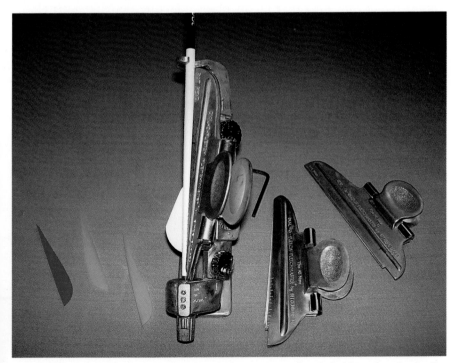

The fletching, whether it is feathers or plastic vanes, is firmly held in place in the jig after being precisely positioned on the shaft. Here, a helical twist clamp is used.

feathers sticking to clamp. After the thirty-minute drying time, gently pinch the clamp open and lift it away from the jig, leaving the feather glued in place. Also remember that the nock is pinched in, but not glued, so be careful not to unseat the nock upon removing the clamp. The nock must remain exactly in place or the feathers will not be equidistant on the shaft. Be sure to turn the rotating knob gently to index it to the next feather.

Clean all the glue off the clamp before installing the next feather for mounting. Do not use a sharp object to remove excess glue when cleaning the clamp. A fingernail is better; if that does not work, try Fletch-Tite remover. Put a tiny drop of glue on the forward tip of the feather to form a lead bead that will dry hard. This bead prevents the feather from stripping back should the arrow fly completely through a target, such as a straw bale. Adding an additional dot of glue on top of the little bead is a good idea. Attach the other two or three feathers in the same way, and you have fletched an arrow.

Glue the nock in place by installing the arrow on the string. A slight rotation may be necessary to align the nock so that the hen feathers lie against the strike plate, or in the case of shooting through the gap, so that a hen feather is line with the gutter between strike plate and arrow rest. While slightly rotating the nock may mildly upset grain direction, if the shaft has a good, straight grain to begin with, this is not a problem. And even if the grain is not perfect, the arrow will be stout enough to withstand the bow's thrust

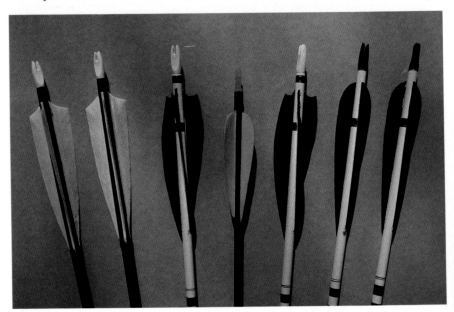

The two arrows on the left are plain, as is the fourth from the left, while the remainder have cresting.

because you chose the correct spine. Once the nock is perfectly aligned, make a small mark from nock to shaft as a witness mark so that the nock will be glued exactly where it should be.

The point taper may have been previously cut. If not, cut it now at the five-degree setting on the tapering tool. Remember that the shaft must be cut at least one-half to a full inch longer than the draw length of the bow so the point will be a little distance from the bow hand. Start the alcohol stove. Melt a small area of the hot melt cement stick. Smear a dab of hot melt on the taper of the arrow. It will dry hard. Now heat the point over the alcohol burner, holding it with pliers. The very warm to mildly hot point is placed on the arrow taper and rotated to evenly spread the hot melt cement inside the ferrule of the point. After setting the point, spin the arrow on the point to make sure it does not wobble. If it wobbles, adjust the point with the pliers (it will still be hot) and spin again until the wobble is gone.

Cresting

This is almost a topic in its own right. Since cresting machines come with full instructions, we'll let those instructions relate how to make the pretty stripes around the arrow shaft. Very early in archery, arrows were crested in various ways for identification. Pope and Young painted their arrow shafts to seal them against moisture. They also painted between feathers already mounted on the arrow to protect glue from moisture. Today, we have waterproof glue, so cresting is simply a decoration.

You have made an arrow.

16

Bowstrings

The traditional archer is much more than a bow-shooter. He or she is a person who thrives on the history of archery as well as on casting arrows. While the bow and the arrow are of major interest, the "simple" string has quite a history of its own. Moreover, while thought of as simple, it is actually a rather complex piece of the bow-and-arrow puzzle, made from myriad materials not only in modern times, but also in the past. Those inventors, not only of the bow and arrow, but of strings as well, were not the slope-headed, knuckle-dragging uncle to a monkey we think of when we envision early humans. They possessed the ingenuitiy and intelligence to use to advantage the natural maerials in their environment—and to bring about advance after advance in their equipment as their experience and skills increased. For example, the Ice Man, who lived five thousand years ago, knew how make a two-piece tapered arrow.

WHAT A GOOD STRING DOES

No string, no bow: the string is as much a part of the bow as the limbs themselves. The string is the life of the bow. Here is how I would describe a good bowstring:

- The string maintains the fistmele (brace height of the bow). A good string does not creep appreciably, thereby ensuring that fistmele remains constant.
- The string maintains the nock set in the same position, shot after shot. This is vital because if the nock set changes the arrow will no longer be in tune with the bow. A good string maintains its length (though not always perfectly) so that the nock set remains in one spot.
- The string efficiently imparts the energy stored in the limbs to the arrow nock, thereby sending the arrow downrange. A string can alter bow performance. However, this is not to say that an older string material, such as B50, is poor. That would not be true.

- A good string is not inordinately heavy, because greater mass re-
quires more energy to move it. This pertains somewhat to the diam-
eter of the string as well, mainly because most "fat" strings will
weigh more than thin strings.
- The good string does not "twang" too much; it is relatively quiet.
You don't want a a string material that "sings a song" when the bow
is shot.
- The good string is abrasion resistant. It does not fray readily.
- The good string is strong. It does not readily break.
- A good string is moisture resistant.

These are some of the qualities and functions of the good bowstring.
Luckily, today's traditional archer has access to the best strings ever, not just
the latest high-tech strings, but good old B50 strings for bows not built to
handle the F-1 type of string. As far as additional arrow speed due to a more
modern string, the difference is not earth-shattering and in fact can be so
small as to be inconsequential.

STRETCH AND CREEP
The best explanation I have found for the difference between these two important terms in the world of bowstrings is by Cleve Cheney, who is a master in the understanding of such matters. Creep, Cheney explains, is the
permanent lengthening of a bowstring, the string not returning to its original
length after the bow is "let down." Pull the bow, and the string gets longer
(minutely) and stays longer: this is creep. Stretch, on the other hand, is a temporary lengthening of the string as the bow is drawn and shot. Afterwards,
the string returns to its original length.

BOWSTRINGS OF YESTERYEAR
What do we know about the first bowstring? We only know that the string
had to accompany the bow because no string means no bow. Both plant
and animal products were chosen to make strings in long-ago days. Many
natural materials are still used in various parts of the world, but most
shooters of composite bows today do not buy or make strings with these
basic materials.

The Plant Kingdom
Linen is made from the fibers of the flax plant and so strings of this material
have been called "flaxen strings." Survivalists know how to make a linen
string from scratch. Archers curious about these basic natural materials can
buy flax seed at the health food store, grow it, and make a useful string. Irish
Seaming Twine, made from linen, is said to be stronger than silk. *Hemp* is

Strings have been built of many materials over time, and still are today. Linen was one option from the plant world.

made from the tough coarse fibers of the cannabis (marijuana) plant native to Central Asia. Ramie, better known as Chinese grass, is a hardy perennial related to nettles. It is a very tough fiber considered by some authorities to be the strongest natural plant fiber, but is not often used due to heavy labor required in processing it. *Nettle* is known for its fibrous content as well as for "stinging." It is a very strong fiber, but like ramie requires considerable labor in processing. *Dogbane* has also been called Indian hemp, bitterroot, and rheumatism weed and like nettle is known for both its poisonous nature and its tough fiber. *Abaca* (pronounced ah-bah-KAH) is a species of banana plant native to the Philippines with a fiber so hard and consequently so strong that it has been used to make fishing nets. Milkweed, iris, yucca, sisal (*agave*), palm, and of course tough bamboo have all been used at one time or another in making bowstrings.

The Animal Kingdom

Saxton Pope experimented with many different materials for bowstring-making, including horsehair. He printed his findings in 1923, rating *catgut* at fifteen pounds breaking strength, while silk ran twenty-three pounds and ramie, thirty-two pounds. *Catgut* has been used for making bowstrings. It is not actually made from cats, but rather from the tough fibers found in the walls of intestines, usually sheep and goats, but occasionally hogs, mules, horses, and other animals. There are other strings simply called *gut*, which may be made from the intestinal material of just about any animal. Believe it or not, there are primitive archery fans making gut bowstrings today, some claiming they relate to the strings made by some American Indians of the

Leather can be cut into long thin strands and then woven into a single string.

past. *Silk* bowstrings date back to the distant past, but are still used in modern times. Useful through the ages in making bowstrings, silk is a fibroin excreted by certain insect larvae, especially silkworms, to form cocoons.

Rawhide is made by cutting wet hide into thin, long strips, then stretching the strips, often by putting a weight on each hanging strand. These "piles" are then twisted together to form a homogenous "rope" that can be turned into a string. Rawhide can be made from any tough hide, such as cow or deer hide. *Sinew* is not gut or catgut but rather the leg tendons from a hoofed animal. After drying, these sinews are shredded into fibers and the fibers woven into strings. A few current primitive archers are making bowstrings from sinew, one reportedly using tendons from a whitetail buck. Also, "artificial" sinew is available. (I'll stick to modern string materials.)

MODERN BOWSTRING MATERIALS

Before you can say "I love traditional archery" some chemical engineer will come up with yet another bowstring material. While it is important for the traditional archer to understand where bowstrings have come from, by far the majority of us will cling to modern materials only. Unfortunately, there are simply too many to delve into each type. And of course, archers cannot agree on which is the "best" bowstring.

Fastflight (Fast Flight)

Fastflight, also known as Fast Flight, which we will simply call F-1 string, came along in the 1990s as far as I can discern from records. It's a polypropylene known as Spectra. The government requisitioned Spectra plants since

Spectra is used in military body armor. Although no longer available, F-1 is mentioned here as a benchmark for comparison.

F-1 lived up to all its promises—stronger, longer-lasting, producing a tad more arrow speed than Dacron, and weather resistant. It had less creep and stretch, and therefore produced higher arrow velocity. However, it was no free lunch: it also broke a few bows because their owners did not heed the instructions for using F-1. F-1 strings were rated at about one percent stretch, which translated to more energy transfer to the arrow nock—but also more energy at the bow tips. Older bows were not always up to it and—Pow! There goes a limb. Bowyers immediately beefed up their bows to withstand F-1. Today, there is Fast Flight Plus but it *not* Fast Flight, as we will soon learn.

Brownell TS-1 Plus

Goodbye Fast Flight, hello Brownell TS-1 Plus! Made with Dyneema, a high modulus polyethylene material, this string material is said to exceed Fast Flight in creep and stretch, lightness, strength, and it will even cook up a nice

Sunday dinner—almost. Dyneema is actually more like F-1 than the F-4 that followed F-1 in that it is has slightly more stretch, which is not all bad, as well as all of the good properties of F-1. Dyneema is "the strongest fiber known to man," according to the literature. And of course TS-1 Plus was not the only string material made with Dyneema: BCY 8125, DynaFlight 97, and of course Fast Flight Plus (which is not made with Spectra like Fast Flight, but is Fast Flight only in name) are made of Dyneema. While many useful string materials have come along, Dyneema seems to be one of the better ideas in archery history.

Dyneema is considered the strongest material currently available for strings such as TS-1 and BCY Formula 8125, shown here, which is 92 percent Dyneema with a smaller than usual diameter. This string is noted for very low creep. PHOTO COURTESY OF BCY.

7-11

Kevlar 7-11 (Aramid) had good qualities, but also problems. It is a liquid crystal polymer that deserves mention for comparison because it is just one example of a high-performance string material that did not satisfy all of us, and it teaches us about the qualities that are desirable in a string material.

It definitely gave higher arrow speed: less energy was absorbed in the string because it was a narrow string with less mass. Less mass meant that less energy was required to move the string. Kevlar was initially thought to be not only viable but desireable. However, after more research and experience, Kevlar was found to produce additional stress on limbs. And it could break without fray warning first—not good for either archer or bow. Meanwhile, 7-11 did not last as long as B50, which remains on the market as a highly important string due to the fact that it serves admirably on bows but is much easier on limb tips than some of the more modern string materials.

B50

B50 is a Dacron string with half the strength of our benchmark F-1 and about two and one-half times more stretch. Regardless, B50 makes into a darn good string and is highly recommended for bows that may fail under the much less forgiving modern Fastflight-type strings. On some of my old self-bows of yew I never used other than B50. I also used B50 on all my older composite bows, such as Bear, Browning, Shakespeare, and other models from the 1960s and even earlier. This is a good, long-lasting string deserving of continued use. B50, per strand, withstands about fifty pounds force strength. While I appreciate the great TS-1 Plus string material, I am also grateful for the continuance of B50.

The ever useful B50 is included here as BCY B500, a polyester string material suited especially to traditional bows not designed for Fast-Flight-type strings.
PHOTO COURTESY OF BYC.

Fast Flight Plus

The name is the same, but the string material is not. Fast Flight Plus is not the Spectra Fast Flight of the past. With Spectra string gone as of 2006, when the U.S. government appropriated Spectra for military use, as in body armor, a new string material was found—Dyneema. A high-performance polyethylene said to be fifteen times stronger than steel, Dyneema has found its way into bulletproof vests, work gloves, and rope as "the word's strongest fiber." Fast Flight Plus string, according to the literature, is "no-creep" string promising increased arrow speed over Dacron strings.

KNOW YOUR BOW

You must know your bow before attaching a string to those bow nocks. Fast Flight Plus, TS-1 Plus, DynaFlight 97, 450 Plus, and others of the F-1 category will add stress to the bow limbs. And that is all right, provided the bow was designed for these minimal-creep and -stretch, high-performance strings. When I first acquired a particular longbow I shoot a lot, I made sure that it was designed for the F-1 type of string. This particular Pronghorn Three-Piece Takedown Longbow is what I call a "deadly sliver." Its feather weight gives the impression that it might not take a beating. But that's a false impression. Super tough micarta overlays afford extra strength at the bow nocks; this bow is definitely made to withstand the extra force applied by the F-1 type of string. The bow nocks will not be cut or broken.

SIMPLE TEST FOR F-1 TYPE STRING MATERIAL

For those making their own strings, there is a material test to ensure that an F-1 type material does not end up on a bow it might break. NZAP, "Your On-line Archery Superstore" serving Australia and New Zealand, offered an easy, quick, and sure way to tell F-1 type string material from Dacron. You can't use it on your bowstring itself because it requires taking a little snip of the material and lighting it on fire. If the tip of string material melts into a little ball on the end that cools hard it is Dacron. Dyneema string material does not do this. Burn the end of string material made of Dyneema and it fuzzes up into an ash and, when cool, crumbles at a touch.

STRING TYPES

The Flemish twist string, sometimes referred to as a reverse-twist string, is the most popular type today. Those who build these strings—and many hobbyists can and do make the Flemish string—will tell you that this type takes a little more time and a tad of extra skill to get right. The reverse-twist string is made up of separate bundles of strands, each one twisted individually in a single direction, then the entire set of bundles twisted in the opposite direction. The result is two excellent features. The string ends up very strong at the loops. Also, it can be twisted considerably to alter fistmele. That is vital. By simply twisting the string (not beyond its capacity to remain in one piece, of course), you can change the brace height up or down so the bow can be tuned.

Describing string types is difficult at best, but also not very important because most traditional archers will buy a string from a bona fide string craftsman and the archer will know the quality will be there—and not only quality, but the string maker's idea of what is best for a given bow. The Flemish or reverse twist string is the choice for most of us who shoot the longbow and recurve of the day. But there are at least two other types of bowstring—the simple and the endless.

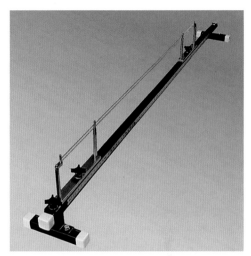

Left: The reverse twist of the excellent Flemish string increases the string's integrity. Right: A jig for making a Flemish twist string can be purchased or made by the archer. The BCY Dream Machine String Jig, shown here, is made of steel and can be mounted on a wall.

To make a Flemish twist string, a single strand is run around the pegs on the jig then cut to form a bundle.

The simple string is nothing more than some form of fiber twisted around until it forms a single unit. They are quick and comparatively easy to construct. But they can also become "untwisted" if not maintained as a single piece. Ideally, this simple string is best kept under tension, such as on a strung bow. This is not always easy as simple strings are often matched to

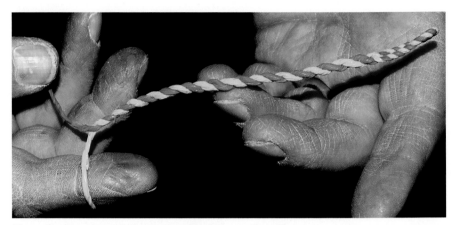

Here, the strands are being twisted to form one bundle.

The Flemish twist string has a superb loop.

simple wooden self-bows, which should not be kept strung indefinitely. Therefore, another means of keeping the simple string intact is necessary, such as keeping it strung on a bow that is no longer in use.

The other string type is the endless loop, made of one or more continuous loop(s) of material. The ends must be served in order to make loops for the bow nocks. These loops are therefore not as strong as the Flemish loops. Currently, Stone Mountain Bow Strings of Orofino, Idaho, offers endless loop strings for recurves and longbows containing twelve to sixteen strands of Dacron. Another company has a two-colored twisted string simulating a Flemish twist but actually in endless design.

I have had endless strings on bows and found that the string had to be the proper length for the brace height, because twisting to change string length is limited with an endless string. The Flemish twist string, on the other hand, allows considerable latitude in growing longer or shorter by twisting. Also, the endless string requires "dressed loops," that is, loops wrapped as a serving on the string. Made of multiple strands of string, the Flemish twist loops are "integral" to the string, more or less formed by being turned into loops. These loops don't need a wrap on these string ends for them to remain intact, so they are stronger than the dressed loops of the endless string. Having said this, there are some archers who insist—never mind what anyone else says—that the endless string is long-lasting and superior in strength due to its design. Wouldn't we be surprised if the individualists who thrive on traditional archery didn't have differences of opinion?

The Flemish twist string, the simple string, and the endless string are only three of the many different variations in building strings that have come along in the last several thousand years. They are the most prevalent styles currently, but some others are still in use. For example, I observed a person making a braided string from flax fibers at an archery show.

STRING MAINTENANCE

String maintenance is pretty simple, really. Clean the string now and then with a damp cloth, followed by a dry cloth. Rub vigorously with the dry cloth to remove some of the old wax as the cloth heats the string. Once the string is clean, apply new bowstring wax. Run the wax over the string and rub it in with a clean cloth. That's about it as far as I know. When storing a string, keep it away from moisture. I have had strings last so long that I finally tossed them out, not because they showed wear, but just due to their age, and this includes strings stored under both fairly hot and cool locations. It is not unknown for an old string that shows no overt signs of wear to snap unexpectedly, and I wanted to be cautious with these old strings.

ORDERING A STRING USING THE AMO STANDARD

A string can be ordered through the mail using the Archery Manufacturer's Organization (AMO) standard. Tammy Joe's Archery Supplies recommends the following in using AMO to order strings:

Take a tape measure, start at the nock/string groove of either end "not the bow tips," run tape down the belly (side facing you when you shoot) of the un-strung bow following the contours of the bow limbs, do not go into the curves of the handle, go straight across to the opposite nock groove and read the measure. Enter the length of the bow into the "additional instructions" field if you will be ordering by the bow length and not the string length.

Some sure ways to get the right string are to buy a few from the bowyer when a new stick is purchased, to write down the string length so you will

The best way to order a string is to go back to the bowyer with a reminder of the specifics of the bow made for you. This light practice and small game bow is 60 inches in draw length with a draw weight of 41 pounds.

always have it to refer to, or to send or bring the old correct string to the string maker.

So simple, yet so complex, the bowstring has been made, over the centuries, of many materials, and today is the best it ever has been, not only in performance but also in many other important traits, such as strength and longevity.

17

Quiet, Please!

Thunderclouds drifted over the tallest peak like smoke billowing from a pirate ship's cannons. I knew what was coming. The sky announced the dropping of its liquid cargo with explosions that reverberated in my chest. The bass drum of thunder in the mountains was thrilling, even intimidating. That night, elk bugled constantly with intermittent messages from coyotes and newly introduced wolves mingling like music for a nature-lover's ears. The wind in the trees joined the gurgling of the creek, a symphony riding on a soft breeze.

Most of nature's sounds stir the senses. But there is one noise traditional archers don't want to hear-ever. It is not the boom of thunder, nor the song of the coyote or wolf. It's the *twang!* of a longbow or recurve "going off." That simple noise can spoil even the best-planned stalk or sit-out, resulting in game "jumping the string," the arrow going where the buck or bull used to be, but isn't anymore.

Quieting stickbows is necessary—and not only for hunters. Even when roving, where the target is a tree stump, it is in my opinion more pleasant to enjoy the *hum* of a bowstring as opposed to a *twang!*

Jumping the string has been around since the first prehistoric

Wild animals, such as this mule deer, can "jump the string" because of their acute hearing ability with those big ears.

hunter sent an arrow toward his Sunday dinner. The major, but not only, culprit is the bowstring, as it launches forward carrying the nocked arrow. Fortunately, this is also one of the easiest noise problems to correct.

The faster the arrow, the easier to avoid game jumping the string. But as fast as modern compound bows are with overdraws and "soda straws" (super lightweight arrows), even they cannot prevent antelope, deer, elk, and other game from jumping the string. And woe to the traditionalist with longbow or recurve firing a dart at around two hundred feet per second, sometimes slower. Whitetails, especially, are masters at jumping the string, ducking low at the *twang* so the arrow passes over their backs. Check it out. Hunting video after hunting video shows hunters missing deer just below their tree stands. Slow motion reveals what happened: the deer instantly "squatted" at the sound of the bow sending an arrow on course. That's why bows must be silenced. Here are eleven ways to say "Quiet, please!" to your longbow or recurve.

LONGBOW VERSUS RECURVE

A major factor determining bow noise is whether the bow is a longbow or a recurve. Longbows, in general, are quieter than recurves for one major reason—the recurve string rests against the working limbs of the bow and the string can slap that area.

There are exceptions to every rule, of course: I have fired a few examples of the normally quieter longbow that sounded like jet planes taking off at the airport. This is due to less than ideal design and fortunately the two offending bows I'm thinking of are no longer on the market. I am not

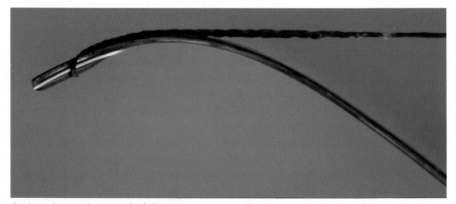

String slap is the sound of the string coming down upon the limbs of the recurve bow. However, a properly tuned recurve with string silencers can be made to shoot with minimal noise.

smart enough to assess exactly why those bows were so noisy—it was something to do with their geometry, of course—but nothing worked well in silencing them.

One solution for a recurve is string groove silencers. These are adhesive-backed strips of calf hair that are sold in pairs, one piece going under each limb tip to cover the string groove. With these in place, the string slaps down on the calf hair rather than on the bow limb itself, resulting in quieter shooting. Another good silencing device is a small piece cut from stick-on strike plate material placed at this same juncture, or even thicker arrow rest material serving as a medium to "soak up" some or most of, the normal string slap that occurs with the recurve bow design. Conversely, the string of the longbow makes no direct contact with the working limbs. This is not a hundred percent accurate, because as the longbow returns to its pre-draw state, the string may make a minor touch on the limb tips, but this is negligible and nothing to cause concern. Do not place any substance where the bowstring of a longbow might make almost imperceptible contact with limb. It's not worth it. Brush buttons (small rubber knobs on the string located where string of recurve initially intercepts the limb) can also help dampen the slam of the string hitting that limb.

FINE-TUNE YOUR BOW

Fine-tuning is an overall quieting factor. Traditional stickbows do not demand the attention lavished on their mechanical brothers to shut them up. But longbows and recurves do demand some tuning. Chapter 7 deals with this important subject fully, but it is important to reiterate here that tuning is a factor in hushing the bow. The well-tuned traditional bow sends its dart on a handsome flight course, neither fishtailing (wagging side to side like the tail of a swimming fish) nor porpoising (undulating through the air like a porpoise through the water). While arrow flight is obviously essential to successful shooting, it is also important to quiet shooting.

BRACE HEIGHT

Brace height (fistmele) is extremely important in terms of string-slap, especially with recurve bows. A very low brace height can contribute to a faster arrow. I believe this based on chronograph tests with my own bows. On the other hand, that very low brace height can cause increased string-slap in the recurve (because it means there is more string lying against the face of the limb). And I have had longbows rap my arm guard a good one with very low brace height, adding to the noise factor. Brace height must be set for optimum performance, of course, but also with regard to noise.

A well-tuned bow with proper brace height will avoid much of the sound usually produced when the string is let go and the limbs fly forward.

NOCKING POINT

Several factors contribute to good arrow flight, a major one being that specific point where the nock set is located on the string. An incorrectly positioned nock set can cause fishtailing and porpoising, both of which add to the deadly *twang*. There is no one correct nock-point for all bows. The best way to determine proper location of nock set on string is by trial and error, moving it up and down until the arrow flies true—and more quietly.

ARROW REST AND STRIKE PLATE

The strike plate and arrow rest can be accused of causing noise. While this is a minor factor, all particulars in quieting a bow are worth addressing. The object of the strike plate and arrow rest is to produce the least possible amount of friction as they guide the arrow and act as a sort of platform for the arrow's takeoff, not unlike the runway for a plane. Any bow is prone to noise when the arrow slams against the rest rather than gliding over it smoothly. In shooting off the shelf (which is the usual method for longbows and recurves even though a raised arrow rest can be incorporated on either type), the shaft of the arrow is very close to the shelf and strike plate. If you are getting noise from these parts of the bow, consider using "quieter" arrow rests and strike plate materials. There are many good ones. The first Bear bow I owned had a fuzzy thing for an arrow rest. It was called Bear Hair and I still see it today. There are many other excellent rests available, including calf hair and leather, which can be very quiet as it "wears in." Don't forget the strike plate. Strike plates are available in numerous materials designed to reduce the noise factor an an arrow gliding alongside the plate. Examples of strike plate materials include Silencer Felt, a soft felt material with adhesive backing which can be cut to size and used as a strike plate. Bear Hair Plate, Rug Side Plate, calf hair plates, and others are available at archery shops.

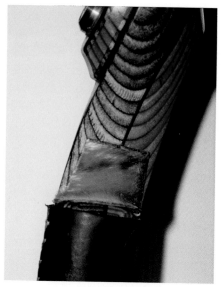

One quieting factor for any bow is a proper strike plate, such as this one made of sealskin.

SHOOTING THROUGH THE GAP

"Shooting through the gap" can promote quiet shooting. A gap is created by leaving a space between the strike plate and the arrow rest (this space is also called a gutter). I learned of this trick when it was promised to promote clean arrow getaway from the bow shelf. The idea is that a hen feather slips right through the gutter, making significantly less contact and therefore contributing to better arrow flight. Arrows shot through the gap did not improve over arrows shot from a standard side plate and rest in my bows. However, I continue using the gutter for a modicum of value in slight noise reduction and perhaps slightly reduced hen feather wear. Animal hearing being what it is, even a slight reduction in sound could be meaningful.

Shooting through the gap does not necessarily make an arrow fly better from the bow, but it may have a mild quieting effect. The two dots of hardened epoxy make a trough, causing slightly less contact between the shelf and the arrow's hen feather.

THE ARROW

Heavier arrows absorb more of the bow's energy than lighter ones. Anyone who has accidentally dry fired a bow has experienced the light arrow syndrome, perhaps without knowing it. The bow twangs like a banjo string when dry fired (and a limb may break). Super light arrows can produce the same effect as dry firing, and should be avoided. This is not to suggest shooting logs with a rainbow trajectory: I have found that arrows in the 500-grain range for bows in 50- to 60-pound draw weight are heavy enough for penetration and also quietness. Going for elephant? Then perhaps the super heavy arrow in a powerful bow, such as Howard Hill used for the movie *Tembo*, is right. But most of us will not bowhunt elephants too often.

FEATHERS

As discussed in the feather chapter, big feathers with consequent great surface area can be noisy. While large fletching tends to straighten an arrow faster during the archer's paradox, the larger surface area also makes a loud *whoosh!* My preference is just enough fletching to stabilize the arrow and no more. Any archer who doubts how much noise over-fletching can cause should try flu-flus. These arrows, intended for short-range shooting, whoosh through the air noisier than a frightened sparrow. Helical fletch with plenty of twist for quick arrow stabilization can also lend increased noise. I find straight offset feathers right for my bows, quiet and totally adequate for point-forward arrow flight.

To assess feather noise, use this test: have another archer stand behind a tree, completely out of danger. Then fire an arrow—*not toward the tree, but to the side of it*. Never loose an arrow anywhere in the direction of a person or anything else you do not want to hit—just like, when shooting a firearm, you never aim in the direction of an object that you do not intend to strike. The archer safely ensconced behind the tree will hear the arrow flying through the air. This is a good test (and a safe one) for discovering arrows that sound like a golden eagle swooping down on a duck.

THE BROADHEAD

Broadheads can add to noise, and certain types make more in-flight noise than others. This is easily tested through trial-and-error shooting. Also, broadheads must be securely attached to the arrow. I lost out on a buck antelope once because a broadhead had partially loosened its grip. The arrow took a spiral flight, which was bad enough. But worse was the whirring noise it made. The 'lope headed for new territory. Current broadheads, while expensive, are also the best the world of archery has ever known. The ones I experimented with recently were aerodynamic and accurate. Out of my bows,

Broadheads may contribute to arrow noise in flight. This factor can be tested quite simply "by ear." Today's broadheads, however, very seldom produce undue noise in flight.

I can count on them to group as well as target points, or at least almost as well. The tried-and-true Zwickey is still going strong. I also find the Steel Force, Woodsman, Elite, Zephyr, Coyote II, and Grizzly heads excellent.

BOW QUIVER

Another factor in reducing shooting noise is the bow quiver. Some bow quivers grip arrows high on the shaft toward the point end. The long and flexible lower part of the shaft is left unsupported, and vibrates when the bow is shot, making noise. The cure is moving the arrow gripper downward from the hood of the bow quiver so as to grip more of the shaft, if the style of the quiver allows. This prevents the flexible part of the shaft from vibrating. If the bow quiver is not adaptable to lowering the arrow gripper, it should be replaced with a different model.

Also, the bow quiver must hold arrows far enough apart to avoid fletching rubbing on fletching, which causes a rustling sound when the bow is drawn or fired. The quiver should also be tightly attached to the bow. Loose, it can rattle when the bow is shot. Overtightening is never the answer, since too much torque may fracture bow glass, but there's nothing wrong with placing washers in between the riser and quiver to provide a better hold. Quiver limb bolts must be tight, but not overly so. "Good and snug" is the byword.

A bow quiver that is not firmly in place can rattle, though this noise may be undetectable by the human ear. Bow quivers must be checked periodically for tightness.

SQUEAK!

Then there's the mouse problem—when your bow squeaks. This happens with takedown bows only where the butt of the limb is attached to the riser of the bow. This juncture between two different elements can cause friction, resulting in noise. The problem is easily cured in one of two ways: lubrication or a buffer. Any mild substance, such as bowstring wax, serves as a lubricant between limbs and riser platforms. The best lubricant I have ever used is NanoLube NDN30-ATM+P. One drop between the limb and the riser platform sends the mouse back to its hole. While harsh lubricants may attack the limb surface, I have found no such problem with NanoLube. The second cure is a buffer, such as flexible cork. Buffers must be very thin, as thicker materials may cause a gap between the limb and the riser. Something as simple as a piece of playing card can do the trick. But I'll go with NanoLube.

THE STRING

The last noisemaker is the string, the number one problem for longbows and recurves, but one with an easy cure. Many different types of string silencers are available. All work about the same way, absorbing (dampening) vibration. Rubber "cat whiskers" have been used since George Washington was in short pants and they work. I cut them in half, having found that four shorter segments dampen noise as effectively as two longer ones, plus the shorter cat whiskers last much longer than full-length ones because they don't suffer so much whip. The shortened rubber strands are mounted with two sets above

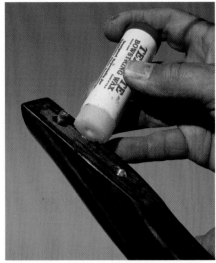

Bowstring wax is useful in lubricating the contact surfaces between the limbs of a takedown bow and the riser. Many other lubricants work equally well, however.

The connection between limb and riser on a takedown bow can make noise and may require either lubricant or a buffer of some sort.

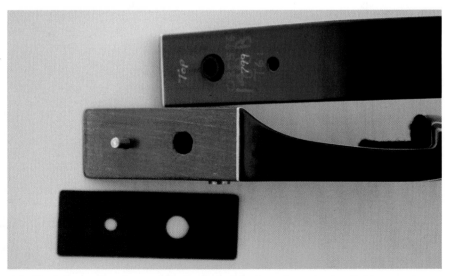

A buffer between the riser and the limb of a takedown bow can be vital to ensuring quiet shooting.

and two sets below the riser. These may be spaced in various ways. One method is locating one set about ten inches from the tip of the top limb, another about ten inches from the tip of the bottom limb, the other two sets three inches inward toward the riser.

Tie Cat Whiskers between the strands of the bowstring. Mounting takes place with the string off of the bow. I slip a rubber band onto each string loop, one going around a door knob (for example), the other around the top strut of a chair—or two chairs can be used—you just need something that will hold the string taut and suspended while you are mounting the silencers. Rubber bands work well because they stretch, allowing give in the string so the silencers can be inserted between strands. Now call on someone to help you. Slip the Cat Whiskers between the center strands of the string and have the helper tug on both ends of these silencers, stretching the set. While the helper keeps the rubber silencers stretched, tie them onto the bowstring with strong nylon thread in a crisscross manner, back and forth a few times in knots to secure them in place. After the silencers are secured, a drop of Super Glue centered on the nylon thread secures them fully. Cat Whiskers attached this way normally last the life of the string.

Cat Whiskers, though good, are not the only string silencers. In checking a list of currently available silencers I found ten on a single page of one catalog, Cat Whiskers included in the number. Muskrat Silencers were noted as water repellent, with "short, thick fur that makes an excellent string silencer."

String silencers are highly useful in reducing the twang! of a bow being shot. The silencers shown here are known as cat whiskers.

Otter Silencers were touted as "about as good as it gets," and Buffalo String Silencers as "elegant, yet simple." There were also Beaver Silencers made of tanned hide, Quiet Wool Silencers, Musk Ox String Silencers, String Leeches (and Super String Leeches) "designed for absolute performance" and maximum silencing, Woolie Whispers, and Puff String Silencers.

Silencing the bow is certainly of immense value to the bowhunter. But I have found that even when roving, a quiet bow is nicer to shoot than a noisier one. And since the methods used in achieving a quieter bow are so simple and effective, there is no reason to go on shooting a bow that makes unwarranted noise when that arrow is released.

18

Stalls, Tabs, Gloves, and Arm Guards

For lack of a nail a shoe was lost. For lack of a shoe a horse was lost. For lack of a horse a soldier was lost. For lack of a soldier the battle was lost. Or something like that. How many archers have lost out on a great rove for lack of a little thing—like an extra bow glove? *Don't know where I set it down, but my glove is gone for good, I guess, and shooting this strong bow without a glove is not going to happen today!* Tackle matters. Besides the obvious bow and arrow, tackle is mainly the archery gloves, tabs, stalls, and arm guards, and these are what I will focus on here. Arrow-making supplies, bow quivers, back quivers, arrow storage boxes, travel cases—these and much more are grist for other mills.

When was the archery glove first used? Nobody knows for sure. The tab? Finger stalls? Bracer or arm guard? All have the same story—their origins are lost in history.

What we do know is that in traditional bow-shooting these little things are big. And they have survived the test of time because they are so valuable. So many "modern" inventions are actually remakes from past ideas. Even the popular mechanical release so-loved by compound bow shooters today had its origin in the 1940s. Releases are good for the wheel bow because extreme let-off (relaxation) can cause hold-back on the drawn arrow; with a light hold at full draw, release can be mushy, with the fingers sort of curling around the string before the arrow can get away. A mechanical release allows for a clean arrow getaway.

Traditional (and primitive) bows have their highest pull at the end of the draw, which can promote a clean release, but also string-burn the fingers. It is true that my archery partner, Ted Walter, never used stalls, glove, or tab, calluses taking their place. He often started the day with Band-Aids on his fingers, but they wore through in no time. Maurice Thompson, in his great book *The Witchery of Archery*, did say, "if your fingers can stand it, shoot without gloves." That advice was given in 1878. And the reasoning was as Ted said, "without finger protection, your fingers feel the string better."

WHY YOU NEED FINGER PROTECTION

As Ted used to say, covering your fingers with anything reduces the "feel" of the string. The problem is, if you shoot without finger protection, you pay the price. With anything but a very low draw weight bow, and even then with repeated shots, your fingers are going to become sore, perhaps much more than sore. And so while it is true that stalls, gloves, or tabs will reduce finger sensitivity on the string, in fact shooting without these protectors will, in the long run, produce poor release as pain increases. I tried the no-glove, no-tab, no-stalls approach and though I taped my fingers at first, as I was instructed to do, I learned quickly that bare-finger bow-shooting was not for me. Furthermore, I quickly learned that the finger protection I liked best did not hamper a smooth release, but rather promoted one.

Maurice Thompson wrote that "the shooting glove is made to protect the three fingers of the right hand from the wearing effect of the bowstring in shooting. It is formed of three thimbles of stiff, smooth leather, having elastic stitches to allow them to perfectly conform to the size of fingers." While this sounds more like stalls than a glove, Maurice did say "glove," not "tab." In chapter seven of Saxton Pope's *Hunting with Bow and Arrow*, there is a perfect example of stalls, lower left-hand corner of the illustration on page 99 in my

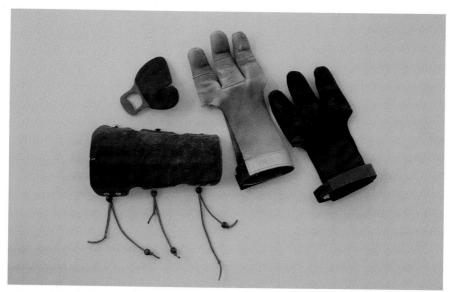

Gloves, tabs, and arm guards—all are to keep the archer from sustaining sore fingers and string-slapped wrists, which invariably lead to poor shooting.

edition. Pope called it a "finger tip." Above the finger tip, the "leather pattern of finger tip" is clearly shown. Pope also made it clear that finger protection was vital: "Doubtless the ancient yeoman, a horny-handed son of toil, needed no glove. But we know that even in those days a tab of leather was held in the hand to prevent the string from hurting." Howard Hill, in *Hunting the Hard Way*, uses the term *stalls* but goes on to describe stalls with a strap, saying "It is not advisable to use finger stalls unless they are made secure to a wristband of some kind, as they are too easily lost when independent of one another." Hill also said in 1953, "The protectors or stalls for the fingertips should be selected with care. A shooting glove works well, but when worn all day it often becomes uncomfortable." This statement clarifies that Hill's "glove" was more of a stall with a strap than a glove.

STALLS

Finger stalls (also called finger tips) covers the fingers only. Stalls are not popular today, but they are not completely gone either. An archer I met at a recent state gathering had stalls on his fingers. He made them himself from pliable leather, stitching them to form a slip-on "tube," as it were. The main advantage of the stall, as best I can come up with, is that it fits so naturally over the finger that in effect it feels as if there is nothing between fingers and bowstring. Properly fitted, they do not slip. But then I never have a glove or tab slip either. In checking through the archery catalogs I had on hand, I found none for sale. I did find a wealth of gloves and tabs. But just because stalls are not popular does mean that they are no good. And an archer interested in them can make them from pieces of leather, forming them into cones, and sewing them to fit snugly over the fingers of the bow hand.

THE TAB

Basically, the tab is little more than a small piece of leather or other material (some are of synthetic construction), usually with a slit near the top. Many tabs available today, however, are far more sophisticated. One option is the tried and true calf hair tab. It has a finger separator, which I find especially useful. And it comes in different sizes so the archer can get a perfect "fit," from small through extra large, made for the right hand or the left hand. The calf hair outer layer makes contact with the string for a "slippery" surface and clean arrow release.

Most tabs are made for archers using the split finger method of holding the string back (also called the Mediterranean draw or Mediterranean release), but some bow-shooters hold all three fingers *under* the nocked arrow on the string. This is a perfectly acceptable method, especially for bows specifically tillered for "three fingers under." And so there are tabs designed for this method of draw and release. One I am familiar with is the 3-Fingers Under Black Widow Leather Tab. Typical of the Black Widow Company, the tab is first-rate in all particulars. It's made of tough but smooth leather and it comes fitted for the right or left hand in sizes small, medium, large, and extra large. There is also a Black Widow 3-Fingers Under Hair Tab (made of calf hair for slick release.)

Another major variable in tab style whether the design has a loop to prevent the tab from dropping away when the arrow is released from the bow. Some tabs have a hole toward the back into which the finger slips. Lacking this finger loop, a tab can have a stretch cord or other means of securing it to the shooting hand—an example of this is the Cavalier Elite Cordovan Tab.

The Skookum Mega Tuff Tab is an example of one of the many different surface possibilities of the tab. This tab is faced with Teflon for a "slippery" smooth arrow release. It also has a rigid composite plate to maintain shape along with suede leather backing to cushion the bow string. It is a far cry from the tab described by Saxton Pope in is book. The Skookum Yellow Jacket Tab is faced with waterproof polyurethane for a smooth release "under harsh conditions."

The long list of tab variations continues with the aforementioned Cavalier Elite Cordovan Tab, which is adjustable to the hand of the individual archer. It has a surface made of cordovan, a very fine leather. Cordovan originated in Cordoba, Spain, and was originally made of goatskin; today it is made of split horse hide, but retains its high quality—and its high price. The cordovan surface promises a smooth release, but that's not all. There is an anodized aluminum plate that provides precise string positioning for every shot, and an adjustable cord-lock attachment provides a wide range of fit for the individual archer. This tab's sister, the Cavalier Ultra Elite Super Leather Tab has suede backing with a lightweight tab plate. It runs at about half the cost of the cordovan Cavalier.

Anyone who thinks that traditional archery is "no big deal" today need only look at the tab to change his or her mind. In my search for various tabs of interest the list grew until it was unmanageable—Cartel, Arco Sport, Gompy, King Archery, Martin Archery, Neet Archery, Browning, Bear, Saunders—and the list goes on. Choosing a tab, therefore, is far more complex today than ever before. While there are some available for only a couple dollars, an upscale tab can cost you thirty dollars; there are many in the ten-to-fifteen-dollar range. The best way to decide on a tab is to begin with a cheaper one just to "feel it out." Give the tab a chance, of course, and try those with finger separators and those without. Both types are excellent, just different.

THE GLOVE

Sometimes an archery glove is just that—a glove, plain and simple. I have gloves of high-grade leather that offer plenty of finger protection. And on colder days they double as hand warmers. I also have gloves with overlays on the appropriate fingers for bow draw and release. And I have made my own by gluing (I use Shoe Goo) small leather pads to regular gloves, turning them into decent archery gloves that serve both to keep hands warm and protect the fingers when drawing and releasing. I have also tried specialty gloves, such as those designed to prevent knife cuts in the kitchen. These, for me, were not satisfactory. They worked in preventing finger soreness but perhaps worked too well in that regard, making "string feel" just about nil.

While many different types of gloves can be used as archery gloves, none take the place of the "real thing," which, due to the modern upsurge of interest in traditional archery, is available in a multitude of designs and is no doubt the best ever. Try several kinds if that is at all possible. As with the tab, it's wise to try a cheaper glove just to see if it is "your cup of tea." Are you better off with a tab or a glove? Good archery gloves can be bought for about ten dollars (at the time of this writing).

One of my favorite gloves at any price is the Damascus style, which you can procure for fifteen bucks. The Damascus is a full-palm glove of deerskin

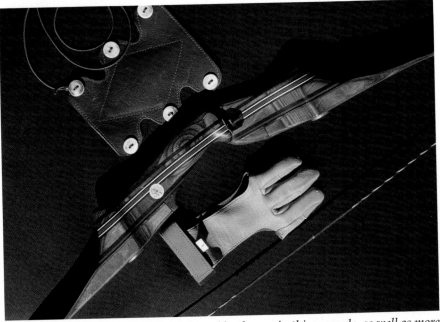

Archery gloves can be made of soft tanned leather, as in this example, as well as more rigid leather and other materials.

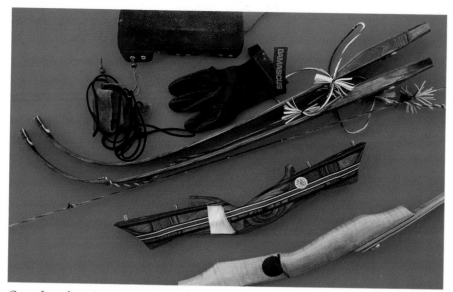

One of my favorite gloves is the Damascus. It offers finger protection while at the same time providing a good feel of the bowstring.

leather, smooth and soft, but with reinforced finger tips. The fingertip rein-forcers are of the same smooth leather (on the Damascus glove I have) for ex-cellent "string feel." The Damascus has a Velcro band that works perfectly to secure the glove to the hand. A similar glove is the Skookum, at double the cost but with synthetic finger reinforcers. It also has the Velcro wrist band. An army of similar designs are available—all with soft body and reinforced finger tips, plus the wrap-around Velcro strap for secure wrist hold.

The most expensive archery glove I found in my search cost eighty dol-lars with shipping—the Full-Shot Glove. It has a buckskin palm, full finger stalls, and slick nylon release pads. The special feature of this glove, aside from superb quality, is the three neoprene knuckles on top that that stretch to fit the archer's hand perfectly. The Full-Shot feels like a fine sports car driving glove but works hard as an archery shooting glove. The American Leathers Big Shot Glove mimics the Full-Shot with the same neoprene knuckle stretch-ers. It runs slightly less dollar-wise at about fifty dollars with shipping for the elk-hide version and sixty-five dollars for the buffalo-hide glove.

There are also "skeletonized" gloves, exemplified by the Cordovan Tra-ditional Glove with adjustable wrist strap. This is, in effect, finger stalls at-tached to straps, very similar to the description that Howard Hill gave of a particular type of shooting glove.

The Wyandotte Closed-End Glove is unlike the Cordovan Traditional Glove in that it does not have the long straps leading to finger stalls. Instead,

This softer Bear archery glove has a Velcro wrist strap, which is typical of many modern archery gloves. The wrist strap holds the glove snugly on the hand.

This Bear archery glove is built to last a lifetime. While thick and sturdy, it does provide a good feel on the bowstring.

This Bear arm guard slips on and off quickly and easily. It is made to withstand string slap from the most powerful bow.

this tanned leather glove has a wide elastic stretch band in between a Velcro wrist strap and the finger protectors. The Wyandotte Open-End Glove is similar but the finger protectors are open rather than closed on the end. It is almost a variation of the Cordovan Traditional, with long straps connecting wrist attachment to finger protectors. But the straps from the finger protectors connect to the same elastic stretch band as on the Open-End model. These three gloves are of the open palm design, while others, like the Damascus, cover all or most of the palm of the hand.

WHY YOU NEED WRIST PROTECTION

Once more we have to backpedal slightly because some archers do not need wrist protection due to their particular style of shooting a bow. The string never slaps the wrists of these bow-shooters, but instead always clears it completely. For the vast majority of us, however, wrist protection while shooting our bows is vitally necessary. I forgot my arm guard once, shot until the wrist-slap of the string took all the fun out of it, and got home with a wrist resembling Grade-A hamburger. Saxton Pope, in *Hunting with the Bow and Arrow,* writes, "the bracer, or arm guard, is a cuff of leather worn on the left forearm to prevent the stroke of the bowstring doing damage."

It doesn't get clearer than that. Pope's arm guard started with a piece of deer hide cut into the shape of an isosceles trapezoid twelve inches on one end and ten inches on the other, eight inches long, so that it folds to form a cone with a narrower end and a wider end to fit the forearm of the archer. Pope then attached straps with buckles to his arm guard. Today, that style arm guard is difficult to find because it is faster and more convenient to use stretch loops or similar means of securing the arm guard onto the archer's forearm. Out of fourteen different arm guards that I reviewed, only one attached with a method other than stretch loops.

Choosing an arm guard begins with length more than design because every arm guard does the job. You can go low-end for about fifteen dollars (at the time of this writing) for an entirely serviceable arm guard made of quality leather (and a few bargain-priced for even less), or buy more sophisticated models that attack the wallet at about sixty-five dollars. Ideally, the archer wants to cover only that part of the forearm where, due to his specific style of shooting a bow, the string slaps. The only other concern is the extremely important aspect of holding back shirt or jacket. Many an archer has missed the target because the string smacked shirt or jacket, causing the arrow to go astray.

The arm guard also serves the extremely important task of holding a shirt sleeve out of the way of the bowstring when the bow is fired. When a collapsing string makes contact with a sleeve, the arrow usually goes errant.

To this end, there is one arm guard specifically made for bowhunters who have found the value of the Shaggie (ghillie suit). This army-designed suit is so effective that when the wind is right a deer or other animal may walk up to within mere feet of a hunter seated on the ground, especially when he or she is backed into a bush to disrupt the human outline with a broken background. The Cat-Guard Armguard is camouflage-patterned, light in weight (only a few ounces), and comes in lengths of eight or fourteen inches. It "breaks" where elbow crooks so that the longer forward portion extends upward toward the wrist, while the shorter back part runs toward the upper arm. This extra-long arm guard prevents string slap against the large sleeves of the Shaggie.

The more standard arm guard will run from a little over six inches to under nine inches. My main arm guard at the moment, the TL-Stretch Armguard, is a simple leather model seven inches long with six large buttons, three on each side, with a long leather thong looped into the right-hand back button. To attach this armguard, you settle it on the forearm and simply wrap the thong back and forth around the other buttons and wrap the loose end around your arm a couple times to tie it off and keep it out of the way. This simple armguard will last a lifetime—the left forward button did break off, but that was the only casualty and the button was easily replaced. Two other

This one little army belt kit contains a number of items useful to the archer in the field, including extra string, bow stringer, nock sets, and nock set pliers.

Left: The two kits shown here are suitable for a rove in known territory, not wandering too far from road or vehicle. For long hauls in the outback, you should carry a larger pack with fire starter and emergency supplies. Right: Small kits, especially belt kits, are handy in the field. Here are two.

particularly attractive armguards (in my personal opinion) are the Archer's Bracer, which is of simple design with speed lace closures and the Medieval Bracer of high-quality leather with brass buckles and studs, decorative as well as functional. The Medieval Bracer, while clearly designed to "call up days long gone," attaches to the arm as securely as any of the modern models.

OTHER TACKLE

I will quickly mention here another little piece of tackle worth having—the belt kit. It's nothing more than any container that fits on belt loops and is capable of holding a few archery accouterments—an extra string waxed and placed in a plastic sandwich bag, a stringer, a few nocks, nocking pliers, a little glue, a couple of string nock sets—whatever the imagination calls for. Missing these little things that can throw a monkey wrench into the smoothly operating gears of a great time shooting the bow. This is not my idea by any means; "The Old Bowhunter," Chester Stevenson, made or had made for him archery kits that closely resembled black powder shooting bags, called "possibles bags" these days.

19

Games and Practice

The compound craze hit like a swarm of bees and I got stung right along with all the others who wanted to find an easier way to shoot a faster arrow. The only real advantage of the new mechanical bow at the time was not arrow speed (the Black Widow recurve bow was faster, as proved by chronograph), but rather the let-off or relaxation factor. Fortunately, I did not sell all of my traditional tackle. I still had one longbow around, but all in all, I set aside stickbows for a spell in favor of the wheel bow. As the compound began to realize its potential, I upgraded several times to faster and faster bows. A four-wheeler Arrowstar was my last compound, later given away as a gift to a cousin. Compounds were interesting, no doubt about it. Sights and let-off allowed precision arrow placement.

But there was something missing. Game-wise, the compound did "its thing" just fine. But one aspect of archery went straight into the abyss: games, especially roving. Roving had been near the top of my list of great enjoyment in archery. Now it was dead. I think I know why: the beautiful flight of the arrow from bow to destination was gone. The compound arrow was too fast for that. That was a compound advantage all right; you couldn't deny it. And yet, the "slow" longbow and recurve have taken game from rabbit to elephant and everything in between for thousands of years, just as they are still doing today in the hands of traditional archers. When I went back to the simpler stick, I also got back into roving and other games. It was fun again, especially with partners, which adds an element of friendly competition to archery games.

ROVING

My favorite archery game is roving, also known as stump-shooting. I like it best because it's an outdoor game, good walking exercise, and ideal practice

Left: The Wiesners, a father and son team, on a day of roving. Here, Bill Wiesner displays a "trophy" beverage can. Right: Roving on a mountain bike affords more than archery practice and fun—it's interesting on its own, plus great exercise.

for hunting. I play by myself, and with friends—with friends is the most fun. You can make the rules up as you go, except of course for safety (know your target). My last rove took place with two friends. As always, we made up our own set of laws. This time, we had a "first shooter." He picked a target. Careless folks had left considerable litter behind, so litter was our goal, especially paper products. The first shooter fires his dart. It's a hit. The next two shooters have to meet the challenge. If we both miss, the first shooter is still "up." Our scoring system was easy enough—each hit earned one point, and a person making a hit becomes the new first shooter. The winner, not the loser(s), buys lunch on the way home. Roving has excellent practice value: you are shooting through brush and trees, at varying distances. It is like the "real thing" in every way.

Mountain bike roving is a variation of roving in which the participants ride mountain bikes. The exercise is not the same and the distance covered on a rove is usually much longer, but the game is otherwise identical.

The only drawback to roving is that finding a place to shoot can be difficult for those who live in a city center. Even this, however, can be overcome if the bow-shooter is willing to drive out of the city limits to farming or ranching area. The quiet short-range bow is no threat to Farmer Jones or his livestock.

One of the pleasures of roving is hiking through interesting country such as this location.

CLOUT ARCHERY

In this game, archers shoot at a clout—sometimes a flag, sometimes a piece of cloth on the ground—for a good distance and the one whose arrows come closest to the target earns points. I have seen this game played only once and never participated in a true clout shoot. However, my brother and I emulated clout shooting by placing an object, such as a flattened cardboard box, on the ground as our "clout."

You can compete informally, or you can play by strict rules. The GNAS Clout (Grand National Archery Society's Rules of Shooting) is played in England, as is the BLBS Clout (British Longbow Society), with longbows and wooden arrows only. There is also the FITA Clout and the Australian Clout. When played in a more formal fashion, a "clout" is a round of three dozen arrows. The "double clout" consists of six dozen arrows to determine a winner of the match. Regardless of your rules, the object of the game is the same—to send arrows in a high arc, having them "rain down" on a distant mark.

Clout shooting is not nearly as transferable to general skill improvement as roving because roving is far more "natural." In clout shooting, the archer tries to "drop" an arrow onto a point much farther than would be reasonable for hunting, perhaps 180 yards away. At the time of Queen Elizabeth of England, the clout distance was twelve-score (240) yards.

ROVING MARKS

Roving marks is supposedly the oldest form of clout and a pastime of King Henry VIII. The archer is moving about on foot, as in roving, but the targets are preselected. The archer moved from station to station to shoot at clout-

A variation of "roving marks" is hiking through an area safe to shoot in, selecting various targets at specific ranges. It's more fun with friends in friendly competition.

type targets which were already set up. The archer shoots at one position, then walks to another position and shoots again, unlike the ordinary rove where the archer walks about choosing targets on the spot. This game is also called roving clouts because it contains aspects of both roving and clouts. While perhaps not providing realistic field practice due to static targets, roving marks is an old and fun game, and of course requires mastery of the bow.

THE YORK ROUND

The York Round has been practiced since at least 1673. According to one set of rules, the York Round consisted of shooting seventy-two arrows at one hundred yards, forty-eight at eighty yards, and twenty-four at sixty yards. There has even been controversy concerning York Round rules, one beginning in the London Field in 1873 when a Mr. Rolt argued that one hundred yards was too far to shoot for accuracy. But his plea to eliminate the hundred-yard aspect of the game was denied. A Columbia Round is similar but with twenty-four arrows at thirty yards, twenty-four at forty yards, and twenty-four at sixty yards.

The York and Columbia rounds have mixed practice value. Maurice Thompson approved of the York, but for best sporting practice he insisted on shooting at all manner of targets, rather than at formal targets with circles.

FLIGHT ARCHERY

The only goal of flight shooting is propelling an arrow at the farthest possible distance—there is no target. The "score" is simply the distance traveled by the arrow. Judges measure how far each archer managed to send his arrow. The 1959 record of 937.13 yards is an example of how far a special arrow can fly; Turkish flight arrows could be very light—one weighed only 191 grains. The Turks were kings of flight shooting, but our own Kansas-born Harry Eugene Drake (1915–1997) proved up to the challenge. Drake designed and built flight bows. One of his bows sent an arrow 1,077 yards on October 24, 1971. Flight shooting is also sometimes called "archery javelin," the connection being that the arrow is thought of as a javelin.

Flight shooting does not hold a lot of practice value for the typical traditional bow shooter of today because the archer is interested in directing arrows to a specific point rather than just seeing how far the arrow can be made to fly. Shooting for distance can, of course, help an archer build strength, since the bows used are normally of high draw weight. Also, shooting for distance could help an archer improve other techniques, such as arrow release and follow-through. Modern flight shooting is as much a competition between specific bows and arrows as it is a competition of the strength and ability of the archers. Flight bows can be very different from "regular" bows: one weighed only twelve and a half ounces, yet it drew at 118-pounds pull, according to one report.

TARGET ARCHERY

Shooting at prescribed distances at standardized targets remains an archery game of high competition. Events are held inside as well as on outdoor target ranges. Targets are marked with a number of evenly spaced concentric rings with point values that go up as you near the center of the target. In the center is the "ten ring," or bull's eye, worth ten points. Target sizes and shooting distances vary depending on the organization putting on the shoot, but here are some examples to give you an idea. Two standard target sizes are 122 cm and 80 cm (48 inches and 31.5 inches). Indoor distances, according to one rule book, are 18 meters (59 feet) and 25 meters (82 feet). Outdoor distances range from 30 meters (98 feet) to 90 meters (295 feet). Another source has men's distances at 90, 70, 50, and 30 meters, while women shoot at 70, 60, 50, and 30 meters. Target archery is very good practice for disciplined shooting since the archer must be in full control of body and bow to score well.

FIELD ARCHERY

This form of archery competition, when the official rules are followed, consists of three different types of shooting: "field," "hunter," and "animal." In field rounds, archers shoot at paper targets, at prescribed distances from "very close" to eighty yards. The hunter round uses varied distances up to seventy yards. Scoring is the same for both field and hunter rounds—archers shoot at paper targets with circles, the innermost circles being worth the most points. Finally, the animal round is shooting at two-dimensional figures of animals in as close to actual size as practical, again at uneven distances. The uneven ranges of the hunter and animal rounds offer valid field-related practice, while the more static field round provides improvement in general bow control.

3-D ARCHERY

This is a highly popular archery game today, a spin-off, at it were, from the 2-D animal round in field archery. The difference is the target. Instead of two dimensional, the "animals" are three dimensional models. For example, I have a 3-D javelina in my back yard that is very close to the general size of these little musk hogs. Some 3-D ranges I have shot on had specific ranges for each target; others did not. Also, target locations varied considerably. At one

3D archery can be formal or just plain backyard fun. The targets are, as the name implies, three dimensional, such as this "deer," and can be set up to represent realistic situations.

Left: I have a proper backstop for capturing fired arrows in my backyard, which makes it a great place to set up a 3D range. Right: Setting up a 3D target to simulate shooting through openings in the brush.

3-D shoot, the archers followed a specific path for obvious safety reasons. However, the 3-D animals were poised differently at each station, some obscured purposely by brush or within trees. The practice value of 3-D shooting is very high, as the targets represent reasonably accurate counterparts of the wild animals most bowhunters pursue.

POPINJAY (ALSO CALLED PAPINGO)

The story goes that this game originated when archers were obliged to shoot birds that were "making a mess" on church steeples. The game consists of duplicating the aim-up-in-the air shot. The archer stands, according to one set of rules, within twelve feet of the base of a pole that is ninety feet tall. The arrow is fitted with a blunt head only. Wooden renditions of birds are fixed to the top of this mast—one cock, four hens, and at least twenty-four chicks. The object is to knock these "birds" from their roost-five points for a cock, three for a hen, and one point for each chick.

I don't know who shinnies up the pole to fasten the birds in place, as I have never witnessed this interesting game. Apparently it still holds some popularity in Belgian archery clubs. Variations are played in Canada and the United States. The practice value of this game is probably quite high for bowhunters who hunt tree squirrels or blue grouse (fool hen), species with a penchant for sitting still on a branch above the archer's head. Otherwise, I don't see a great deal of transfer from knocking birds off the top of a post to field shooting.

ARCHERY GOLF

This game can actually be played on a golf course, although it had better be when golfers are not out and about! Those dedicated to archery golf could set up their own range, provided there's space enough with all safety provisions in place. You'll need three different arrow types: a flight arrow (not the true flight arrow of the flight shooting game), a "medium approach" arrow for shots not far enough to demand a flight arrow, and a flu-flu for "putting." The hole is not a hole; according to the set of rules I found, it's a tennis ball resting atop an aluminum beverage can, or something similar.

The game can be played solo or with up to four people (the limit set in the rules I read). There is a tee-off spot from which all participants must begin. Distance to the "hole" is from one hundred to five hundred yards. Shot one is from the tee-off spot; following shots, from wherever your arrow got buried in the turf. As in golf, the low score wins, in this case the person who knocks the ball off the can with the least number of shots. In my opinion, the most important thing about archery golf is the safety factor. The range must be totally free of people, animals, or anything we never want to hit. There is some practice value in having to deliver arrows downrange to eventually knock out a small target.

ARCHERY PITCH AND PUTT
A variation, archery pitch and putt, is the same as archery golf, but played on a smaller scale, a "Pitch and Putt" course. As with archery golf, the practice value lies in having to direct an arrow to a specific spot with accuracy.

ARCHERY TIC-TAC-TOE
Draw up a tic-tac-toe board, a large one, at a distance you chose. One archer is black, the other red. On your turn, you shoot for the desired square. If your arrow lands in your opponent's square—oops! You lose the shot. No second chance. Otherwise the rules are the same as tic-tac-toe; your goal is to get three arrows in a line. The practice value of this game is dependent upon the distance you shoot at, but even at close range the archer is obliged to control the bow well to arrows into the squares of choice.

ARCHERY DARTS
Make up a standard dart board on a large paper background set it up at an agreed-upon distance. The rules are exactly the same as a regular game of darts. The practice value of archery darts is developing full bow control to place an arrow in a very specific spot on a target. Since the distance to the target is set by the players of the game, the practice value can be enhanced by setting the target up for longer as well as closer shots.

SKI ARCHERY
This game is very much like the biathlon, where players ski from one set of targets to another, competing for skiing speed and shooting accuracy, except that players use bows instead of guns. Specific stances are required, such as standing or kneeling, and at no point may the archer remove the skis, although unfastening the binding for the kneeling shot is acceptable as long as the foot remains in contact with ski. The rules I came across place the distance of the shot at 18 meters (59 feet) on targets 16 centimeters (6.3 inches) in diameter. Specific rules vary, one being that an archer who misses the mark may have to ski a 150 meter penalty loop (495 feet). If a bowhunter wishes to pursue game on skis, this game would be perfect for practice. It also has value in that the archer is somewhat hampered by being forced to stay with the skis rather than shedding them for a shot. Otherwise, there is not much transfer value to the regular field.

THE WAND SHOOT

Reminiscent of stake-busting in blackpowder competitions, where the shooter must cut a stake in the ground in half with bullets, the wand shoot is a tradition among English archers. Archers take turns shooting at a vertical stake (piece of wood) called a wand. Stake may be around six feet tall and three to six inches wide. Hit the stake and earn points. Miss and you get a zero. There was a Cherokee Indian game called "cornstalk shooting," which was similar to wand shooting, just with a cornstalk for a target. Vertical arrow placement is about nil in the wand shoot, but horizontal arrow placement becomes essential to success, especially with a narrow wand. To win this game, an archer has to have full bow control.

AERIAL TARGETS

My friend Shannon Thomas built a little catapult to launch wooden disks into the air at close range. With practice, he got pretty good at smacking the disks with a flying arrow. Most of us won't shoot birds on the wing, but it has been done and will be done again. Regardless, the aerial targets provided a great game. The practice value of this game is very high for any archer intending to go for birds "on the wing."

It's not all arrow-shooting. A rove takes the archer outdoors for exercise and to enjoy nature as well as for shooting practice. Here, two archers plan a long roving trek through some rather wild country.

COMBAT ARCHERY

I include this game only because a reporter has to report. While it may be hard to believe, there is as sort of paintball war for archery in which arrows are fired at people! There are "heavy" and "light" classes. You guessed it, heavy means the participants wear armor, light means they do not. The arrows are cushion-tipped (fortunately). Participants must use longbows (according to the rules I found for the game) and there is a 30-pound draw weight maximum. Maybe I am a stuck-in-the-mud. But I find the practice value of this "sport" nil and in fact would encourage the reader to avoid playing the game—ever. Bows are not toys.

Out of all these games, I see a clear winner: roving. It's pure and simple-going into the field with a bow and arrow, selecting safe targets, and shooting in the most natural way. It is, arguably, the finest practice for the archer interested in procuring a bit of protein for self and family, and it is, in its own right, a grand sport. It's so good that Dr. Errett Callahan wrote an entire book, short at 128 pages but a book nonetheless, called *Roving Handbook*. "Dr. Errett Callahan offers a new world to many of us: the wonderful world of roving," the description reads. I buy that "wonderful world of roving" part. I have a large back quiver made beautifully of leather, capacious to pack many arrows into the field, mostly blunts with an assortment of Judo points as well. My goal: walk or bicycle around the countryside in search of no special targets, but a very special pastime.

20

Stickbows for Kids

A limb cut from my grandparents' oleander bush, a length of string, reeds from a swampy place across the highway, chicken feathers, and pieces of broken glass were the materials for my first bow and hunting arrows. For months I pursued a particular jackrabbit with my deadly tackle, until one day the aging hare made a mistake: he let me get too close. Over a decade passed before I felt that same thrill at age eighteen with my first trophy Coues deer, and it was much later still when I felt it again with my first Cape buffalo. All my friends in the neighborhood made our own bows. We didn't have commercial examples, so we made our own, rude and even comical as they were. Today's kids are privileged with a much brighter beginning—if we put them on the right path.

The first step is simple: buy that boy or girl a stickbow designed for kids. I prefer getting them started with a stick, but if a compound is easier for a youngster to handle, go with it—but leave the sights and other accouterments off. I am all for letting the young person "go natural." It's called instinctive, or reflexive, shooting. It's that built-in ability to pick up a stone and toss it at a can or pitch a baseball across a plate. Those who shoot with sights may think I am handicapped because I don't use sights. I look at it the other way around. I have to get closer than they do with their mechanical arrow-launchers. But in a tangle of brush or patch of black timber I can send an arrow accurately from just about any shooting position. I want to pass that legacy on to the young archer.

Nowadays, there is no need to pirate a limb from a bush or make arrows from reeds. The practice might make an interesting do-it-yourself project for Boy Scouts or Girl Scouts, but there are plenty of high-class, well-made longbows and recurves designed for youth. Many are scaled down "real" bows. They draw smoothly. They handle great. They are handsome. They also shoot

The length of a traditional bow for kids does not matter much. What does matter is draw weight and the bow's "manners." Autumn Villwok can handle this bow very well. It is a custom bow made just for the very young shooter by Pronghorn Custom Bows. Autumn will "grow into" this bow in time, shooting it for several years, unlike a "kiddy bow" that will soon be discarded.

an arrow many times better than anything created from bushes and reeds. Where to buy them? That's easy. Every custom bowyer in the country has the ability to make a good youth bow. Not all of them do, but the potential is there. I have two from Pronghorn Custom Bows in Casper, Wyoming. These bows have been used not only by family children, but also by those of friends who borrowed them for their sons, daughters, and grandkids to learn on.

THE BOWS
It's true that some, perhaps even all, of the following bows for "kids" may be replaced in time with newer models. However, it remains very important that the reader knows such bows do exist, and are currently available, along with appropriate arrows and tackle. I warrant that kids' bows will not disappear any time soon.

Commercial bows designed for kids abound. They range in price from twenty bucks to full custom bows that can run a few hundred dollars. But mostly, these bows are fairly priced by companies and custom bowyers because both are interested in promoting the sport of traditional archery for young people. Here are a few examples for dads, moms, uncles—or whoever—to think about buying for that budding archer.

The Traditional Only Company has, as this is penned, four fine "little bows." The Pilgrim Squirt Longbow runs about a hundred dollars, a handsome recurve in shape but not in function, as the string does not lie along the limbs but rests only in the bow nocks. The Pilgrim Squirt has a solid bacote riser with birdseye maple limbs and horn overlays at the tips. The AMO length is 34 inches, and the draw weight falls between 10 and 12 pounds at 16 inches. It comes in right- and left-handed, and is suitable for children four to six years old. The Pilgrim Longbow (not a Squirt) is about double the price of the Squirt and has an AMO length of 48 inches and a draw weight of 20 to 24 pounds. It also comes in right- or left-handed versions, and is designed for ages six to sixteen.

The Crusader Youth Recurve is solid fiberglass at 51 inches with a 24-inch draw for ages seven to ten, and costs around twenty dollars. The Titan Youth Recurve is also solid glass and measures 60 inches with a "working limb." The draw weight is 30 pounds, and it is recommended for ages ten to eighteen. It costs under fifty dollars. These solid glass bows are good for "testing the waters" to see if the archery bug bites or not.

In a whole different category of youth bows, the hundred-dollar Mohegan T/D is a handsome no-tools-required takedown that comes in 48-, 54-, and 62-inch lengths for ages seven to ten, ten to fourteen, and fourteen to

It may be hard at first, but this little girl will soon draw her bow with ease, thanks to its low draw weight and manageable size.

eighteen. Draw weights range from 20 to 24 pounds at 24 inches; 24 to 28 at 26 inches; and 36 to 40 pounds at 28 inches. The Nirk Rebel Recurve costs over four hundred dollars, with its beautiful bubinga riser and maple limb laminations. It draws 25 to 50 pounds at 28 inches.

ARROWS

It is just as important to match arrow to bow for the little folks as it is for grown-up archers because the finest little bow in the land will perform badly with mismatched mongrel arrows. So we must ensure that the arrow matches the bow. This is no problem. The Traditional Only Company has a set of quality 5/16-inch diameter arrows for fifteen dollars a half-dozen. They have three feathers and target points already installed, are suitable for up to 35-pound draw, and come in 26-inch and 28-inch lengths. Along with wood arrows, there are 27.5-inch fiberglass arrows at twenty dollars a half-dozen, built to take a reasonable blow if the arrow happens to miss the straw bale. They come with tips, nocks, and fletching ready to go, with a white cap wrap for show. NASP (National Archery in the Schools Program) Youth Arrows come in a six-pack as "the only arrow approved by NASP for tournament use." And of course, the mentor can make up any number of excellent arrows for the budding bow-shooter as described in chapter 12.

TACKLE

Proper tackle is also essential. An adult-size quiver, for example, is not a boon to a young archer; it is a burden. There is a wide range of fine tackle available today, including numerous scaled-down back quivers. One of the older and still excellent models is the Lil' John Back Quiver, which a young shooter showing promise deserves. It costs over fifty bucks currently. But it's made of quality leather, holds a dozen target arrows, and runs about 18 inches in length. On the other end of the back quiver spectrum is a service-able Youth Side Quiver for less than ten dollars. In between are several quivers ranging twenty to thirty dollars as well as a youth-size takedown bow case from Traditional Only Company.

If an outsized back quiver is a drag for a smaller archer, imagine trying to outfit that boy or girl with a full-size archery glove or tab. Kids' gloves and tabs are available for as little as three dollars for a tab to under ten for a good glove with Velcro wrist attachment and smooth leather tips. Arm guard choices are also abundant for the young bow-shooter, and also well-priced at under ten dollars. Two that I like are the Kids Armguard with a simple hook to make putting it on and taking it off easy and a Youth Leather Armguard with two hooks instead of one. These are available from 3 Rivers Archery.

Ready or not? How about the form of this six-year-old boy? Is he ready to shoot a bow instinctively? Obviously, yes.

READY OR NOT?

There is no such thing as a "toy bow," although the term is bantered around in an almost playful way. Even a "toy bow" can inflict harm when misused. No kid is ready for any tool, be it a knife, a BB gun, or a bow, unless he or she is sufficiently mature to handle such a tool.

Responsibility is the key word. If the boy or girl cannot carry out a simple routine task without mishap, such as taking out the garbage on a regular basis or working with a parent on a project, it might be well to hold off on the bow until a higher level of responsibility is achieved. There is also a level of desire that has to be assessed. Not every young person will want to shoot a bow. It might be best to give every young person a chance and then leave it up to them whether they continue with training.

When starting kids in archery, don't overlook the girls. We originally bought .22 rifles and bows for our boys, but not for one girl. She expressed a great deal of interest, however, and eventually got her bow and rifle. She quickly outshot her brothers with both. So let's be careful, especially as dads, that we do not shortchange the girls. I have yet to train a female, young or old, who could not shoot well.

GETTING THEM STARTED RIGHT

Before even looking for a bow, be sure of the young person's dominant eye. While left-hand youth bows are not readily available, it can be very worthwhile to have a bowyer build a nice left-hand model for a youngster who just may go on to shoot bows for the rest of his or her life. Finding the dominant eye is easy. Do this yourself first so you will be familiar with the method when checking eye dominance with a youngster. Hold your right arm straight out in front of you with index finger extended. The index finger becomes a "sight." Pick an object, such as a picture on a wall. Point your finger directly at that object as if it were a front sight on a rifle. Keep both eyes open. Now blink your left eye shut. If your right eye is dominant, your finger will remain optically "pasted" right on that object. Now blink your right eye shut. If your right eye is dominant, your finger will optically "jump" right off of the object. The reverse of this little test also works for left-eye dominance. If your finger is still pointing at the object when you close your right eye, your left eye is dominant.

Let's say you have procured a decent little bow, along with proper arrows, arm guard, quiver of some sort, a proper-fitting glove and protective arm guard. Now the training begins.

TRAINING NEW ARCHERS

The following steps for helping new archers succeed in enjoying the longbow and recurve with the instinctive shooting method are not chiseled in concrete. They represent one method that has worked well for the author. But it is not the only method. Other "coaches" may use different, but just as reliable, tactics.

Step 1

Before going forward with lessons, teaching respect for the bow is important. Young people, especially very young children, may have gotten the idea that the bow can be a toy, rather than a tool that, when used improperly, can inflict harm to people, animals, and objects. Take your own bow into a safe

A 3D target like this bison is ideal for teaching respect for the power of a bow. The young shooter sees graphically that his arrow has the ability to penetrate deeply into the target.

shooting area, explaining why you chose that place to shoot arrows. Demonstrate what an arrow can do penetration-wise by setting up a target that has visual impact, such as a plastic gallon milk container filled with water. While there will be no explosive effect, as would occur with a bullet striking this target, the arrow smashing through the container will illustrate penetration vividly.

Step 2

Begin with the feet for a newcomer to the bow. A right-handed shooter must learn to angle his or her feet to the right. There is no precise angle. About 45 degrees is a good starting point, but the student may find a greater or lesser angle more comfortable. Along with pointing the feet slightly away from, rather than directly toward, the target, encourage the student to unlock his or her knees in a slightly relaxed manner. At this point, the deep knee bend assumed by some successful archers should not be encouraged. If the archer assumes that posture later on, fine. But in the beginning mildly bent and relaxed knees are preferred over the deep bend because we do not wish to have the new archer thinking that he or she *must* crouch to be good with longbow or recurve.

Step 3

Without an arrow at all, have the newcomer hold the bow out in front of him or her in a straight up and down position. At this point, the bow is not drawn. It is simply held in the hand straight up and down. At this time, with

Start with the feet. This young archer already has that part of instinctively shooting a traditional bow down pat. His feet are perfectly positioned for a right-handed shooter.

the bow in front of the student, you may wish to go over the names of the various parts if that has not been accomplished earlier. Point out the riser, the grip, the limbs, bow nocks, string grooves if the bow has them, shelf (some kids' bows will not have a shelf), arrow rest if there is one, and so forth.

Step 4

The bow remains in the hands of the student, pointed straight up and down. At this point teach the student to tilt the bow on an angle. The right-handed archer will tip the top limb of the bow to the right. Show the student how tilting or tipping the bow creates a V-shape for the arrow to rest in, even when there is no specific shelf. Help the student to create *just enough* angle to form a V for a solid resting place when the arrow is attached to the string. Although later the archer will learn that the bow can be managed even from the horizontal position, at this stage the goal is teaching just enough angle to support the arrow. The student will easily and quickly see that tilting the upper limb of the bow creates this arrow "valley." Be aware that as the student continues to develop his or her own personal style of shooting that he or she may adjust the tilt of the upper limb more or less than first instructed, because instinctive shooting is personal.

Step 5

Now have the student nock an arrow on the string. This arrow is *not* to be shot away. The point of this exercise is to demonstrate how tilting the upper limb has created a place for the arrow to rest upon. The bow need not be drawn at this point to show that the V-shape created by angling the upper limb has indeed made a solid resting place for the arrow. The only point of this step is to show the student that because the bow has been tilted, a valley for the arrow to rest in has been created.

Step 6

This step requires the student to remove the arrow from the string. The arrow is no longer nocked at this point. However, the nock of the arrow is positioned *next to* the nock set. The arrow is retained in this position by the fingers of the drawing hand holding it in place. Have the student assume the shooting posture-feet angled, head tilted to the right slightly for a right-handed shooter. The student is encouraged to draw the arrow back. Just the arrow. The arrow is not on the string at this point because we want to concentrate on how the bow will "look" when it is drawn. The arrow will be resting on the V-shaped valley. By *not* having the arrow nocked, the student does not have to be concerned with actually pulling the bow, but rather only on how that arrow looks when it is properly located. While not teaching the anchor point at this step, do encourage the student to bring the unstrung

arrow to a point on his or her face. If necessary, position the student's hand by moving it with your hand so that the student is "looking down the arrow." Keep in mind what this step is for—to show how the arrow will look when it is properly aligned on the bow.

Step 7

Now the student can nock the arrow on the string, tilting the bow as learned previously, so that the arrow is properly aligned with the V-shaped valley. Start with the Mediterranean method of securing the arrow on the string, this being with the index finger above the arrow nock and the next two fingers below the arrow nock. In this method, the arrow nock is pinched between the index finger and the second finger, with the third finger situated below the second finger. The

A perfect Mediterranean method of securing the arrow on the string is easily taught and easily learned. This young shooter has it down perfectly.

bow is not drawn during this step. The point of this step is to teach the student how to properly secure the arrow on the string.

Step 8

Now teach the student simulated shooting. In this step, the arrow is *not* nocked on the string because it is not time for the student to send the arrow away. The point of this step is for the shooter to learn how to control the bow itself, the left arm for a right-handed shooter securing the bow at the grip of the handle. Have the student relax the elbow of the left arm slightly. Remind that the bow is to be tilted. The arrow nock is pinched *alongside* but not actually on the string. In this manner, the arrow can be drawn back to the face without concern for actually pulling the bow. This is simulated shooting. It's a very important step in beginning to learn how to coordinate all aspects of instinctive management of the bow without having to actually pull the string back under pressure. As the arrow is drawn back, the student clearly sees how the nock comes back toward his or her face and how the nock of the arrow will be located at an anchor point on the face. Some target archers use an under-the-chin anchor point. Do not instruct this anchor point because the goal is to teach the student how to draw and anchor in the manner of archers shooting fluidly. The under-the-chin anchor point is more rigid and often used when sights are on the longbow or recurve; sights are not used in instinctive shooting.

Step 9

Help the student concentrate on an anchor point at this time. The arrow still should not be nocked on the string. We are not interested in "pulling" the bow for this step. Our only interest is teaching an anchor point. By not having the arrow nocked, but only pinched in the fingers, the student only has to use the force to move the arrow to "draw" the bow to an anchor point. The student can see how the arrow glides back toward his or her face smoothly. Suggest a specific anchor point, remembering that this point may, and probably will, change. A reasonable, but not the only, starting point is anchoring with the second finger of the right hand directly at the right-hand corner of the mouth (for a right-handed shooter). As the archer gains more experience and practice in shooting the bow, he or she will naturally and normally gravitate to personal shooting stances and shooting methods.

Step 10

Now it is time to "load" an arrow on the bow and shoot it away. It is best to show the student the straight pull-back method because it is easier than the push-pull style where the bow is thrust forward at the same time that the arrow is drawn back. The bow is extended in the left hand with the elbow slightly relaxed. Note that the bow is tilted as instructed earlier. The nocked arrow is drawn straight back toward the anchor point. The anchor point is reached. Ideally, the anchor point is held for a few seconds. It is true that many good archers release the arrow at the split second that the anchor point is reached. However, if only as a starting point, *holding* the anchor point (for as long as a count of ten) is desirable because it gives the archer a little time to *control* the bow before turning the arrow loose. The newcomer's bow should be light enough that he or she can concentrate on all the aspects of form that are being taught, rather than having to concentrate on forcing the bow to full draw. As part of this step, teach that a strangle hold on the grip of the bow is not necessary. You might use the old cliché about the correct grip on a sword being like holding a bird: only tight enough so the bird cannot fly away. Have the student hold the bow only tightly enough for control.

Step 11

The release of the arrow is absolutely vital to the arrow taking a true course of travel to the target. The two major release styles that I know of are the "flower petal" and the "pull-through." If the student can master the flower-petal first he or she can always go later to the pull-through. In the flower-petal release, the arrow is at full draw, of course, and nocked properly on the string, the fingers of the right hand (for a right-handed shooter) controlling the arrow-and then, like a flower's petals opening, the fingers relax and the arrow "slips away" as the bow arm continues following-through by remaining as close to the pre-shooting position as possible, rather than the arm "falling downward" as the arrow is released. In the pull-through release method the fingers holding the nocked arrow draw back against the archer's face a short distance before the arrow is released. It's not unreasonable to think of the flower-petal as part of the pull-through because as the fingers retaining the arrow come back toward the face in the pull-through method, those fingers must relax and allow the arrow to "take off."

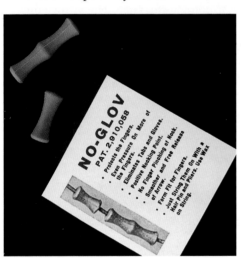

Some young shooters have a difficult time with a tab or shooting glove. One remedy is the No-Glov, which protects the fingers, but eliminates the use of glove or tab.

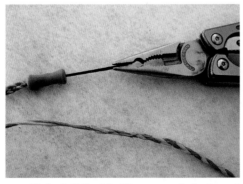

To install the No-Glov, use a hairpin and pliers and wax the string well.

Step 12

Follow-through is important. One method of instructing follow through is to gently hold the extended arm of the student, with one hand on the student's upper arm. Then when the arrow flies, the student's arm, being mildly restrained by the instructor, *cannot* fall. It will remain reasonably close to the position held before the arrow flew.

The major problem facing any archery coach is the fact that in order to master the traditional bow in instinctive shooting, the archer must be able to perform all the proper functions *simultaneously:* left elbow (for a right-handed shooter) slightly crooked, bow tilted to form the V-valley for the arrow, feet positioned at an angle to the target, knees unlocked, head tilted to the right (for a right-handed shooter), proper grip on the nocked arrow, a smooth draw, a good anchor point, the release, and follow-through. This is a lot to handle all at once, which is why it is best to teach these things separately at first.

A FEW CLOSING IDEAS

Don't be too concerned about accuracy in the beginning of a new archer's training. Form is much more important at this stage. Start the student up close—five to ten yards from archer to target is far enough. A bale of straw with a balloon pinned to it makes a good target. The balloon serves as a point of concentration for the new archer, and when hit gives a satisfying pop!

Talk safety whenever appropriate: safe shooting area, stringing the bow safely, checking the bow and arrows for any possible defects before shooting, identifying a target before sending an arrow toward it.

And have fun with the newcomer. Enjoy the teaching experience. It can be quite rewarding, not only when the arrows start finding the target more often than not, but much more when you see that the new archer is truly enjoying the experience of shooting a traditional bow in a natural instinctive way.

Make it a family affair. Archery is fun and bow-shooting, especially roving or 3D-shooting, is good exercise for everyone.

21

Bow and Arrow Maintenance

There is a little gremlin that follows archers no matter where they shoot their bows. This gremlin belongs to Murphy, and it works hard to ensure that Murphy's law functions flawlessly—*if something can go wrong, it will, and at the worst possible time.* The best way to thwart the efforts of the gremlin is maintaining your bow, arrows, and all related tackle. Something as small as a chipped or broken arrow nock can destroy an otherwise perfect shot. As Robert Burns put it, "the best laid schemes o' Mice an' men, Gang aft agley [often go wrong]." So no matter how well a bow may be set up, or how fine the arrow it shoots, or how perfect every piece of tackle may be, without proper maintenance our best plans may go astray and, as in Burns's poem, "lea'e us nought but grief an' pain for promis'd joy!"

BOW EXAMINATION AND MAINTENANCE

Before leaving for practice, roving, or hunting, pass a quick visual checkup over all tackle. Consider the whole bow first, looking quickly for any separation of laminations, as unlikely as that is, or cracks. Being practical about this, I doubt that any of us will give our bows the once-over every time we take them out. But it can't hurt, and even if we don't do it every time, we should at least check our bows out when they leave storage for action. The arrow rest and strike plate can come unfastened, for example. Since these make a launching pad for the arrow, clearly they must be intact for best performance. If either or both are loose, a touch of contact cement is good for repairing them. Contact cement will not harden like epoxy or fletching glues. And I have yet to see contact cement attack bow finish.

There are many different methods of securing the limbs to the riser in a takedown bow. Bear Archery, for example, has the Fred Bear Supreme Takedown Bow, which functions on a latch system—no tools needed. Most, however, have the limbs bolted to the riser platform. These bolts must be "good

226

and tight," but never cranked down so hard that the glass is cracked. This checkup is especially useful after a long shooting session. Admittedly, finding these bolts loose is rare. But it can happen and does every now and then. Eyeball the limbs of the recurve bow. Does the string lie perfectly within the string grooves on both limbs? Sometimes a cockeyed limb can be made straight; often not. And when not, a trip to the bow doctor is in order. The worst news the bowyer can give is "I'll have to make another set of limbs."

Limb bolts can loosen. If a limb bolt becomes extremely loose it could strip out when the bow is pulled back. You may be able to detect this problem by drawing the bow slowly the first time out and listening for a creaking sound. Better yet, make sure that limb bolts are properly tightened.

Tug back on the bowstring before going to full draw. Pulling back gently on the string to about half draw will usually reveal any further need to silence the bow. And the tug-back is also useful should there be damage unseen by the eye that can be picked up by the ear. While a full-scale examination of the bow before every shooting session is more wishful thinking than reality, the tug-back on the string should be done every time to ensure that the bow is sound before shooting. It only takes a few seconds to do this.

One of the worst things that can befall a composite bow is to be left strung in the trunk of a car, especially on a hot summer day. The bow will be delaminated, the limbs are back where they began, as separate pieces. And it is not reparable. The bow doesn't have to be strung for

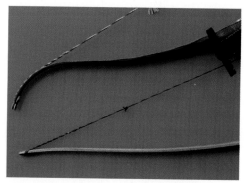

Bowstrings require visual inspection, not only on the "body" of the string, but also, and even especially, at the bow nocks. This goes double for the recurve bow, where the string lies right on the limb end and smacks the limb every time the bow is drawn and fired.

this to happen, but stringing makes this problem even more likely because it adds tension on the limbs. And it need not be a hot car trunk. Nor even summertime. I've heard of a bow being delaminated inside a vehicle as its owner

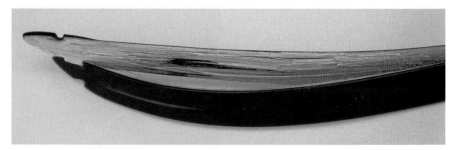

Leaving a composite bow in a hot spot, such as a summer car trunk, can cause delamination, as shown here—a fine bow limb ruined.

ran business errands in town. A bow left in direct sunlight is also asking for trouble. Carrying the bow in the sun is not the culprit. Leaving it in the heat is. Good maintenance says not to do that.

STRUNG BOWS

You should store bows unstrung. However, proper maintenance also includes unstringing a bow that may be subject to a string-cut, no matter how remote the chance. When the string on a strung bow is cut, the limbs flash forward with great force. That bow has just been dry-fired and a limb may break. Self-bows should always be unstrung when not in use as part of their maintenance routine. The strung self-bow can take a set, the limbs failing to return fully to the unstrung position. This will mean a power loss as well as possible arrow flight problems.

Self-bows like these should be stored unstrung to avoid the limbs taking a set.

A little wax on a bow's surface is normally sufficient for maintaining the finish. This process also helps identify cracks or other potential problem.

MAINTAINING BOW FINISH

Clean the bow first with a damp cloth. Now and then, apply a hard paste wax—not spray wax—very sparingly and rubbed it in well on all surfaces. Repair minor checks, small dents, and nicks with a light coating of polyurethane finish. If you find a nick, dent, or check of sizeable area, take it to a bowyer.

EXTREME COLD

I have carried and fired bows in below-zero temperature and so far have not had one break. These were composite longbows and recurves, all laminated. While this book is not really about self-bows, which are usually counted as "primitive" rather than "traditional," there are traditional archers who also shoot the bow made of one material only—wood—and for those I have a warning. I know of a fine yew bow that cracked in very cold weather. The owner said, "Yew has a reputation for freezing and breaking," adding that it could be a characteristic of that particular wood. Of that I am not sure. But I am sure that self-bow archers should consider extreme cold and those of us carrying traditional sticks might pay the same heed.

RAIN AND SNOW

To date, not one of my traditional composite bows has ever shown the least effect of either rain or snow. I have brought them into tents, cabins, and homes, drenched. I dried them off, wiped the string down, perhaps applying a bit of string wax, and that was that.

A COLD WEATHER BOW

Herb Meland of Pronghorn Custom Bows came up with an All-Weather Bow with all-glass limbs. This type of bow was attempted in the past by a number of bowyers but they never quite achieved best results. This all-glass-limb bow, however, has the advantage of both advanced geometry as well as the best materials for bow building of all time. Does the All-Weather Bow take the place of Herb's regular bows? No. Herb's Three-Piece Takedown Longbow is number one in sales and most recommended by this bowyer. But for the archer going into truly harsh weather conditions, the All-Weather Bow might be just the ticket, being constructed of phenolics and other modern materials that are impervious to temperature variation and moisture.

ARROW MAINTENANCE

Straightening a crooked wooden arrow can be done by hand quite successfully. I have had more trouble with making crooked aluminum arrows straight again, but it can be done as well. Wooden arrows go back straight "by eye" quite well, but there are also tools you can use for taking the warp out of a wooden arrow, such as the Ace Roll-R-Straight. As the name implies, this arrow straightening tool rolls over the shaft to bring it back to true. The Shaft Tamer is another arrow straightening tool. It uses the compression method, fits any size shaft, and works well. There are also arrow-straightening tools for aluminum shafts.

To straighten a wooden arrow, start by using a clean cloth to burnish the arrow shaft. Burnish simply means rubbing vigorously to heat the shaft. When the shaft is good and warm, "aim" down it visually, holding the nock end close to the eye. Seeing the warp is easy enough—so bend the shaft in the opposite direction of the warp back to straight again. After straightening the arrow, either with a tool or by hand, you can check if the shaft is straight and the point properly aligned—especially important with broadheads—with a little device known as the Large Spin Tester. It also shows the archer whether the nock of the arrow is properly lined up with the shaft. Simply spinning an arrow on its point on a hard surface is a lot better than nothing, but a spin tester is a more sophisticated method.

The little device that retains the arrow on the string can cause untold mischief. I know. When I have failed to do proper arrow maintenance, I have missed broken nocks and actually had a bow dry-fire because of my lack of attention. Today, the nock has evolved from a simple notch cut into the back of the arrow to the numerous designs we have now—a long list of types. Having made self-arrows, I can attest to the fact that those early self-nocks must have broken easily. Even though today's arrow nocks are made of high-impact materials, they can, and sometimes do, break, especially when roving where a hard tree stump may be the target. There are nock collars today that help in reducing the jackhammer effect of an arrow smacking hard into an unforgiving target. The nock collar is a preventive maintenance item.

Broken nocks are easily replaced. On wooded shafts, heat the nock—I use an alcohol burner—twist it off with pliers, clean the nock taper with fine sandpaper, and glue a new nock in place. Sometimes a nock can be shaved off with a hobby knife or sharp jackknife. Nocks on aluminum arrows can also be heated with the alcohol burner, then twisted off of the nock taper. On carbon shafts, the damaged nock may be of the insert type. Again, heat the area and pry the nock loose with a wood screw or the point of a knife until you can grab it. If necessary, a new taper can be cut on the wood shaft, only shortening the overall length of the arrow a small degree. However, if the nock end of an aluminum or carbon arrow is damaged, that arrow may be a candidate for the scrap heap.

Wooden arrows are easily checked for cracks by simply bending by hand—just flexing enough to ensure that they are sound. This is quick and easy maintenance. If an arrow breaks upon simple flexing—good—that's a lot better than having it snap when fired from a bow. Flexing arrows is important because a defect in a wooden shaft may be hidden within the grain structure itself.

FLETCHING

Feathers are tough, but they are not completely impervious to damage. At the Buffalo Bill Historical Society in Cody, Wyoming, there are Plains Indian arrows that go back to the time when Bill himself was shooting bison for the railroad. The feathers on these arrows are intact, mainly because they are not subjected to excesses of anything—cold, heat, even strong lighting. Outside of special museum cases, however, feathers can mold and rot. They can perish left in a hot and humid area. Maintenance of feathers includes rubbing duck oil into them from time to time. Recall that little dot of glue at the foremost part of the feather? That was preventive maintenance for feathers. A tiny drop can be added here to refresh the glue spot.

In keeping with the continued advances in traditional archery, there is Gibbs Spray Lubricant which is useful on almost all types of equipment from knives to boots. Gibbs claims that it "waterproofs and lubricates almost anything." There is also Fletch Dry Waterproofing, a waterproofing agent in powder form. While not an oil, Fletch Dry serves the same purpose as duck oil—to waterproof feathers. It also tends to stiffen a feather that may have become limp due to exposure to moisture. A small container of Fletch Dry will treat about a hundred three-fletch arrows. Deformed feathers can be brought back into shape with steam—but use it judiciously. Too long under steam

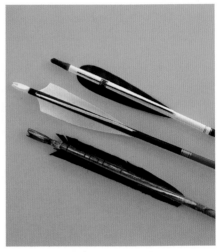

Keeping fletching dry promotes feather life. The way to do this is first to prevent contact with rain or snow. It is also helpful to apply a feather coating, such as Fletch-Dry or a similar product.

Feathers are tough, but in time can become ragged. They will last much longer, however, if arrows are stored properly in racks or boxes where feathers do not smash against each other or anything else.

and the glue attaching the feathers may fail. A little steam from a kettle does the trick. It softens the feather so that it can be pressed and coaxed back into its original shape.

Feathers can also be replaced when they become tattered, although as mentioned in chapter 14, a feather has to become pretty well wrecked before it ceases to guide the arrow, partly because even a ragged feather has drag. I still have my Saunders feather stripper, purchased some years ago. It's a tool that strips feathers from the shaft cleanly. If you're careful, it works on aluminum and carbon shafts as well as on wood. After the broken feather is removed, a light sanding with fine sandpaper will remove the glue from the surface of the shaft. Now a new feather can be installed with the jig just the way it was done the first time. Also part of fletching maintenance is proper storage, as described in chapter 22.

STRING MAINTENANCE

Replacement is part of any string maintenance program. When a particular part of an engine wears out, it is replaced. The same goes with the bowstring. It's not wrong to do a little maintenance—replacing the serving on the string or applying a drop of fast-drying glue to stop a little fraying. This is a safe practice as long as the string itself is intact. But if one strand of a string breaks, discard that string and replace it with a new one. That is wise maintenance.

Maintaining a good string so it stays that way calls for a wax job. Bowstring wax is cheap and performs at least three major functions. First, wax helps to maintain the integrity of the string by sticking the strands to each other. Second, wax prevents the string from drying out. Even though the materials employed in string building today are the best ever, they can suffer what we might call "dry rot"—the string can become so dry that it fails. Third, wax is great preventive string maintenance because it prevents the invasion of oils or other elements that may cause trouble—including water. While we don't want a string to dry out, neither do we want it to take on moisture. Wax keeps the string supple while protecting it.

LEATHER QUIVER MAINTENANCE

A leather quiver of any type is subject to scuffing and drying out. There are many leather treatment products on the market. I find good ones at feed stores that sell saddles or offer saddle "soaps" and other cleaner-preservatives. Ordinary neet's foot oil is useful in protecting leather, but may darken the quiver more than desired.

BOW QUIVER MAINTENANCE

Loose quiver bolts cause vibration and noise. Vibration can also lead to stripping out the female thread in the riser of the bow. Simple maintenance means checking from time to time to ensure that "good snug fit." Also, the bow quiver can develop a crack. The foam underhood on some bow quivers can eventually wear out from insertion of arrow head after arrow head. These can be replaced as part of maintenance. The arrow grippers are also subject to wear. They, too, can be replaced.

LEATHER TACKLE

Arm guards, tabs, and leather bow handles should be handled the same

Leather is easily maintained. A leather quiver will last lifetimes when treated occasionally with leather cleaner and conditioner.

way as the leather quiver—wiped clean with a damp cloth, allowed to dry thoroughly, and then treated with a leather preservative.

INSECT REPELLANT AND OTHER CHEMICALS
I do not know what insect repellant will do to *all* bow finishes, but I do know what insect repellant did to one bow—it softened the finish and caused damage. Along the same lines, cleaning a bow with paint thinner or any relative thereof should be avoided. Clean as described above—with a damp rag followed by a touch of hard paste wax.

TACKLE BOX
I recommended keeping a tackle box containing a few tools—arrow straighteners, feather strippers, a little paste wax, bowstring wax, extra nocks—anything and everything useful in maintaining all manner of bows, arrows, and tackle.

IT'S EASY
Maintaining our valuable bows and everything that goes with them is simple, requiring a very small time investment. Traditional bows and arrows are built right to begin with and almost take care of themselves. They require only a little care to avoid exposing them to extreme heat and perhaps cold, along with a watchful eye for the little things that the gremlin loves to foil us with—broken nocks, overly tattered feathers, and so on.

22

Transporting and Storing Bows and Gear

Although traditional composite longbows and recurves are rugged, with the best adhesives holding iron-clad laminations, anything short of a steel ball can break in transit if you do the wrong thing to it. While today's bows are the best ever, they also cost more than ever. Bowyers offer warranties but of course cannot be responsible for breakage that is not their fault. And so it is important to learn how to get a bow and its arrows from Point A to Point B and have them arrive just as they were when they left home—intact and operable. Operability is the major concern in some cases. You get off the airplane in Happy Arrow Valley for a fun shoot only to find that your one-piece longbow is now in two pieces. The fun is over before it begins.

HOW BOWS BREAK

The bowyers I talked with were exceedingly happy to relate how their best work was destroyed. One just had a bow delivered to his shop, a takedown he built for a customer in another state. He showed me the box it came in—it was *smashed*. Something big had literally run over the package. That was carelessness on the part of the shipper, but not entirely. The bow was wrapped as you might send a jacket or pair of pants:

This bow was forced into a mailbox when the delivery person found no one at home. The force was sufficient to break the bow. While the delivery person should not have forced the bow into the mailbox, the shipper also should have used more care, by shipping the bow in a much stronger container.

235

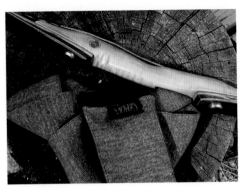

in a soft container with little internal padding. It didn't take much to break it. Had that bow been shipped in one of the many excellent hard cases built today it would have arrived intact. Bowyers said the number one limb destroyer on car trips is closing the car door or trunk on the bow.

The bow sock, in this case the excellent Sack-Ups, will not protect a bow from breakage, but it will keep the scratches off in transportation and protect against humidity.

Here, the Sack-Ups is shown with a longbow inside.

THE BOW SOCK

Having just said that a hard case would have saved the bow that was crushed in shipping, it's important to add that sometimes a bow sock makes more sense. A particularly excellent sock is the Sack-Up. While these are more for storage than transport, as long as we make sure not to close the car door or trunk lid on our bows they work just fine for protecting a bow during a car trip. Made of cotton, the Sack-Up is impregnated with silicone to resist moisture and thwart corrosion. These traits are more important to firearms than to bows, but the cloth case does protect against scratches and dents as well as humidity. Along with the Sack-Up sock, there are also polar fleece and poly-cotton blend bow socks.

SOFT CASES

Soft cases are more protective than socks because they often have internal padding. They do not fit over the bow like putting on a sock, but instead are case-shaped. Soft cases work wonderfully for transporting a bow from home to field, as well as for storage. There are also takedown soft bow cases. These are excellent for compactness. My full-length one-piece recurve soft case is sixty-five inches long, and my takedown bow case is significantly shorter, at thirty-six inches. A good feature of these cases is that they can hold both bow and arrows. The long case noted above holds two dozen arrows. Soft cases may also be decorative, with Indian-style patterns and names such as

Chippewa and Navajo. Soft cases come in numerous types. The Bear Padded Bow Case, for example, is made of heavy-duty Cordura with foam layering within, and is more or less rectangular. It comes in two sizes: 70 inches for longbows and 62 inches for recurves. Then there are soft cases shaped for holding strung bows. These are nice cases in that they offer protection against "reasonable" contact with offensive objects, but take up no more space than the bow normally would without the case. While not "airline approved," any soft case, including a sock-style case, will work for car transport (with care) and all are fine for storage.

AIRLINE-APPROVED TUBE CASES

Many companies make tube cases that are "airline approved," that is, suitable for air travel (not approved by the airlines, who will let you bring your bow in a sock and pick up the pieces at the end of the flight, if you really want to). A prime example of an airline-approved tube case is the 3 Rivers Archery Standard Longbow Case. It has a hard, impact-resistant Cordura nylon outer casing that surrounds an inner shell of the same strength as PVC pipe. The interior of this case is padded with soft cloth; some tube cases have a cloth divider inside. The end caps are also padded. This tube case has double zippers which can be locked together for security. The tube itself is solid—no zippers. An example of the recurve model is 6 inches in diameter and 59 inches long; the takedown type is only 39 inches long, but still 6 inches in diameter. A longbow tube for traveling is thinner, only 4 inches in diameter, but can be from 69 inches up to 73 inches long for one-piece bows; the takedown longbow case is the same diameter, but only 39 inches long. All have web handles. Short webbing pieces allow the archer to attach an arrow case to avoid paying for an extra bag when traveling by air.

Here is an airline-approved tube case. It will take a hit and still protect the bow, short of being run over by a truck. There are many different styles of tube cases. This one has a zippered end and inside separators.

Tube cases are also made for arrows. The features are the same as those of the bow cases—top grade materials, this time with foam dividers inside. Most hold a dozen arrows. A typical example is an arrow case I have had for years. It is 37 inches long and 6 inches in diameter, and has a strap that can be used to attach it to a bow case. Many other hard arrow cases are available, especially for archers who need to transport more than a dozen arrows. One of these cases I use is 36 inches long by 9 inches by 5 inches and holds as many as thirty-six arrows. It is made of high-impact polypropylene and is lockable. The hard arrow tube offers more protection, but for anything like normal travel, these rectangular plastic arrow cases are excellent.

THE HARD BOW CASE

Hard rectangular cases, for the most part, have greater capacity and are built to withstand terrific abuse. There are dozens of excellent hard cases on the market from numerous companies such as Kolpin, Plano, SKB, and—one that I happen to own—the Hardigg Storm. This is a large case with wheels, and if the airlines could have broken it, that case would be squashed by now, having traveled to Africa several times—but it still shows no damage. These cases are airline approved and lockable, defying every abuse short of, perhaps, being run over by a piece of heavy machinery—and even then, some of

This rectangular arrow case from Hoppe's Company is tough and hard, and will take a formidable blow while still protecting its contents, although it is not noted as airline approved.

This is an airline-approved hard case that was purchased for the long haul to Africa. It will withstand the most careless and aggressive treatment.

The Americase is a super case capable of withstanding immense torture by baggage handlers as well as long hauls into the backcountry by horse and mule.

these cases might survive. My Black Widow hard case was run over—by a baggage transport vehicle at an airport. It bounced off the vehicle somehow and under it went. The bow inside survived.

CUSTOM CASES

Custom bow cases are available in many different styles from handcrafters who put art first, although protection is also considered. I found over fifty custom case makers in a short search, mostly dealing in leather. The leather custom case can be built to withstand everything but a real onslaught. There are even hard leather cases that will take air travel reasonably well.

CASES FOR SHOW

The show cases I own are all from one source, an artisan who lives in Idaho and thrives on Indian culture—Dave Iron Neck Carrick. Iron Neck, who got his name following an industrial accident that caused him to wear a metal neck brace for a while, has worked at Indian villages teaching his talents to young people who are not familiar with the culture of their forebears. Dave

This interesting bow and arrow case is patterned after American Indian cases and handcrafted by expert Dave Iron Neck Carrick of Naples, Idaho. It is not meant to fully protect either bow or arrow from extreme force; however, it does serve to prevent scratches and other damages.

These two artistic bow cases also built by Carrick are reminiscent of Indian culture. They are good cases not only for protection from minor hazards, but for display as well.

can turn a moose hide into an Indian bow case that will hold a strung bow and a set of arrows. There are many other craftsmen working to make all manner of artistic archery cases.

THE SIMPLE ARROW BOX AND BOW RACK

The ideal method for storing arrows is a cardboard box made specifically for this purpose, with separators to keep the feathers from "attacking" one another. These boxes are available from catalogs and archery shops. For bows, the bow rack is ideal. It's reminiscent of the old-time rifle rack on the wall. An arrow rack can be made from pinewood panels and dowels with a few tools.

TRANSPORTING IN THE FIELD

My favorite way of enjoying the outdoors has been the backpack adventure. When I first got into that game on the survival hunts that my late friend Ted Walter and I mounted several times a year, suffering was the byword. Our gear made us pay a high price for the joys of hiking into seldom-seen, out-of-the-way places. We got the idea of making our own pack frames from wooden struts, with clothesline cord to form the "cushioning" part that lay against the hiker's back (the word "cushioning" here meaning "digging in"). They were rough but they worked. Our sleeping bags were military-issue, filled not with nice goose down but chicken feathers. It's a wonder that the soldiers who were issued those bags could rise in the morning to march on. We carried water in five-quart bleach bottles. Considering that a gallon of water weighs over eight pounds, these were not easy to carry when full. Our shelter against wind, snow, and rain was a tent—a two-man affair that seemed to be made for a couple of 95-pound soldiers (Ted weighed 200 pounds and I weighed 175). Our cooking gear was a grate we commandeered from a stove in a junkyard and we had one pot that strapped onto one pack frame and one frying pan strapped onto the other frame. Learn the lesson we learned from these unpleasant trips—buy the top-grade pack gear of the day and be happy. Especially, forget about making your own pack frame.

DAY HIKE TRANSPORT

The modern day archer can now go light but with gear that works many times better than what we had in the past. For a daypack, I continue to use and enjoy my Rancho Safari CatQuiver, which can hold not only arrows but all I need for a day in the outback, including the all-important fire-starting equipment I go nowhere without—especially lifeboat matches that flare up even in a wind. This outfit allows you to transport arrows in a dry environment, along with essential gear for hiking away from car or camp. The CatQuiver III.5, which I don't have, is my next goal—this model adds two worthwhile 7- by 9- by 3-inch side pockets.

FAR COUNTRY TRANSPORT

This could be the most important chapter in the book because it could save the reader's life. To me, the most interesting archery outing is heading into territory far from roads. I use a modular kit to transport arrows (the bow I

The fine and useful CatQuiver, on the left, completely protects arrows from damage, while also keeping fletching dry. It also serves as a pack for minor supplies and small but important gear, such as fire-starter. I added the small leather pouch on the side for extra carrying room.

carry) in the field on my long-stay hikes. Here is how it works. The main unit is a Badlands Monster Fanny Pack. A full array of gear goes into this pack—the list is long, including those lifeboat matches for emergency fire starting and fire-starter of different kinds from petroleum-jelly-soaked cotton balls to commercial military surplus from Cheaper Than Dirt Company. In this pack are also my light sources—I like to bring two on backpack treks. Coincidentally, my current flashlights are both from Browning—the larger one (mine is no doubt outdated by the advances in handheld lights) takes two C batteries and puts out more than enough light for finding your way without falling down a crack in the earth. This old model was probably superseded by one of Browning's Flashpoint or similar models. The second is Browning's Microblast—small, handy, and putting out far more light than its size would suggest. This fine out-of-the-way pack is large enough to pack all gear necessary for getting along in the wild. But these essentials, though they are just that—essential—are not enough.

The three-piece modular concept continues with a Blackhawk Blacktrail daypack, just the right size for me with a width that stays within the breadth of my shoulders. This excellent pack carries food and other supplies, and sometimes my sleeping bag. The two packs are joined by my tent and ground pad—I use the Cabela's Hunter Bivouac Seclusion 3D Outfitter one-man tent and the Cabela's XPG Ultralight Ground pad. The groung pad is important

This is the highly important three-piece backpack kit I use in wilderness settings. It contains what I need in rain, wind, snow, and other dangerous storm conditions.

not only to "soften" the ground but also as added insulation. My sleeping bag is Coleman's Exponent Cloudcroft Goose Down FP 800, the darndest mummy bag I have ever slipped my bones into. The Cloudcroft is good for 20 below zero when coupled with medium-weight sweats, a watch cap, warm socks, and light gloves—all stuffed easily into the Blackhawk Blacktrail daypack.

I carry arrows in various ways with this outfit, including in a standard bow quiver carried in the stretch cords on the daypack. This manner of transport of archery tackle and gear comes recommended by experience. It has kept me warm, fed, and safe even in big mountain storms.

GPS AND RADIO DEPENDENCY

Today's handheld radios are smaller than ever, have greater range than ever, and though they remain somewhat dependent on line-of-sight communication, are strongly recommended for treks into the hinterlands. When you go with a partner, which is the only way to go, the two of you (or more) can use these devices to keep in radio contact when separated. I depend even more on the GPS. The GPS does not fully take the place of a good compass, but I must admit that I have not broken out my compass for a long time, relying instead on GPS navigation to find my way back to camp or vehicle. I carry two because, as foolproof as they are, GPSs are still man-made instruments. I have a Garmin Geko 301 Personal Navigator and a Coleman BackTrack at all times; the latter is the simplest unit to use that I have ever owned.

GOOD WEATHER HIKING

On good weather hikes, my plan changes a little. I locate a great camping spot and leave my Blacktrail pack there, along with the erected shelter, the ground pad, and the sleeping bag. I only keep the fanny pack on for a hike around the area, and now my bow and arrows are easily handled. When the afternoon sun bids return to the campsite, it's a simple matter of GPS navigation to the spot. And should the unexpected occur, like a surprise storm materializing out of a sky that was cloudless when I set out from camp, the fanny pack still has fire starter, a few food essentials, and a water bottle or two.

In case I ever need more potable water, I carry a PUR Hiker Microfilter that "strains" to 0.03-microns (a micron is one-millionth of one meter—very small). This filter traps Giardia, cryptosporidium, and bacteria (but not viruses). There are various portable water filters these days that do a good job of filtering out the bad things. They can be indispensable when hiking into country that has streams or other sources of water that should not be drunk without treatment.

The individual archer will have to arrive at his or her own plan to keep not only bow, arrow, and tackle safe, but also the archer.

OTHER GEAR AND GADGETS

A multi-tool such as the Leatherman or one of the Buck Knives Company models is always handy on the trail. I also have a very small but also very handy Gerber Clutch with blade and tools. I also carry fire pistons for their touch of antiquity (they also work), a fine little Coleman one-burner pack stove that weighs little but works hard, a bit of food, my totally waterproof Woolrich rain parka, minor extra clothing, a Purcell Trench grill (which weighs a couple ounces), small stick-free frying pan, a little fishing tackle, and of course my ever-present walking stick. I make mine out of dead (never cut live) *agave* cactus stalks.

MAKE YOUR OWN TRANSPORT AND STORAGE PLAN

Transportation and storage of archery equipment and other gear is a "to each his own" subject. I store my bows on pegs in a dry place with a fairly constant temperature, and I go by plane only with airline-proof cases—but you should develop a system of transport and storage personally suited to you. Luckily, there is seemingly no end to the good cases for storage and transport, along with modern lightweight gear that allows the archer to enjoy a romp into those outlying places where a simple rove or hunt takes on a special touch of adventure.

23

Bow Safety

One day, one of my friends got itchy to shoot his bow. The archery range was not open until the weekend, and the archery shop was shut down pending new ownership. So he decided to fire a few darts in his own back yard. He rested a target against the fence. An arrow from his heavy-draw recurve bow careened off the target and leaped right into his neighbor's back yard across the alley. Due to the angle of the fence, the arrow flew high, smacking into a wall with sufficient force to bury the target point. All our archer could do was face the music, walk over to the neighbor's yard to get his arrow, and pray for no damage. When he entered the yard, he had a surprise waiting for him: there was a barbecue going on. All our archer could say was, "Excuse me" as he plucked up his arrow.

Shoot only in safe places. This 3-D range was designed with safety in mind. Every 3-D figure is placed to capture a missed arrow.

The only enjoyable shooting is safe shooting. Even in a wide open expanse like this, know your target and what is behind that target.

The point of the story is that you should *shoot only in safe places*. Here's one more quick and unfortunately true story illustrating another point: *know your target*. Two bow-benders were roving a field on grounds adjacent to their college campus. They were thoughtfully picking up litter that they shot at. There was a bright something lying on the ground. It was long and some-what narrow, and in order to put an arrow into it, the dart had to arch over a fallen tree—an interesting target. Something told one of the archers that they had best be sure of the target, thinking it might be a valuable object that had been forgotten or blown in the wind to the spot. It was a good thing they did, because the "object" on the ground was a co-ed sunbathing. A small pair of easy-to-carry binoculars are a good way to fully identify any target before sending an arrow away.

The only enjoyable shooting is safe shooting. That's a given. Another safety rule that will help you achieve safe and enjoyable shooting is *use a stringer*. Archery is safer than taking a bath. But a good way to add to the dangerous side of archery is stringing a bow by the step-through method or, worse yet, the push-pull method. Step-through, where you start with one loop of the string pulled down around the bow and the other in the nock and brace the bow against your leg as you slide the loop up the bow, is not so bad. About the worst thing that can happen is the bow slipping before it is strung, and seeing that it's in between your legs. . . The push-pull is where the lower bow tip is settled against the inset of the shoe, right-hand for a right-hander pulling back on the riser, left hand pushing top limb away as the string slides up to the bow nock.

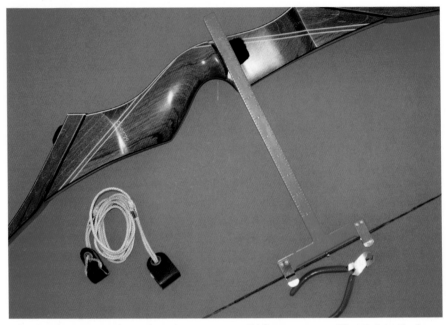

The simple stringer shown here is easy to use. Different types will attach to the bow differently. Always follow the instructions for each stringer.

Not taking the time to use a stringer can have serious consequences for both archer and bow. The old cliché about familiarity breeding contempt proved true for a bowyer I once knew who, especially while working on a bow, hated to take the time to use a stringer. One day, he was working on a bow and needed to string it, so he stuck the lower limb against his shoe and proceeded to use the push-pull method. He had done it hundreds of times before. But this time the upper limb of the bow slipped, springing back into his face and cracking the tempered lens of his eyeglasses. He was lucky not to lose an eye. Another bowyer told of a delivery person arriving with a package to his shop. The bowyer went to get his checkbook to pay for the goods. He got back just in time to see the delivery person attempting to string an expensive custom bow by putting the tip of the lower limb on the cement floor and pushing down on the top limb with all his weight. If the bow had slipped, the bow could have been ruined.

The stringer is safe for bow and archer. It may only be a length of strong, small-diameter rope with pouches at the ends or a bumper for the top limb. But the stringer does a huge job. It safeguards the archer because the bow is held at the horizontal as he or she bends over to string it. The archer lays the stringer flat on the ground and stands in the middle, with feet perhaps a foot or so apart. Then the archer pulls up on the riser of the bow simply by rising toward a standing position. As the riser is pulled upward, pressure is put on the pouches or the pouch and buffer and the limbs begin to bend, eventually bending enough that the string can be slipped onto the bow nock. Slowly, the hand on the riser relaxes—*slowly,* to ensure that the string is truly secure. The bow is strung. *Use the stringer safely.* The pouch retaining the lower limb must be perfectly in place and the string on the lower limb secure in its bow nock groove before you pull the riser up to bend the limbs.

Another safety rule worth observing is *make the first draw slow and easy.* Test the bow to be sure the string is securely in the bow nocks and the bow is sound. Of course the string will be in the bow nocks. And of course the bow has received no damage since last use. Or has it? Maybe the string isn't secure. And you don't know for sure that the bow hasn't taken damage, perhaps a crack that cannot be seen. So pull back gently a few times. Yes, the string is in place and the bow is springing to life as it always has. The little checkup only took fifteen seconds. Modern traditional bows exploding upon draw are rare as finding a hundred dollar bill stuck to the bottom of your shoe. But it can happen when there's a crack in riser or limb. It's especially important to inspect bow tips for damage.

Checking arrows before shooting is one of those safety practices that few of us observe although we all should. A cracked wooden arrow can splinter, finding a path through a hand. This is why wavy-grain shafts are used for starting fires and not for making arrows. One easy checkpoint is the arrow nock. A cracked nock can deal out a good bit of mischief, perhaps causing to a dry-fire as the string goes by the nock, slapping forward with no arrow on it.

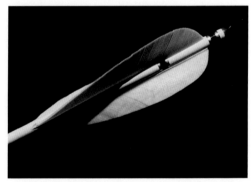

Another rule tantamount to law is *never dry-fire a bow,* and this one is good for any bow. Shooting a bow without an arrow can cause it to break. The weight of the arrow obviously impedes the forward progress of the string. In effect the arrow dampens the string's zap forward. No arrow means no weight on the string. The extra energy is going to go somewhere else. That somewhere else is going to be a limb and maybe even the riser.

A break in an arrow can cause a great deal of mischief, including sending a piece of shaft into an arm or other body part.

Respect your bow is an important *law,* rising above a simple rule. Even a low draw weight target bow can inflict damage. Consider it a tool that when used safely is safer than a saw or hammer. But when not respected, it can inflict serious damage. A bow can send an arrow on a ricochet course, the dart bouncing off a hard object and sailing in an unwanted direction. Ricochets are common in roving, especially when an arrow glances off of a stump or other hard surface. But by observing the simple rules of shooting in a safe place and in a safe direction, you will ensure that an arrow that glances away will harm nothing—though you may still have trouble finding it.

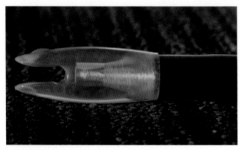

As part of respecting a bow, respect the arrow, right down to the nock itself. Ensure that nocks are intact, not cracked.

The bowstring is tough—it has to be in order to survive the forces a strung and then drawn bow put upon it. But strings are not infallible. They can and sometimes do break. The safe course of action is to *discard obviously worn strings* and replace them. Strings reveal weakness by fraying, especially at the loops.

Another safety rule is *don't overdraw a bow*. The bow was constructed with a certain poundage at a specific draw length, usually marked on the bow itself. If a bow is marked as 55-pound draw at 28 inches, but the archer decides to pull that bow to 31 inches, all bets are off. A related rule is *be sure to use the right arrow for the bow*. This pertains to spine, as an arrow not stiff enough to withstand the archer's paradox may break, but also to length. A friend of mine shot a "kid's arrow" from his hunting bow. It broke (luckily, he did not get hurt). Shooting an arrow too short for the bow can send it into the bow hand as the arrow is drawn past the shelf and is no longer supported.

Strings can break. The best insurance against this is checking for fraying, and throwing out any string that is starting to fray. A broken string can cause a "dry fire," which in turn can damage a bow.

Another good rule—*be extra careful with very old bows*. It is impossible to tell just by looking when an old bow has hidden damage and may break next time it is drawn. Sometimes the wise thing to do is put that old one on the wall to admire but not shoot.

Old bows are great for collecting, but shooting them may not be wise, especially when they are self-bows made only of wood.

You should always *check self-bows especially carefully before shooting.* Bows made of only one material, usually but not always wood, do not have laminations, although they may be backed for strength. I had retired a very old York self-bow of my youthful shooting days. One of our boys saw it and strung it. One tug and—wham! The top bow limb broke in half, took to the air like a curve ball from a world class baseball pitcher, and whacked the archer right in the back of the head. Luckily, the only lasting damage was to the bow, which was given a proper farewell in the fireplace.

One of the most beautiful sights in archery is watching an arrow ascend toward the heavens. In flight shooting, firing a dart at about 45-degrees into the sky is safe because the grounds are prepared to ensure that no person, animal, or treasured object is downrange. The area is large and open with great visibility. The rest of the time *never fire an arrow into the sky.* That is the rule. The Henry Wadsworth Longfellow poem comes to mind:

> I shot an arrow into the air,
> It fell to earth, I knew not where;
> For, so swiftly it flew, the sight
> Could not follow it in its flight.

Old Henry was right. Shoot an arrow into the big blue sky and it may very well go out of sight, and the long-held rule pertains—what goes up must come down. The trouble with the skyward arrow is *where* it might come down.

Another worthy rule is *protect your body.* Shooters of firearms are constantly admonished to wear safety glasses. This rule is far less often observed in archery because it is so seldom that anything will shoot back at the archer. But even a broken string could conceivably do damage. The arm guard, another piece of protective gear, is not always necessary for all shooters, but my

Especially for self-bows made only of wood, unstringing the bow when putting it down for a period of time is good maintenance. The self-bows shown here are unstrung by rule, and restrung only when being used.

Protect your body. An arm guard like this prevents the bowstring from slapping the arm.

shooting style certainly demands one. I learned that the hard way when I forgot mine on a rove and decided to fire arrows anyway. My left arm told the tale in crimson red. Any form of finger projection is also wise for most of us. My partner on those survival hunts never wore glove, tab, or any other finger protection. He shot with bare fingers protected by built-up calluses. Not me.

As part of taking care of yourself, never forget that in archery we often use things that cut. I have a nice white scar on the inside of my left leg that I got from a properly sharpened Bear Razorhead. Actually, I was sharpening it at the time. I turned to talk to someone in the room and inadvertently levered the arrow point into myself. It was very embarrassing, but a good lesson. It could have been worse if I had hit anything important, like the femoral artery. Sharpening broadheads requires great care, as does carrying arrows with these heads in the field. And while on the topic of doing damage to self, take care making arrows. The alcohol stove, if upset, can cause great damage to you or to a valued wooden worktable.

In some areas it is unlawful to carry a strung bow in a vehicle. Even if it isn't illegal in your area, it is a good rule to follow. The odds of the string being cut are slim to none. But strange things do happen. If that string does let break, the two limbs are going to uncoil like striking snakes and with considerable force. As an addition to this rule, remember that leaving a lami-

Going into the "outback" is great. But getting lost or injured is not so good. Keep a keen watch on the elements as well as on any terrain that could lead to a fall.

When reaching into the brush or rocks for that lost arrow, look before you grab.
Something might be lurking right next to it, such as this rattlesnake.

It's not only rattlesnakes that can cause the archer a problem as he or she reaches into bushes or rocks to retrieve an arrow. While normally docile, a gila monster like this one can grab a finger and hang on.

nated bow in a hot place, such as a summertime locked up vehicle, can cause delamination of the limbs. What's worse, the limb laminations may hold just long enough for that next shot and then break.

Be careful when roving for many reasons, including having so much fun that you have no idea where you are as the sun descends on the western horizon. I like to roam when roving, but I carry two GPS units—a Garmin Geko and Coleman Back-Track. Watch out for sunburn, poison oak, poison ivy—lots of not-so-fun-things that can happen. So be prepared. Take along a pack with lifesaving contents: matches, flashlights, and a little food and water.

A more likely way of sustaining bodily damage on a rove is reaching for an arrow and getting more than the arrow, such as a snakebite. Twice (and I know the odds are astronomically in my favor) out of the hundreds (or thousands?) of times I have

Many great adventures, such as horseback treks into wild places, are enjoyed by archers who love traditional bows. Always keep in mind, however, to be careful on the trail.

reached for an arrow half hiding in the brush my ears have been met with *buzzzzzz*! The warning of the rattlesnake. The first time I already had the feathers of the arrow in my grasp so I pulled it free and left the snake to its own designs. The second time, which was much more recently, I waited for the snake to move off because its head was no more than six inches from the arrow. I've also discovered scorpions under something pierced with an arrow while roving. I recall a wayward roof shingle that I had shot a few arrows into. When I picked them up, I found one of the more toxic members of the scorpion clan taking shade underneath.

Shooting as a group demands rules—whether you're shooting at 3-D targets or roving or hunting small game, decide ahead of time that everyone will know where everyone else is before turning a dart loose.

Bow-shooting is one of the safest sports, or for that matter, activities of all. It only demands a little "heads-up" to remain that way. Something as "small" as maintaining a little distance from a drawn arrow tipped with a broadhead can end the day on a happy note instead of with a bandaged hand.

Stickbow Myths

A heavy-draw bow always shoots a faster arrow then a lighter-draw bow.
Arrow speed depends on bow efficiency, not draw weight. It is possible for well-made modern recurve or longbow at 55 or 60 pounds draw weight to shoot the same arrow faster than a heavier-draw bow that is not as well de-signed or is not made of the best materials. The law of diminishing returns is also a factor: bows beyond 60- to 65-pound draw weights do not produce ex-tremely higher arrow speed. There is no positive correlation between an in-crease in draw weight and arrow speed because the arrow must match the bow. This is not to rule out very heavy draw bows as high performers, be-cause a heavy bow will be capable of shooting a very heavy arrow, which will penetrate better than a lighter arrow. But that arrow may not be any faster than a suitable light arrow shot from a light bow. The bottom line is: arrow speed depends more on bow efficiency than on bow draw weight.

Bamboo is the best bow limb material.
Bamboo is an excellent choice in a longbow or recurve (one bow I tested that had Tonkin bamboo laminations in the limbs proved smooth-drawing and shot a fast arrow), but to date no specific material has been proved to be the absolute best in bow building.

A bow can produce a high-velocity arrow but have poor cast.
It is the speed of the arrow that produces cast. A comparison to firearms will help dispel this misconception: a bullet at higher velocity travels farther than the same bullet at lower velocity. The same is true for arrows.

Right-handed archers should always use arrows with right-wing feathers.
This notion is readily proved false when an archer tries arrows fletched with right-wing feathers and arrows fletched with left-wing feathers in the same bow. Both kinds of arrows will fly to the same point.

Only large feathers stabilize arrows from longbows and recurves.
Ideally, an arrow should have only enough feather surface to stabilize the arrow in flight and no more. More surface area than required for stabilization slows an arrow down and produces more noise as the arrow flies downrange. Super large feathers are useful for flu-flu arrows, which are designed to fly only a short distance for easy recovery. However, helical (twist) fletching, along with greater feather surface on an arrow, may be absolutely necessary to stabilize an arrow, perhaps because it has a very heavy broadhead or due to a particular archer's shooting style.

All traditional bows must be more than 60 inches long.
In the past, due to their design, short bows were problematical; the shorter string caused a sharper angle in the center where the archer grasped the string, resulting in finger pinch. Even today, though we have some of the finest traditional bows ever scientifically designed, a bow can simply become "too short." Still, there *are* shorter bows that "behave" well and fit nicely in a ground blind or tree stand situation. There are many 58-inch bows that prove the point.

Leaving a bow strung over a long period of time will cause it to lose poundage.
The self-bow of the past, being made of wood and wood only, could "take a set," thereby reducing its "power." These bows had to be unstrung after each shooting session to avoid the problem. The modern laminated bow can be left strung over long periods of time without the limbs taking a set.

Shooting through the gap produces better arrow flight.
Shooting through the gap or trough created by separating the strike plate and arrow rest to make a space for the hen feather to glide through with less friction may help preserve that feather from a little bit of wear. However, tests with a shooting machine have proved that shooting through the gap will not improve the grouping of arrows at the target.

Recurve bows are trickier to shoot than longbows.
Once this may have been true, but there are many excellent recurve bows on today's market that handle excellently and are not "tricky" to shoot. At the same time, the longbow, due to its narrow limbs with thick cores, plus the fact that the string makes no contact with the tips of the limbs, is so stable that exhibition shooters, such as Byron Ferguson, choose longbows over recurves.

Compound bows are inherently more acurate than traditional composite bows.

Test a well-made traditional bow and a compound bow in a shooting machine to remove all human error and both will produce tight groups with properly matched, straight arrows. At the same time, due to the fact that the compound bow is usually shot with sights and the traditional bow does not use sights, it is common for compound bow shooters to create smaller groups on target than traditional bow shooters. The compound bow also an advantage with release because the mechanical release allows for a more consistent arrow release than fingers on a string can normally achieve. However, a practiced archer with a longbow or recurve can do wonders. Recall Howard Hill placing an arrow on target at well over 150 yards—with regularity.

Glossary

Accent stripe. Laminations running through the riser for decoration. They can also be for added strength.

Actionwood. A laminated rock-hard maple, popular as a limb core wood. Not colorful, but strong and reliable, producing particularly hardworking longbows and recurves.

Anchor point. Any specific point, such as the corner of the mouth, used as a locator for the archer's drawing hand, for consistency. Once called anchorage.

Archer's paradox. The natural bending of the arrow as it warps around the riser of the bow—this can be quite pronounced. The arrow straightens in flight a short distance from bow if the arrow is of the correct spine.

Arm guard. Also known as bracer in the old days, any stout covering of the forearm of the hand that holds the bow, used to protect the arm from string slap.

Arrowhead. Any head, whether a target point, broadhead, blunt, or any other fixture, attached to the point end of the arrow.

Arrow nock. The groove into which the bowstring fits when the arrow is "nocked."

Arrow plate. See strike plate.

Arrowsmith. In the "old days," a person who put points on an arrow. Today, the term is used more generically to indicate anyone who crafts arrows.

Arrow rest. A piece of material residing on the shelf of the longbow or recurve for the arrow to slide over. This was once known as an arrow plate, a term that may come up in older archery literature.

Atlatl. An ancient instrument employed to throw long feathered darts, more like arrows than spears, used to increase the user's throwing power.

Back of the bow. The part of the bow limbs that faces away from the archer when he or she holds the bow in the shooting position.

Backing. A layer of material that is attached to the back of the bow used to strengthen that part of the bow and increase cast (in some cases).

Backset. A bow with limbs that bend forward from the riser when the bow is unstrung. When the bow is strung, the limbs are "pre-loaded," that is, they are under pressure that will result in energy when the bow is fired.

Bamboo. A grass of numerous types, used as a lamination in some bow limbs. Tonkin bamboo is a variety found in some modern traditional bows.

Banana fletch. A feather cut high in the middle and tapering at both ends, usually of large surface area. It is useful in quickly stabilizing an arrow following the archer's paradox, but can also slow an arrow due to drag.

Barebow. This term refers to shooting a bow that does not have sights.

Barred fletching. A feather with a striped appearance, natural with wild and other "dark" turkeys and artificially colored on white dyed feathers.

Barreled shaft. An arrow shaft tapered on both ends and therefore having a thicker center section.

Belly of the bow. The opposite side of the bow from the back; the belly faces toward the archer as the bow is held in the shooting position.

Blunt. Any arrowhead with a flat surface, often may be rubber. Blunts are useful for hunting small game and certain informal target shooting.

Bois d'arc. French for "bow wood," referring most often to Osage orange wood, pronounced bow-dark.

Bow tip. The very end of a limbs.

Bowyer. One who builds bows.

Brace. To string a bow.

Bracer. An older word for arm guard.

Brace height. Distance from the throat of the grip of the bow to the string. See fistemele.

Broadhead. Any arrowhead with cutting edges.

Brush button. Rubber button-shaped device that slips onto the string of a recurve bow and is positioned where the string just meets the limb. Its main use is to prevent foliage from catching at this point, but some archers feel it can be a silencing factor as well.

Burn. A full-length feather shaped with a burner.

Cap dip. Color applied to the back part of the arrow shaft in various lengths up to about a foot but usually shorter. Also known as a crown dip. The cap dips helps an archer find the arrow in grass or brush; it is also used for decoration.

Cant. To tilt the bow at an angle, creating a V-shape at the point where the arrow rest and strike plate meet. The V serves as a platform to retain the arrow in position before flight.

Cast. The farthest distance a bow can launch an arrow. Also thought of as the inherent efficiency within a bow.

Center line. The line that runs straight up and down the entire length of the bow, defining its center point.

Center-shot. Also centershot, where the window of the riser (the portion containing the strike plate and arrow rest) is cut past the center line of the bow so that the arrow rests more in line with the center of the bow rather than offset to one side of the riser. The nocked arrow is now aligned with the longitudinal axis of the riser. Considered to reduce the archer's paradox.

Clicker. A device that can be attached to the string and makes a clicking noise when the bow has been drawn to its proper draw length. Can be helpful to archers who are working on achieving a full draw instead of short-drawing the bow.

Cock feather. On an arrow with three feathers, this is the feather that protrudes outward from the bow, facing away from the shelf when the arrow is nocked on the string. Usually, but not always, it is a different color from the other two feathers.

Composite bow. A bow made from two or more materials, as opposed to a self-bow.

Compressed shaft. An arrow shaft that has been "squeezed down" over its full length to strengthen it, reduce the diameter, and promote straightness.

Core. The material between the laminations in a traditional composite bow. The long-bow is known for narrow limbs with thick cores; the recurve bow, for wider limbs with thinner cores.

Cresting. Narrow colored lines that go around the nock end of the arrow. Cresting is mostly for decoration but can also be used to identify the arrow through the colors of the bands and how they are arranged.

Crow bills. Horn arrowheads found on some English arrows of the Middle Ages.

Crown dip. The colored portion of the arrow extending forward from the nock toward the point, usually about nine to ten inches long.

Dacron. A trademarked name for a synthetic polyester fiber used in making bowstrings, especially the popular B50 string.

Deflex. Deflex bow limbs curve inward toward the archer when the bow is held un-strung in the shooting position. Compare reflex limbs.

Deflex-reflex. See reflex-deflex.

Delamination. When the glue in the limbs of a composite bow fails and the limbs fall apart. A common cause is a bow being left in the trunk of a car in summer.

Draw length. The distance in inches from the front of the riser to the arrow string when the bow is drawn. This is different for each archer, but often around 28 inches, a draw length that most archers can adapt to readily through adjusting shooting stance.

Draw weight. The force required to draw a bow to a specific draw length. A 50-pound bow with a 28-inch draw would require a force of 50 pounds pull applied to the string to bring the arrow back to a full 28 inches.

Dry fire. Drawing a bow without an arrow and letting the string go. This can break a bow.

Efficiency. The amount of the stored energy in a fully drawn bow that actually propels the arrow when it is fired. It can be thought of as the relationship between a bow's draw weight and the arrow speed it produces.

Elevated arrow rest. A rest attached to the window of the bow that the arrow rests on.

Fadeout. The part of the bow that allows for a smooth transition from the riser (rigid) to the limb (flexible). This change must not be sharp or it will concentrate stress in a small area, leading to failure. In the one-piece bow, fadeout is at the end of the riser and must be paper thin. In the takedown bow, fadeout serves the same purpose but is located within the limb itself, which allows for a solid and rigid riser.

Fast flight string. A trademark name for a specific bowstring that offers very little stretch or "give," for improving arrow velocity. Not all bows are built for Fast Flight strings. Those that are not may be damaged if you try to use these strings with them.

Fistmele. Brace height, the distance from the throat of the riser grip to the string, mea-sured in inches. Originally, this distance was the breadth of the fist plus the length of the extended thumb. Some archers will still use this as a gauge for brace height, but it is not precise.

Ferrule. The tubular portion of any arrowhead intended to slip on to the pointed end of the arrow. It is the ferrule that makes contact with the taper.

Finger-pinch. A problem that may arise with very short bows, where the angle of the pulled-back string is too sharp, squeezing the fingers of the shooting hand together. Finger pinch is also accentuated in bows that are too heavy for the archer's draw.

Fishtailing. When the arrow wobbles side to side in flight.

Fletch. To put fletching on an arrow.
Fletching. The guidance system on an arrow—mainly feathers for traditional archers, but it can also be made of other materials.
Fletcher. The person who applies fletching to an arrow.
Flu-flu. Also floo-floo, large fletching that purposely creates extra drag, impeding the flight of the arrow for short-distance shooting, such as shooting at aerial targets and hunting small game. The feathers may be completely spiraled around the shaft or normally positioned.
Following the string. When bow limbs remain in the strung position rather than returning to their unstrung position. This is mainly seen in self-bows that were left strung and took a set.
Footed arrow. An arrow with a piece of hardwood spliced into its forepart or pile end for additional strength.
Glove. Also shooting glove, usually a three-fingered skeletonized glove made of leather or synthetic materials to protect the fingers of the shooting hand when the bow is drawn.
Grip. The handle of the bow.
Hand shock. Vibration felt in the hand when an arrow is released.
Handle. The non-flexible grip part of the riser of the bow.
Heeling. Shooting a bow with the heel of the hand pushing against the handle, often with a very loose finger grip. This method of shooting is used by some archers to reduce torque that may be applied to the handle by the fingers wrapped firmly around the handle.
Hen feathers. In three-feather fletching, the two feathers opposed to the cock feather.
Helical twist. A style of mounting feathers on the arrow with a mild twist, credited with quickly overcoming the archer's paradox.
Instinctive shooting. Shooting a bow without sights. The archer directs the arrow through the natural ability of hand-eye coordination. Instinctive shooting improves dramatically with practice.
Laminations. Thin layers of material built into risers for added riser strength and improved limb performance
Locator. Any indentation on the riser of the bow that a finger falls into, ensuring that the bow hand is always in the same position shot after shot.
Nock. A groove cut in the back of the wooden arrow to notch onto the string. In traditional archery, the nock is of many designs and is glued in place on the arrow taper. The term is also used to identify the notch in the tip of the bow that retains the string, the "bow nock."
Nock set. Any small device attached to the string to indicate the precise point where the nock of the arrow will come to rest. Mainly made of strong plastic today.
Parabolic fletching. A feather where the back is rounded and the front slopes to a point.
Pile. Also pyle, a medieval term still in use to indicate the forepart of an arrow.
Porpoising. When the arrow undulates through the air in an up-and-down motion (that looks like the movement of a swimming porpoise).
Plucking the string. Releasing the arrow with an outward motion of the fingers, the fingers of the shooting hand moving forward before the arrow is sent off.
Push-pull draw. A style of drawing the bow where the bow hand pushes the riser away while at the same time the shooting hand pulls the string back.

Push-pull stringing. Stringing the bow by placing the lower limb tip into the inset of the boot or shoe, then puling the handle section back toward the archer while sliding the string up the top limb toward the bow nock. Bowyers working with bows every day can get away with using this method. The rest of us should use a stringer.

Quill. The centermost part of the feather that is split in half to form a base for gluing onto an arrow.

Quiver. A holder for arrows.

Recoil. The tendency for a bow to lurch forward when it is shot.

Reed. From woodworking language, meaning the stronger aspect of the shaft's grain.

Reflex. Unstrung reflex bow limbs curve slightly outward, away from the archer who is holding the bow in a shooting position.

Reflex-deflex. A style of limbs combining deflex, where limbs curve inward toward the archer, with reflex, where limbs curve away from the archer. In a reflex-deflex bow, the bases of the limbs, near the riser, curve inward, toward the archer, while the rest of the limbs curve outward. This style of limbs is popular today among bowyers and credited with promoting stability in a bow.

Release. The act of turning the arrow loose from a drawn bow. There are mechanical devices, also called releases, that can be attached to the string to take the place of a finger-release.

Reverse handle bow. Longbow or recurve in which the handle rests flush with the belly of the bow, giving the appearance on some longbows that the bow is strung backwards. This kind of bow may have a lower brace height in relation to limb length.

Riser. The entire middle section of the bow that separates the limbs and serves as a handle.

Roving. The game of hiking through an area for the sole purpose of shooting a bow at various inanimate objects, such as pinecones. It can be an interesting informal competition.

Royal Toxophilite Society. Founded in 1780 in England, this organization lays down shooting rules for bow competition and keeps records of membership, events, and points of interest to the society.

Self-bow. Also selfbow, a bow constructed of only one material, usually wood, although other materials have been used for self-bows.

Self-arrow. An arrow made of one material only with the nock cut into the back as a simple notch.

Serving. The thread wrapped around the midsection of the string, creating a strong wear point for the nock set. The arrow nock fits onto the serving.

Shaft. The "body" of the arrow, sometimes also used to refer to the whole arrow.

Shelf. The part of the bow that forms a platform for the arrow rest.

Shield cut. Feather fletching with a concave profile at the back, and a normal taper to a point in the front.

Sight window. The section of the riser that is cut to bring the arrow more toward the center line of the bow. Sights can be mounted at this location, but today's traditional archer is mainly an instinctive barebow shooter.

Spine. The stiffness of an arrow, expressed as a number that corresponds to bow draw weight, although spine is usually selected a bit heavier than the actual draw weight of the bow.

Spine tester. A machine or device used for determining the spine or stiffness of a given arrow shaft.

Silencer. Anything intended to lessen the hum a bowstring makes when released.

Stacking. Build-up of drawing force toward the end of the draw rather than a continuous building from the initial drawing of the bow to full draw.

Stalls. Also finger stalls, leather fingertip coverings that look like a shooting glove without the straps.

Static recurve. A recurve of an older design where the tips of the limbs bend dramatically toward the back of the bow; the tips on this kind of bow are rather solid and inflexible.

Stave. An older term referring to the long piece of wood used to make a self-bow.

Straight fletch. Feathers mounted parallel to the shaft without helical twist.

Straight offset fletch. Fletching where the feather itself is straight but mounted angled on the shaft, not parallel.

Straight grip. Also called a broom handle, a grip with very little throat or inset part of the riser.

Strike plate. Material on the side of the bow's window that works in conjunction with the arrow rest. The side of the arrow makes contact with the strike plate when the arrow is nocked on the bow in preparation for shooting.

Stringer. A device used to string a bow. There are many kinds of stringers, but the most common is simply a strong cord with pouches on each end that fit onto the bow tips.

Stump shooting. Roving.

Tackle. Equipment for shooting a bow.

Tapered arrow. An arrow that narrows toward the nock end, usually for about 9 to 10 inches, reducing the shaft from $^{11}/_{32}$- or $^{23}/_{64}$-inch diameter to $^{5}/_{16}$-inch diameter (for $^{5}/_{16}$-inch nocks).

Target panic. The inability to loose an arrow at the appropriate time, or allowing the arrow to fly before reaching full draw. Once called "archer's catalepsy."

Tab. A flat leather finger protector for the shooting hand, now available in numerous styles.

Takedown bow. A bow that "breaks down" into three parts—a riser and two limbs.

Throat. The deepest part of the handle section of the bow.

Tiller. To bring the limbs of the bow into balance with each other during the building stage of the bow.

Toxophilite. An old term meaning a person with a strong interest in archery.

Tune. To bring a bow to an ideal balance, mainly between brace height, arrow, and nocking point, for best arrow flight.

Underspined. When an arrow is too flexible for a bow.

Vane. Today, plastic fletching. In the past, vane referred to any type of fletching on any arrow. Also used to identify the softer part of the feather as opposed to the harder quill section.